The book addresses a topic that is well-established a.. .. ....
(common factors [CF]) but has suffered from having too little guidance regarding
practical applications. Over the years I've heard many colleagues speak their concerns
to the effect of "I understand and agree with CF theory, but how do I apply it?"
Something I really like about this book is how well it balances theory and practical
applications. Too many books in psychology overemphasize theory and leave readers
without guidance on practical applications. This has been needed for a few decades now!

—**Tony Rousmaniere, PhD**, *Cofounder and Program Director, Sentio University,
Los Angeles, CA, United States*

This is the right book at the right time. The field of psychotherapy is starting
to transition from the question of *who* is right to *what* is right. This volume
provides a description and illustration of those transtheoretical principles
that comprise the foundation of all schools of therapy. The implications for
research, practice, and training are indeed exciting, and this volume should
be required reading for experienced and beginning professionals alike.

—**Marvin R. Goldfried, PhD**, *Distinguished Professor, Psychology Department,
Stony Brook University, Stony Brook, NY, United States*

In this book, Russ Bailey and Benjamin Ogles describe a common factors (CF)
approach to psychotherapy based on five principles of change—the therapeutic
relationship, motivation, corrective experiencing, insight, and self-efficacy. Most
important, this book moves beyond a simple description of CF theory to detail a
comprehensive approach that can be used by CF therapists. The authors' guidance
will be helpful for therapists, trainees, and researchers. As I read it, I found myself
wishing that I would have had access to this book early in my training and career.

—**Joshua K. Swift, PhD**, *Department of Psychology, Idaho State University,
Pocatello, ID, United States*

The book is a rediscovery of psychotherapy principles on the basis of common
factors: a fresh, open-minded, and systematic introduction to the world of
psychotherapy. It is an invaluable resource for psychotherapists who do not want
to confine their professional identity to a single school but who wish to capitalize
on the essence of what works in psychotherapy. Like a Swiss Army knife, the book
represents a versatile tool for the everyday work of a psychotherapy practitioner.

—**Tomáš Řiháček, PhD**, *Masaryk University, Brno, Czech Republic*

As trainees and experienced clinicians feel increased pressures to integrate a
wide range of evidence-based practices, this much-needed book offers a model
of therapy based on principles of change that cut across different theoretical
orientations and provides detailed guidelines, methods, and examples for
implementing them flexibly and effectively. Bailey and Ogles have opened a new
and promising avenue to learn and improve how to conduct psychotherapy.

—**Louis G. Castonguay, PhD**, *Liberal Arts Professor of Psychology,
Department of Psychology, Penn State University, University Park, PA, United States;
former president of the Society for Psychotherapy Research*

# COMMON FACTORS THERAPY

# COMMON
# FACTORS
# THERAPY

## A Principle-Based
## Treatment Framework

**RUSSELL J. BAILEY | BENJAMIN M. OGLES**

 **AMERICAN PSYCHOLOGICAL ASSOCIATION**

Published by
American Psychological Association
750 First Street, NE
Washington, DC 20002
https://www.apa.org

Order Department
https://www.apa.org/pubs/books
order@apa.org

In the U.K., Europe, Africa, and the Middle East, copies may be ordered from Eurospan
https://www.eurospanbookstore.com/apa
info@eurospangroup.com

Typeset in Charter and Interstate by Circle Graphics, Inc., Reisterstown, MD

Printer: Gasch Printing, Odenton, MD
Cover Designer: Anne C. Kerns, Anne Likes Red, Inc., Silver Spring, MD

Library of Congress Control Number: 2022034211

https://doi.org/10.1037/0000343-000

Printed in the United States of America

10 9 8 7 6 5 4 3 2 1

*To the many therapists I've known who show me on a daily basis
their commitment to relieving suffering: I admire you.*
—RJB

*To the many scholars and theorists, too many to mention by name
but hopefully cited liberally in this work, who formed the foundation
and framed the discussion of effective therapy ingredients,
both specific and common, over the past 90 years.*
—BMO

# Contents

# Preface

This book began with an argument. Three psychologists, including the two authors, all interested in psychotherapy research and in understanding how common factors figure within the practice of psychotherapy and even committed to the idea of common factors, disagreed about whether an established therapeutic orientation based on common factors was necessary or even possible. The question lingered long after the argument. We (RJB and BMO) began to meet to discuss this question and how best to answer it. This book is a positive answer to the question of whether a defined theoretical orientation based on the common factors hypotheses can exist. However, our answer seems unlikely to be the authoritative, definitive, never-to-be-amended answer to the question.

Eclecticism and integration may seem on the surface to be practical answers to therapists' arguments regarding theoretical orientation. Integration reflects synthesis, the bringing together of ideas. Certainly, the idea of common factors as an integration or eclecticism represents just such a bringing together of ideas. We hope that the effort of this book is combined with a wider effort to bring ideas together for discourse in the fields of psychotherapy practice and psychotherapy research.

A closer examination of any synthesis of ideas may yield many more arguments and questions than answers. Apparently discrepant ideas are joined into a body that may seem out of joint. Where this is the case, we hope for time and patience so that our proposed model can be refined and the rough corners smoothed so the model holds together and operates more effectively—both practically and theoretically. May there be many more fruitful arguments in the name of progress.

## ACKNOWLEDGMENTS

Many thanks to our shared mentor, Mike Lambert, who made our careers possible and sparked our engagement in psychotherapy research. We acknowledge his help in getting us started. Many thanks also to the research organizations where the ideas found in this book have been discussed for decades and where fertile ground has been provided for the development of these ideas, namely the Society for Psychotherapy Research and the Society for the Exploration of Psychotherapy Integration.

For feedback to guide thinking through the process, we acknowledge Alex Vaz, Tomas Rihacek, Davey Erekson, and Tony Rousmaniere. For reading and editing help, we acknowledge Heidi Vogeler, Rob Dixon, Wyatt Capener, Brick Ellis, Josh Allen, Tatiana Leroy, and David Dodini. Special thanks to Jadzia Holland for her work creating appealing figures and illustrations. We thank Susan Reynolds for shepherding the book creation process in an efficient and very kind way and David Becker for leading and Catherine Malo for executing an extremely helpful editorial process.

# COMMON FACTORS THERAPY

# INTRODUCTION

*A Common Factors Approach to Therapy*

In this book we show how common factors (CF) therapy offers a novel lens for the practice of psychotherapy. The therapist can focus their attention, interactions, and interventions through the lens of change principles that are shared in common with many theoretical orientations. CF therapy, as a specific type of integrative approach, focuses on a few identified change principles rather than a strict allegiance to a single theoretical orientation. These principles line up with common factors, which are consistent across theoretical orientations as well as associated with rich psychotherapy research literature. The CF therapist is guided by a focus on the following factors: the therapeutic relationship, motivation, corrective experiencing, insight, and self-efficacy.

Over its history of more than a century, the field of psychotherapy has seen a steady proliferation of general theoretical orientations and specific therapeutic approaches. Common factors as a concept was hatched as a sort of metatheory of psychotherapy and—though altered and refined in many ways (e.g., the contextual model of Frank, 1961)—has remained as a metatheory. The CF therapy we describe here represents the common factors as a departure from metatheory and an entry into the practical strategies of a theoretical orientation. When a theory of change is specified along with

https://doi.org/10.1037/0000343-001
*Common Factors Therapy: A Principle-Based Treatment Framework*, by R. J. Bailey and B. M. Ogles

interventions associated with this theory, CF therapy can be an actionable treatment approach. The change principles form the CF therapy framework, the lens through which a clinician can practice. These principles undergirding the overall approach have been identified based on our preestablished inclusion and exclusion criteria.

As we show, the global concept for the CF hypothesis has suffered from one particular problem: how its ideas, when they remain in the abstract, tend not to be as actionable as they could be. If a therapist identifies CF therapy as their primary theoretical orientation, what does that mean? By making CF therapy a specified, actionable approach, we hope that this book serves as a guide to enacting the common factors change principles. Definitions and interventions are included, which hopefully will lend well to operational definitions in research endeavors. By including deliberate practice suggestions, we hope that the CF therapy approach can be taught in a straightforward manner, with trainees learning a framework for therapy and more experienced practitioners learning to enhance their practice around the change principles.

We write with many audiences in mind but one audience in particular. Psychotherapists currently in training may especially benefit from the contents of this book, as we present how CF therapy offers a route to make sense of the vast universe of therapy approaches via several key change principles. In addition to this audience, we believe psychotherapy researchers with an interest in eclecticism and integration will find useful content within. Seasoned therapists may find our framing of the common factors to be useful and practical and hopefully will find resonance with the work they are already doing. We hope our model for CF therapy gives a practical framework for helping others in the endlessly complex human interaction that is psychotherapy.

## HOW TO USE THIS BOOK

We first give a detailed overview of the hypothesis and metatheory related to common factors to help us make our case for a specified model of CF therapy. The remaining chapters detail how each change principle can be enacted by a person seeking to practice CF therapy. Please consider it as an overall guide for CF therapy, likely to be less prescriptive than most treatment manuals in its lack of session-by-session instructions for intervention. With the notable exceptions of discussing how to form a therapeutic relationship (which tends to occur at the beginning of therapy) and how to work toward the termination of therapy, all of the change principles are relevant at the beginning, middle, and end of therapy. The change principles mentioned first (therapeutic relationship and motivation) may be especially relevant at the beginning but continue to be relevant in the middle and at the end. Self-efficacy, our final change principle, is often seen as an outcome and may therefore be especially relevant at the end of therapy though it applies throughout all phases of therapy. The change principles of corrective experiencing and insight may be sandwiched in the middle but can occur in the beginning and end. In short, session-by-session instructions would be overly prescriptive for this approach and belie the reality that common factors play a role throughout the process of therapy. Instead, each change principle is a sort of rubric, offering guideposts for the practicing therapist to focus their work.

We note that we often use the term *common factors* to refer to the intermediate-level change principles or processes (see Goldfried, 1980), and therefore we use the terms *change principle* and *common factor* as largely interchangeable. A CF therapist can call to mind each of the change principles when meeting with a client, framing each principle as a category with representative interventions. Common factors, or change principles, form the framework of CF therapy.

This book is organized around five identified change principles, with each treated in its own chapter. Within each chapter, the change principle is first presented conceptually with an overview of the relevant ideas. We then subject each principle to our established criteria for inclusion in the CF therapy model followed by presenting a CF therapy definition for the principle that evolves out of this conceptual background. These sections are designed to be informative, offering a big picture view of how the principle plays out in the practice of therapy. Each chapter also reviews language used to describe the change principle, with the intent of arriving at a working definition and a description of the change principle. CF language avoids being tied to a single theoretical orientation.

The remainder of each chapter describes the implementation of the change principle and associated subprinciples as a general guide in clinical practice. We describe examples of key interventions that evoke the change principle, including concrete tasks, sample therapeutic dialogue, and strategies for engaging in deliberate practice to improve one's application of the change principle. As the journalist Miles Kington is reported to have said, "Knowledge consists of knowing that tomato is a fruit. Wisdom is not putting it in a fruit salad" (McSmith, 2008). Knowledge of the change principles can be helpful, but the wisdom of how to apply them clinically will require thoughtful care and practice according to the intervention suggestions we have included.

We repeat the following concept frequently throughout this book: The change principles are a lens, a framework, or a heuristic for guiding treatment. Whenever a CF therapist is interacting with a client, they can hold the change principles in mind and make intervention decisions based on these principles. Throughout this book we refer to various manuals and resources, all of which represent the broad spectrum of theoretical orientations. All of them can be used to deepen a therapist's understanding of how to enact the change principle.

## CF THERAPY PRINCIPLES

We recommend taking a brief moment to memorize the five change principles of the CF therapy model. A CF therapist uses these five principles as a guide:

1. Therapeutic relationship
2. Motivation
3. Corrective experiencing
4. Insight
5. Self-efficacy

Here we pause to consider how the principles fit together to form a cohesive whole that is therapy, and Figure 1 illustrates this whole with the image of a house. The first two principles may be considered support factors, using Lambert's (2013) categorization of common factors. The therapeutic relationship and motivation factors form an essential foundation, the context in which therapy can occur. The next two may be considered learning factors based on Lambert's groupings. Corrective experiencing and insight

**FIGURE 1. Common Factors Therapy as a House**

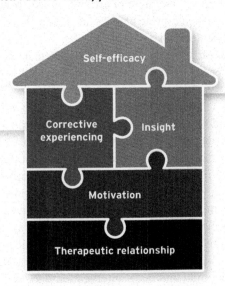

represent key activities during the course of therapy that encourage learning by the client and, in our image, rest on the foundation of the support factors. And finally, self-efficacy, an action factor, represents the roof of the building. As the client moves forward with the gains of therapy, remoralized, they are actualizing the self-efficacy change principle.

Each intervention section also contains many deliberate practice recommendations. These are based on the work of Rousmaniere (2016), who gave several principles for therapists wishing to engage in deliberate practice to improve their therapy. These may be used by therapy trainees or by fully licensed and experienced therapists, or anyone who hopes to improve their effectiveness as a therapist.

Too often, therapy training and supervision occur only through didactics, with the trainer describing how therapy is to be conducted with a client. To use a sports metaphor, the coach (the supervisor) hopes the basketball player (the trainee) will be able to make the free throws if they just tell them how to properly place their feet, raise the ball with their hands, and shoot the ball through the air and into the hoop. Any basketball player will tell you that it takes far more than an explanation of free throws to learn to shoot a free throw. It takes practice, and then the coach's role is to give feedback and assistance with improving the technique and practicing effectively. Practicing deliberately can improve the likelihood that the player will hit the free throws in the more difficult scenario, an actual basketball game. The work in the gym, it is hoped, will pay off on the court at game time.

In similar fashion, deliberate practice can be used to improve when the therapist uses several principles. Following Rousmaniere's (2016) ideas, the therapist can view videos of their clinical interactions with clients and pay attention to their muscles, sensations, and emotions to more closely approximate what occurs when face-to-face with a client. We have included suggestions for what to pay attention to in each section in order to implement the change principle with deliberate practice. The therapist seeks feedback from a consultant and sets small, incremental goals to practice. The therapist then engages in solo deliberate practice. For example, they could say aloud the interventions they have been practicing, addressing them to a video of the client, while monitoring how they are performing and adjusting practice as needed. The therapist uses progress feedback on outcome measures to inform treatment decisions.

Overall, this book can be used as a reference guide for learning about the change principles or as a framework or rubric to inform treatment with clients. It can also be used to enhance one's practice according to the change principles.

# 1

# COMMON FACTORS

*Hypothesis to Metatheory to Theoretical Orientation*

The common factors (CF) hypothesis is not a new idea. Therapists approach their work from any of a multitude of theoretical orientations. These orientations help them to ground their conceptualizations of clients, including what language they use to describe their clients' concerns and the interventions they use to benefit their clients. Therapists can be trained in a single orientation or can learn to approach therapy from several different orientations (though the time allotted us as mortals certainly allows only a discrete, limited number of them). Too often these orientations have been silos, with the practitioners of an orientation affiliating primarily with fellow practitioners of the same stripe, using their own language, conceptualizing clients from the same perspective, and implementing the same interventions indicated by the orientation's originators. Freudians follow Freudians, Rogerians enact Rogerian practices, cognitive behaviorists implement carefully delineated cognitive behavior interventions.

The CF hypothesis highlighted how therapists of differing stripes may unwittingly be practicing the same strategies. The hypothesis originated

https://doi.org/10.1037/0000343-002
*Common Factors Therapy: A Principle-Based Treatment Framework*, by R. J. Bailey and B. M. Ogles

with Rosenzweig (1936) and was carried on in different forms by J. D. Frank, M. R. Goldfried, B. E. Wampold, and others, as is discussed later. The common factors may be inherent to all forms of psychotherapy, regardless of whether they are explicitly named or whether they are labeled with unique terminology across different orientations. The genius of the idea is that these common factors that cut across orientations, by virtue of their ubiquity, likely exert a strong influence on outcome (see Wampold, 2001). Because most forms of psychotherapy tend to be relatively equivalent in terms of their effectiveness, what they share may represent the key ingredients of psychotherapy. Think of common factors like a distillation lab assignment in a high school chemistry class when you boil salt water to separate the salt and the water. With common factors, when you boil down the major approaches to psychotherapy, you may distill the elements that make the most significant difference.

The CF hypothesis shares roots with eclectic approaches to therapy. Eclectic therapists tend to care less about allegiance to a particular model or theoretical orientation and more about bringing ideas together in a hodgepodge of models. Technical eclecticism, theoretical eclecticism, and integrative approaches to psychotherapy are examples. As you read our description of CF therapy, you will notice the bringing together of ideas from different models in the spirit of eclecticism. One might ask, if eclectic approaches already exist, why then this book dedicated to CF therapy?

Around a decade ago, we began hearing therapists refer to themselves as CF therapists as though this were their theoretical orientation. One of us (RJB) considered himself just such a therapist, viewing his practice through the lens of a few common factors. The other (BMO), however, published a piece (Lambert & Ogles, 2014) taking issue with this view, arguing that common factors were a post hoc explanation for the results of empirical research, not a defined approach. This argument laid bare the fact that no defined CF therapy, as such, existed. Yes, there were some interesting proposals related to common factors as a therapy (Arkowitz, 1992; Weinberger, 1995) but none that went so far as to establish themselves as bona fide, definitive orientations to therapy.

Why? We asked ourselves why CF therapy did not yet exist. What makes a bona fide theoretical orientation? If one were to create a treatment manual for CF therapy, what would it contain?

Through our discussions, we uncovered the abstraction problem (more on this later). As we show later, the abstraction problem arose from the status of the CF hypothesis as a metatheory. A metatheory differs from a bona fide, actionable theoretical orientation. For it to become an actionable theoretical orientation, CF therapy needs to overcome the abstraction problem. To overcome the abstraction problem, it needs specified elements.

The book you are now reading represents just such a solution, giving specified elements for defining CF therapy as a bona fide theoretical orientation. Is it *the* solution? We hope so, though it feels strange to claim as proprietary an idea that is more than 90 years old. Rather, we hope that our framework, built using the ideas of many previous scholars, helps to capture, in an actionable way, the main components of a CF version of integrated therapy.

## HISTORY: COMMON FACTORS AS A METATHEORY

Rosenzweig (1936) was the first to articulate the concept of common factors. He suggested that even apparently highly discrepant approaches—separated by canyons between the orientations—are in actuality operating with the same factors, with the same rocks and water that make up the landscape of each orientation. He wrote:

> It is justifiable to wonder (1) whether the factors *alleged to be* operating in a given therapy are identical with the factors *that actually are* operating, and (2) whether the factors that actually are operating in several different therapies may not have much more in common than have the factors alleged to be operating.
>
> Pursuing this line of inquiry it is soon realized that besides the intentionally utilized methods and their consciously held theoretical foundations, there are inevitably certain *unrecognized factors* in any therapeutic situation— factors that may be even more important than those being purposely employed. (p. 412)

His proposal was less about identifying which common factors were at play and more about decrying the use of a successful treatment outcome as evidence for proving true a theoretical orientation. He was the first to use Lewis Carroll's Dodo bird verdict as a statement on the general equivalent efficacy of therapy regardless of the different orientations: "At last the Dodo said, '*Everybody* has won, and *all* must have prizes'" (Rosenzweig, 1936, p. 412).

Rosenzweig (1936) suggested some common factors, including social reconditioning and catharsis (p. 413). He wrote about the therapist's personality as well, which in today's jargon would be termed *therapist effects*. He also pointed out that it may not matter what doctrine is espoused by a therapist (e.g., how the diagnosis and treatment are explained), but the "one-sidedness of an ardently espoused therapeutic doctrine might . . . have a favorable effect" (p. 414). One need only have an identified therapeutic orientation, and the common factors will play out anyway, inherent to the work that all therapists do regardless of their specified orientation. He argued:

> In conclusion it may be said that given a therapist who has an effective personality and who consistently adheres in his treatment to a system of concepts which he has mastered and which is in one significant way or another adapted to the problems of the sick personality, then it is of comparatively little consequence what particular method that therapist uses. (Rosenzweig, 1936, pp. 414–415)

A prescient argument. The ground was set for the development of the contextual model of therapy.

Jerome Frank first wrote *Persuasion and Healing* in 1961 and highlighted common elements of therapy, but it was with later editions (first in 1973, then in 1991 coauthored with Julia Frank, his daughter; both were psychiatrists) that the contextual model for psychotherapy was described definitively. Though different from the CF hypothesis in some key ways, it showed enough consistency with Rosenzweig's idea, such that in contemporary parlance many seem to treat the contextual model and the CF hypothesis as roughly interchangeable terms for the same idea (see Wampold, 2001; Wampold & Imel, 2015).

Frank and Frank (1991) noted common components for psychotherapy that came to be known as the contextual model. According to this model, all forms of healing generally—and psychotherapy specifically—contain the following elements:

- "an emotionally charged, confiding relationship with a helping person" (p. 40);

- "a healing setting" (p. 41); and

- "a rationale, conceptual scheme, or myth that provides a plausible explanation for the patient's symptoms and prescribes a ritual or procedure for resolving them" (p. 42).

In recounting this model, Wampold (2001) emphasized that the ritual needs to be accepted by the client and therapist; it need not necessarily be "true," but it needs to be consistent with their worldview, attitude, and values. If the ritual is not accepted by the client, he emphasized, the therapist assists the client to be led to believe in the rationale and the treatment. The emphasis here is primarily on the client and their belief in the treatment and investment in the treatment procedures through their actions. Regardless of the specific actions, the belief and investment in proactive change are likely to lead to change. The therapist's role is to assist with this, but the therapist's beliefs are secondary. Just as Rosenzweig suggested with his idea of a therapist with an effective personality, the contextual model posited that it matters less what orientation the therapist operates under than that it is believed.

All treatments reflect the contextual model by definition, with the core elements present in all. These elements can be thought of as incidental aspects of all therapies (see Wampold & Imel, 2015) that are common but not necessarily based in the theory used by the therapist. These authors conflate the term *common factors* with *incidental aspects* in a manner that is not consistent with a CF integration approach (Goldfried, 1980; Norcross, 2005). We discuss this discrepancy later in this chapter. Incidental aspects of treatment would provide insufficient foundation for a fully fledged theoretical orientation. For this reason, we point out how the contextual model is necessary but insufficient to fulfill our purpose of constructing CF therapy.

Some may point (and have pointed) to the contextual model (Frank & Frank, 1991) as highlighting that one need not form a CF therapeutic orientation. For this reason, Wampold (2001) explained that one "cannot construct a manualized contextual model treatment" (p. 27). Perhaps such an endeavor would be futile, if only based on incidental aspects of all treatments. By making his point, Wampold highlighted the abstraction problem—that a metatheory is at a different level of abstraction than a theoretical orientation. CF therapy must resolve this concern if the CF hypothesis is to move in the direction of actual, bona fide treatment. As will be seen with the next aspect of CF hypothesis history, the idea takes steps in the direction of treatment but falls short of the threshold of establishing CF therapy.

The CF hypothesis gained more conceptual clout through the work of theorists/researchers interested in eclecticism in psychotherapy, most notably Goldfried (1980) and Norcross (2005). To illustrate, Norcross showed common factors as a type of eclectic approach, in contrast to three other eclecticisms: technical eclecticism, theoretical integration, and assimilative integration. These strategies focus on practicing multiple approaches and choosing the treatment based on the ailment (technical eclecticism), bringing together theories to form a combined theory (theoretical integration), or adding elements from one to another (assimilative integration).

Common factors as an integration approach could focus on the intermediate level of abstraction somewhere between theory and technique (Goldfried, 1980). The therapist focuses on change processes (and principles) at this intermediate level of abstraction. A change process "can be thought of as a heuristic that implicitly guides experienced therapists" (Norcross &

Newman, 2003, p. 13). These change processes are what discrepant theoretical orientations share, their common factors. It is hoped that they also represent what works best, presuming from their equivalent outcomes. Notably, the work that established the CF hypothesis as an integration approach presented it as a conceptual guide and not as an established therapeutic modality with treatment rationale and interventions.

Regarding equivalent outcomes, Wampold (2001) used the contextual model as a frame for understanding in his seminal volume, *The Great Psychotherapy Debate* (see also the most recent edition coauthored with Imel; Wampold & Imel, 2015). They used extensive evidence from meta-analyses examining comparisons of effectiveness between therapies. They found a lack of differences among the variety of treatments, showing that if one expected a specific treatment's ingredients (specific effects) to have a greater relative benefit, one would expect to see larger differences between treatments. The uniform efficacy of treatments highlighted how the contextual model is more strongly supported by effectiveness research taken as a whole, compared with a medical model of specific treatments for specific diagnoses (Wampold, 2001). They make a persuasive case for Rosenzweig's Dodo bird verdict to remain in place, highlighting how common elements are most likely to be responsible for change.

## DEFINING SPECIFIC, NONSPECIFIC, AND COMMON FACTORS

Over the past few decades, researchers and theorists have explored several aspects of common factors that are relevant to our purposes. Here we highlight some important considerations for vocabulary to be used. We aim to clarify the terms we use, especially relative to how these terms have been used in the past. We also explore different conceptions of common factors from the past few decades, including lists of possible factors. We highlight how each conceptualization of common factors proposed a way to understand and organize common elements. By doing so we aim to illustrate how our proposal for CF therapy situates itself as similar to but distinct from past conceptualizations.

Regarding important vocabulary, we distinguish between specific and nonspecific factors and how they relate to the term *common factors*. The distinctions between these three terms are not universally agreed upon, due to how the terms have been used over the past decades. *Specific factors* as a term has referred to elements (theory and interventions) of a treatment that are specified by the proponents or practitioners of the treatment. For example, a behavioral therapist will likely use exposure therapy with a client with a specific phobia. Systematic desensitization, as an element of exposure therapy, has been specified by the treatment and would be a specified factor. The term *nonspecific factor* in this same behavioral treatment would refer to an element that is essential to the treatment but has not been specified in particular by the treatment, such as the relationship between the behavioral therapist and their client with specific phobia as they interact in a treatment setting. This definition is consistent with the contextual model (see Weinberger, 2014, on how the term *nonspecific factor* has confused discussion).

Confusion arises, however, as we specify what these so-called nonspecific factors are, which renders the term a misnomer. Further confusion arises when the term *common factors* is used interchangeably with *nonspecific factors*. For example, Wampold and Budge (2012) wrote:

> The distinction between common factors and specific ingredients, unfortunately, is a false one. Specific therapeutic actions are common; Jerome Frank (1961, 1973) was one of the first to describe how a therapeutic ritual was necessary for all treatments. Without specific therapeutic ingredients, there is no treatment. On the other hand, the specific ingredients cannot be delivered without the common factors—they are delivered in the context of a relationship, usually a face-to-face meeting in which the therapist and the patient are talking to each other. (p. 602)

Wampold and Budge's (2012) interchangeable use of the terms appears to reflect their adoption of the contextual model as interchangeable with the CF concept. Because there has been no CF therapy as such (as we show later), we find this conflation of ideas to be unfortunate.

We use the term *common factors* to refer to intermediate-level change principles or processes (as Goldfried, 1980, described) that are shared across therapies. Many of these principles may be specific, as in already specified within a therapy (e.g., empathy is a specific ingredient of client-centered therapy). Many of these principles may have been previously known as non-specific, due to being reflective of the contextual model and inherent to every treatment (e.g., motivation in therapy may be considered as inherent to most therapies). We aim to make these principles specified within the framework of a defined CF therapy.

## COLLECTIONS OF COMMON FACTORS

Our effort to identify the most relevant and pertinent common factors was far from the first. We pause here to recount many relevant efforts in this endeavor, showing how each pertains to our current proposal.

Metatheories of psychotherapy have been few. Wampold (2001) distinguished between the contextual model and a competing model he called a medical model for psychotherapy. Orlinsky and Howard (1987) outlined a generic model of psychotherapy as a metatheory that is related to but distinct from the contextual model. Notably, this was designed not as a "clinical practice theory" (Orlinsky, 2009, p. 320) but as a framework common to therapies to allow for comparison and contrast between therapies. Elements of the generic model include the therapeutic contract, therapeutic interventions (i.e., the procedures of therapy, much like Frank's ritual), the therapeutic bond, self-relatedness of client and therapist, in-session impacts (originally called *therapeutic realizations*), and temporal patterns or events related to the progression of therapy. As a metatheory, the contextual model has been more applicable to our purpose—the construction of a CF therapy.

Wampold and Imel (2015), rather than seeking to create a list of common factors, used the contextual model to highlight three pathways that take place in all therapies to facilitate change. These principles were descriptive and not prescriptive, but they highlight how the metatheory of the contextual model plays out in most therapies, much like Frank and Frank (1991) showed. To illustrate, the first pathway to change, according to Wampold and Imel (2015), was the forming of a bond between therapist and client, a real relationship (see also Gelso, 2009). Following this, the second path to change occurs through explanations of treatment and expectations of treatment. The third path to change, according to the authors, includes the carrying out of treatment actions. Much like the generic model (Orlinsky & Howard, 1987), this conception remains as metatheory rather than an attempt to create a specific treatment approach.

In addition to offering the framework that became known as the contextual model, Frank and Frank (1991) also proposed a list of common factors. Their six elements that are common to the rituals and procedures used by all psychotherapists are as follows:

- "combating the patient's sense of alienation and strengthening the therapeutic relationship" (p. 44),
- "inspiring and maintaining the patient's expectation of help" (p. 44),
- "providing new learning experiences" (p. 45),
- "arousing emotions" (p. 46),
- "enhancing the patient's sense of mastery or self-efficacy" (p. 48), and
- "providing opportunities for practice" (p. 50).

Empirically derived lists of common factors were made by gleaning from theoreticians' hypothesized lists of factors. Notably, Grencavage and Norcross

(1990) reviewed published empirically derived lists to identify which common factors were identified by researchers. They narrowed these down to a few categories: client characteristics, therapist qualities, change processes, treatment structures, and relationship elements. Their top selected factors were as follows: development of a therapeutic alliance, opportunity for catharsis, acquisition and practice of new behaviors, and clients' positive expectancies. In *The Heart and Soul of Change* (Hubble et al., 1999), the factors that received attention were extratherapeutic change, the therapeutic relationship, expectancy, and therapeutic technique. One can see through many lists that similar factors emerge.

Our shared mentor, Michael Lambert, embraced the CF concept based on extensive evidence in support of it. In his most recent version of this list, Lambert (2013) sorted lists of possible common factors into three categories: support, learning, and action factors. He also highlighted a conception of factors responsible for therapeutic outcome in a pie chart (previously postulated in Lambert & Bergin, 1992). By this estimation, client factors—or experiences in the client's life external to the events of therapy—contribute to or explain 40% of overall change. Common factors explain 30%, client expectancy or motivation 15%, and techniques or interventions only 15%. Attempts to empirically substantiate these estimates have supported the pie-chart breakdown nearly exactly as was proposed in 1992 (see Cuijpers et al., 2012).

## Earlier Attempts to Create a Common Factors Therapy

Very few researchers went so far as to propose a CF therapy. We found two: Arkowitz (1992) and Weinberger (1995). In both cases, their proposal was a single chapter or article without claims to being definitive. Arkowitz (1992) noted that it was unfortunate that there was not a developed manual associated with the study of common factors in therapy. He focused a version of CF therapy (the first we know of that was branded as CF therapy) on how it could help depression, utilizing the supportive elements of therapy. He pointed out how placebo treatment included these supportive elements and could be a treatment in its own right. His treatment proposal was based on a National Institute of Mental Health placebo treatment or clinical management manual (used in clinical trials for depression as the comparison treatment), and Arkowitz expressed a hope for this to become a bona fide therapy. Given that it relied heavily on a Rogerian approach, it seemed less likely to enjoy broad support from psychodynamic and cognitive behavior camps.

In principle, the second proposal seemed most similar to our effort in that it focused on intermediate-level change principles. Weinberger (1995) proposed a CF therapy and gave the following list of factors: (a) the therapeutic relationship, (b) expectations of therapeutic success, (c) confronting or facing the problem, (d) providing an experience of mastery or cognitive control over the problematic issue, and (e) attribution of therapeutic success or failure. His rationale was to choose factors that were "emphasized by one school and relatively neglected by others" for all of the factors but one, which was "not addressed by any school" (p. 46). In so doing, he highlighted inclusion and exclusion criteria but also despaired that a complete theoretical integration could be "a practical impossibility" (p. 59).

Recent proposals have continued to give lists of common factors. As much of our work has been inspired by Goldfried, his recent piece reiterated his list that has served as a springboard for CF therapy (Goldfried, 2019). His list consisted of the following:

- promoting client expectation and motivation that therapy can help,
- establishing an optimal therapeutic alliance,
- facilitating client awareness of the factors associated with his or her difficulties,
- encouraging the client to engage in corrective experiences, and
- emphasizing ongoing reality testing in the client's life. (p. 488)

However, he recommended that clinical work focus on these change principles instead of theoretical orientations (see Starreveld, 2021, for a similar example in development). We feel our approach is mostly consistent with his proposal, though we aim to describe a theoretical orientation focused on change principles. The model we describe began with the work of Frank and Frank (1991) but moved quickly in similar directions as Goldfried (2019), focusing on change principles. Our model is certainly highly influenced by Goldfried, though there are key differences in our proposal, most notably a focus on the establishment of a defined theoretical orientation.

Fault lines within the proponents of common factors were evident. Perhaps no one articulated the discrepancy better than did Lundh (2014). In this conceptual work, the author underscored discrepancies in how common factors are discussed, with basically two different conceptions or models: (a) relational–procedural persuasion (RPP; e.g., Frank & Frank, 1991; Wampold, 2001) and (b) methodological principles and skills (MPS; e.g., Goldfried, 1980; Norcross, 2005). The first focused on the form rather than the contents of the treatment, emphasizing the "need for a good therapeutic relationship . . . as a means for engaging the client in a certain therapeutic procedure and to persuade the client of a new explanation that gives new perspectives" (Lundh, 2014, p. 132). The second focused on the content of therapy as generally defined change principles, with Lundh's summary of its assumptions that

> effective psychotherapy relies on methodological principles which may be manifested in various forms in different kinds of psychotherapy, and . . . that successful psychotherapists are characterized by their skills in applying these methodological principles to a variety of clinical situations. (Lundh, 2014, p. 136)

Contrasting the two, Lundh (2014) surmised that the former model (RPP, consistent with the work of Frank & Frank, 1991, and Wampold, 2001) was more "pessimistic" with regard to the future, having "little prospect for improving the practice of psychotherapy, beyond the Dodo verdict" (p. 141). In other words, if the contextual model applies in all forms of therapy, then all future therapies will continue to show equivalent outcomes. However, the latter model (MPS, consistent with Goldfried, 1980), based on methodological principles and skills (our intermediate-level change principles), showed promise and optimism for Lundh in the further development and improvement of therapeutic interventions.

Some proponents of the CF idea used CF language while showing the shortcomings of the empirically supported treatment movement (Laska et al., 2014). By so doing, they referred to "the CF approach," even as they used the term as roughly interchangeable with the contextual model. By describing "*the* CF approach," it seemed that there was a reifying of the perspective as a treatment approach. Lambert and Ogles (2014) took issue with this suggestion that there was in general or in evidence-based practice an existing CF approach. In a separate piece, however, Laska and Wampold (2014) reiterated a clarification that "there is no such thing as a 'common factors' treatment" (p. 520). They pointed out that this would be equivalent to a therapy "without *any* explanation [for the client's distress]" or "simply a relationship with an empathic therapist" (p. 520). Their point clarified that the CF hypothesis was still seen as the contextual model, as metatheory rather than a treatment approach.

Rather than finding a definitive model of CF therapy as a therapy or a definitive list of the relevant common factors that would be included in such an approach, we found a few intrepid attempts at both of these. More to the point, we found experts giving a resounding "no" to the question of whether a CF approach exists. Some even suggested that such a thing would be an impossibility. Yet we persist in this book to show that it can be a practical, actionable principle-based treatment approach.

## Summary of Common Factors History

From this brief recounting of the history of the common factors, we gleaned several key concepts. We highlight them here, noting that a proposed model of therapy based on common factors will require consistency with these concepts:

- *CF hypothesis.* As Rosenzweig first observed, shared components are active in divergent models of therapy, with or without the therapist's explicit awareness. The original concept focuses on what is shared or common.

- *Contextual model.* Frank and Frank (1991) described the key elements common to all therapies. We abbreviate them here: relationship, setting, myth, and ritual. Without all of these, a treatment will fall short of a bona fide treatment. Because the contextual model applies to all treatments and because of the rough equivalence of outcome for all therapies (Wampold & Imel, 2015), we can expect a newly defined treatment based on common factors to be reasonably effective in the same way.

- *CF integration or eclecticism focusing on intermediate-level processes or principles.* Goldfried (1980) and later Norcross (2005) took the hypothesis to imply that an eclecticism could be constructed, focusing on the intermediate level of abstraction. These principles are neither theory nor technique; rather, they give a focus for a defined therapy. A list of factors can be established based on empirical support, whether they are broadly espoused across theoretical orientation fault lines and whether they are specified by the treatment or inherent to treatment and identified post hoc.

We will continue to refer to these ideas as we present our proposal. Our review and thinking through the challenges of common factors led us to the conclusion that CF therapy did not yet exist. It also led us to uncover a central obstacle for it to exist: For the CF hypothesis to transform into the CF therapy, it needed to overcome the abstraction problem.

## THE ABSTRACTION PROBLEM

We have previously referred to the abstraction problem as an obstacle that needs to be overcome for CF therapy to exist and have written about this at length (Bailey & Ogles, 2019). We illustrate our reasoning here, as it seems crucial to understanding how CF therapy can exist at all. Indeed, given that many have indicated that it is impossible, we aim to show how it is possible for CF therapy to be created in a manner that is actionable and useful.

Consider for a moment how we use our minds to conceptualize ideas—from ideas that are general, abstract, and broad to ideas that are specific, concrete, and narrow. This is evident in the popular saying "I couldn't see the forest for the trees." A single tree would represent a lower level of abstraction, and many trees taken together form an idea at a higher level of abstraction (i.e., a forest).

Abstraction is evident in the history of science; as pioneering chemist John Dalton pointed out, all matter is made up of indivisible atoms (matter = more general material, atoms = more specific constituents). Both of Dalton's levels of abstraction continued to be valuable in everyday life—most of us humans interact with matter on the scale of visibility rather than on the scale of atoms—but Dalton's showing a lower level of abstraction yielded the field of modern chemistry. In the 20th century, even these atoms were shown to be constituted of subatomic particles as small as quarks, muons, and gluons, extending the level of abstraction to an even smaller scale. Chemistry on the level of atoms continued to be useful, but atomic physicists continue to extend our understanding at the subatomic level of abstraction (Sutton, n.d.).

Levels of abstraction can be seen in many fields, scientific and otherwise. The taxonomic levels of biology (kingdom, phylum, etc., as shown in Figure 1.1) show useful levels of abstraction based on shared qualities at each level of abstraction. The kingdom animalia consists of members that have shared characteristics, including that all animals are multicellular, possess no chlorophyll (as plants do), and possess cells with DNA in chromosomes in nuclei (i.e., are eukaryotic). This high level of abstraction can be very useful to biologists in understanding animals and what organisms have in common. The lowest level of abstraction (in this example, the species alpaca) can also be useful, as an alpaca expert would specialize in studying one of the most adorable organisms on the planet. Figure 1.1 also shows how our biological understanding of organisms proceeds in distinct and useful levels of abstraction. Human social relations can be abstracted as well, as we show with a popular character from Tolkien.

Let us take the levels of abstraction and apply them to our purpose of understanding psychotherapy. Orlinsky (2009) used the taxonomic levels of genus and species to highlight how his metatheory, the generic model of psychotherapy, could be thought of as the genus in the genus–species pairing: "e.g., within genus *Homo* such related species as *Homo habilis*, *Homo erectus*, *Homo neanderthalensis*, and *Homo sapiens*" (p. 320).

Perhaps already evident from our discussion thus far, CF theorizing and applications have focused on the metatheory aspects of the hypothesis. This metatheory level of abstraction has been extremely useful. Perhaps its most

**FIGURE 1.1. Levels of Abstraction in Various Domains**

| | Zoology | | Human Anatomy | | The Lord of the Rings | |
|---|---|---|---|---|---|---|
| *Kingdom* | Animalia | *Organism* | H. sapiens | *World* | Middle Earth |
| *Phylum* | Chordata | *Organ systems* | Nervous system | *Wider city or nation* | Gondor |
| *Class* | Mammalia | *Organs* | Brain | *Community* | Minas Tirith |
| *Order* | Artiodactyla | *Tissues* | Neural tissue | *Partnerships/ families* | Fellowship of the Ring |
| *Family* | Camelidae | *Cells* | Neurons | *Individuals* | Aragorn, Arwen |
| *Genus* | Vicugna | *Molecules* | Myelin protein | | |
| *Species* | V. pacos (alpaca) | *Atoms* | Carbon | | |

(left margin label: **Levels of Abstraction**)

useful application has been through Wampold and Imel (2015) showing persuasively how common factors as a metatheory can help explain the general equivalence of therapy outcomes for different theoretical orientations. Common factors as metatheory has been useful in identifying what is shared between therapies, from Rosenzweig to Frank to Goldfried (see the History: Common Factors as a Metatheory section). We applaud these developments as foundational for understanding common factors. Abstraction itself is not the problem.

The problem lies in how the ideas, when they remain in the abstract, tend not to be as actionable as they could be. Specifically, they could be more actionable for therapists. What is needed is to move from the more abstract to the more concrete and specific so that the CF idea can be used in practice. To become a bona fide theoretical orientation, CF therapy needs to be more than a metatheory. In our earlier piece (Bailey & Ogles, 2019), building on a previous chapter (Anderson et al., 2010), and as seen in Figure 1.2, we highlighted the different levels of abstraction as they relate to the practice of psychotherapy. The levels we use are as follows, in order from most abstract

**FIGURE 1.2. Levels of Abstraction, Moving the Common Factors From a Higher, Superordinate Level of Abstraction to the Level of a Theoretical Model of Psychotherapy**

| | *Metatheory* | | Contextual Model | | |
|---|---|---|---|---|---|
| *Theoretical orientation* | Cognitive | Behavioral | Psychodynamic | Humanistic | **Common factors** |
| *Theory/ principles* | Maladaptive cognitions | Avoidance/ reinforcement | Core conflictual relationship | Experiential, acceptance | **Specified factors (e.g., alliance, corrective experiences)** |
| *Techniques/ interventions* | Cognitive restructuring | Exposure | Interpretation | Empty chair dialogue | **Trans- theoretical, focus on factors** |

(Row label, left vertical axis: **Levels of Abstraction**)

to most specific: (1) metatheory, (2) theoretical orientation, (3) theory or principles, and (4) techniques or interventions.

Past writing on common factors has sometimes obfuscated the levels of abstraction between metatheory and theoretical orientation. Wampold (2001) partially distinguished common factors from the contextual model but denied that they could be separated, then argued against classifying the contextual model as a psychotherapeutic theory rather than a metatheory:

> First, the characteristic ingredients discussed by Frank and other common factor conceptualizations are shared by all theoretical approaches. In this sense, all treatments are characteristic of the contextual model. . . . Second, the contextual factors and common ingredients of the contextual model, which are considered incidental by psychotherapeutic theories, cannot be removed from the treatments prescribed by the various theories. . . . Third, the contextual model dictates that a treatment be administered but that the particular components of that treatment are unimportant relative to the belief of the therapist and the client that the treatment is rational and efficacious. (pp. 26–27)

In the revised edition, Wampold and Imel (2015) described Frank's contextual model as the most comprehensive model of common factors, noting that their usage of the term *contextual model* is derived from Frank's model. Clearly, their thinking shows common factors as a metatheory, equivalent to the contextual model. With even more recent commentary on the topic, Wampold and Ulvenes (2019) wrote, "The contextual model is not a common factor therapy as such, but rather an explanation of why specific interventions may be effective. . . . The common factors give potency to the specific ingredients" (pp. 76–77).

If common factors remains as metatheory, as Lundh (2014) showed with his two models of common factors, Wampold's pessimism about CF therapy would make sense. Model 1 is the metatheory version, based on Frank and Wampold. Lundh's Model 2, however, focused on methodological principles and skills, based on the work of Goldfried and Norcross in that it focused on the intermediate level of change. This second model does not yet exist in practice, most likely because of the restraints from the Model 1 idea, which effectively say it not only does not exist but cannot exist.

To illustrate the problem, let us suppose that a therapist calls themselves a CF therapist. What do they do that makes them a CF therapist? According to the metatheory argument, any therapist regardless of persuasion will enact the contextual model, so every therapist would be a CF therapist. However, this does not allow us to develop the CF idea any further. Metatheory does not allow us to describe (or prescribe) in detail what a CF therapist actually does.

This reasoning brought us to a thought experiment, a question that could show how the CF concept could move from metatheory to a treatment approach. Our thought experiment was as follows: What would a CF therapy manual look like? On the basis of metatheory only, we would not be able to construct a contextual model treatment manual (because it is inherent in all forms of treatment). However, a CF therapy manual could be constructed by overcoming the abstraction problem, by making the metatheory concrete with specific elements. Specific elements would transform it into a bona fide treatment approach. Here we describe this potential solution in detail.

## A POTENTIAL SOLUTION: WHAT IS NEEDED

For the CF concept to become a bona fide therapy, thus overcoming the abstraction problem, it needs specified components. But what components are needed? Wampold and Imel (2015) described a definition of *psychotherapy*, which seems to be what may make it bona fide:

> Psychotherapy is a primarily interpersonal treatment that is a) based on psychological principles; b) involves a trained therapist and a client who is seeking help for a mental disorder, problem, or complaint; c) is intended by the therapist to be remedial for the client disorder, problem, or complaint; and d) is adapted or individualized for the particular client and his or her disorder, problem, or complaint. (p. 37)

This was similar to what Wampold et al. (1997) used in their meta-analysis to include or exclude bona fide treatment approaches. They required that the treatment was delivered by a trained therapist, was based on psychological principles, was offered to the psychotherapy community as viable treatments (e.g., through professional books or manuals), or contained specified components.

Recall Frank and Frank's (1991) contextual model, in which all therapeutic approaches contain a theory of change, which includes a myth to explain pathology and rationale and a ritual or procedures to evoke change. Myth and ritual may be considered as ingredients in a recipe for any new theoretical orientation; that is, each of these elements needs to be specified and enacted. We propose that these are the ingredients needed for CF therapy, to comprise its specified components. We take each of these in turn and lay the groundwork for CF therapy.

Recall also Goldfried's (1980) emphasis on the intermediate level of abstraction, that is, change principles (referred to by Lundh, 2014, as Model 2, which focused on methodological principles and skills). To overcome the abstraction problem, we submit that CF therapy needs to focus on these principles of change. CF therapy must maintain fidelity to this conceptualization of the common factors to be actionable. These principles become our common factors in CF therapy, the organizing ideas for the specified components of treatment.

Recall common factors as but one of several approaches to psychotherapy eclecticism or integration, as outlined by Norcross (2005). He pointed out how eclecticism and integration differ (divergent vs. convergent). Our proposed model can, by this description, be considered an integration. However, the spirit of eclectic psychotherapy is highly relevant, as it is based on the fact that there is a wide proliferation of therapies, that any one specific therapy is inadequate, and that the differential effectiveness of one therapy over another is lacking (Norcross, 1986). The focus on what is shared across theoretical orientations honors this eclectic movement in therapy. CF therapy, as we propose its framework, needs specified components that are truly representative across the broad spectrum of theoretical orientations. As we describe the framework, we aim to maintain fidelity to the idealism of integration.

## SPECIFIED COMPONENTS

To reiterate, CF therapy requires specified components. These components include a theory of change, which includes a myth, in other words, a rationale or theory of the problem that is to be addressed (i.e., a theory of pathology) and a ritual or procedures that evoke change. We offer here our myth that includes a rationale for the client's problems to be addressed with a transtheoretical theory of pathology and a rationale for treatment based on common factors. The ritual or procedures that evoke change are described later in this chapter and in succeeding chapters.

## A Transtheoretical Theory of Pathology

We offer a CF therapy definition for *pathology* as follows: Psychological, social, behavioral, emotional, cognitive, and biological factors combine to create disruptions in a person's life and associated demoralization. The first specified component needed is pathology—in other words, a description of the clinical problem to be addressed in therapy. Frank and Frank (1991) described the metatheoretical contextual model for treatment using a global conceptualization of distress: *demoralization*. They explained the term using dictionary definitions, with synonyms such as deprived of spirit or courage, bewildered, or confused. They wrote,

> The state of demoralization, in short, is one of hopelessness, helplessness, and isolation in which the person is preoccupied with merely trying to survive. . . . Overall, demoralization may be a cause, a consequence, or both, of presenting symptoms, and its relative importance differs from patient to patient. (p. 35)

Note the relationship between demoralization and symptoms, that these are not synonymous terms, nor are they directly proportional to one another, nor is the causal arrow fixed in one direction. One or both may be present, and as a consequence one or both may be the subject of treatment.

Demoralization relates strongly to common factors. For example, the therapeutic relationship as described by Frank and Frank (1991) emphasizes the roles of helper and the one who is helped. Expectancy, the hope that treatment will be of benefit, relates strongly to motivation for entering treatment and making changes while in treatment. Most treatments do not focus on demoralization, per se, but aim to relieve distress or symptoms as defined by the treatment.

A counterargument for using demoralization may be that treatments do better when they focus on specific elements. In other words, treatments may do better when matching specific treatment elements to the specific symptoms they are designed to alleviate. This counterargument rests on diagnosis, which rests on the accurate and valid description of symptoms as distinct categories. However, critics of categories would point to the usefulness of dimensions rather than categories and the helpfulness of transdiagnostic approaches (see McCabe & Widiger, 2020; Shear et al., 2007;

Wigman et al., 2017). Specificity seems intuitively desirable in the sense of matching treatments to problems, yet even the most vocal proponents of specificity seem to move toward transdiagnostic understanding (Barlow et al., 2010). In a departure from strict specificity, Barlow et al. (2010) combined emotional disorders (depression, panic disorder, generalized anxiety disorder, social anxiety disorder, and obsessive–compulsive disorder) and focused on the fact that these disorders are less specific than one might think:

> Through this research we have learned that the disorders just discussed actually have much more in common than their separate diagnostic labels might lead you to think. At their core, all of these disorders arise out of a tendency to experience emotions more frequently, more intensely, and as more distressing than someone without these disorders. (p. 12)

This transdiagnostic framing seems especially apt for CF therapy and a focus on what is shared across perspectives. Though demoralization can be thought of in a transdiagnostic sense, it seems especially amenable to a dimensional understanding of pathology. Proponents of a dimensional approach to psychopathology point out how categories (e.g., discrete diagnoses such as obsessive–compulsive disorder or alcohol use disorder) tend to reduce explanatory power (Forbes et al., 2016). Better to focus on how individuals fall on a continuum, or the degree to which they experience symptoms that line up on defined dimensions (e.g., internalizing concerns, such as what Barlow et al., 2010, combined under the term *emotional disorders*). The latest diagnostic manuals—*Diagnostic and Statistical Manual of Mental Disorders* (5th ed., text rev.; American Psychiatric Association, 2022) and *International Classification of Diseases, 11th Revision* (World Health Organization, 2019)—contain dimensional approaches to the diagnosis of personality disorders. Notably, the prominent dimension, negative affectivity, corresponds to neuroticism on the five-factor model of personality (McCabe & Widiger, 2020) and seems very similar to our understanding of demoralization in its dimensionality and in its capturing of distress.

Regardless of the shortcomings of specificity and the push for transdiagnostic and dimensional understanding of pathology, most working therapists likely use diagnostic categories in their work. Though in many settings it is not required to diagnose clients, insurance companies and medical settings typically require a diagnostic category to be given by the therapist at an initial evaluation or very soon thereafter. Therapists may also use the language of diagnosis in describing to a client what they are experiencing and the interventions they choose to use. It can be useful to highlight factors from multiple domains to a client, such as showing them explanations for how they think, feel, or behave. Even though the movement away from specificity is notable and helpful from a CF therapy perspective, a truly transtheoretical perspective need not limit pathology in ways that exclude physiology, behaviors, cognition, or emotion. A more holistic, global perspective can be held paramount while also allowing for specificity as needed.

Taking into account the need for therapists to often move into specific content related to a clinical presentation of symptoms, the focal point for CF therapy emphasizes a global view through demoralization inspired by the contextual model. Here we reiterate the definition of pathology to be treated by CF therapy as given previously: Psychological, social, behavioral, emotional, cognitive, and biological factors combine to create disruptions in a person's life and associated demoralization.

Therapists may choose to emphasize elements from the first aspect of the definition, as each relates to a different aspect of the client's experience. Overall, however, a CF therapist would focus globally on the demoralization associated with these aspects and aim for remoralization or a restoration of self-efficacy and a sense of mastery in their lives. Clients often come to therapists seeking hope through relief and reengagement with their lives in meaningful ways.

## A Rationale Based on Common Factors

The central premise of CF therapy, as we proposed previously (Bailey & Ogles, 2019), is "that a collection of principles or processes of change across therapeutic modalities can variously be applied to help resolve psychological, social, behavioral, emotional, cognitive, and biological factors that disrupt and demoralize" (p. 248). As described already, this rationale maintains a focus on intermediate-level change principles (based on Goldfried, 1980) that are common across therapeutic modalities. The change principles must meet several requirements to be validly regarded as change principles held in common across treatment orientations and to be a useful framework for CF therapy. We present our requirements for selecting change principles, which we have expanded and refined since our earlier piece (Bailey & Ogles, 2019; note that "factors" refers to common factors that we later describe with greater detail in other chapters as "change principles").

Our selection criteria for CF therapy change principles comprise both inclusion criteria and exclusion criteria. The inclusion criteria are as follows:

- The factor has been identified and supported with persuasive evidence from psychotherapy research, with a reasonable level of consensus among researchers that the factor is positively associated with psychotherapy outcome. As the evidence base continues to evolve, these factors may continue to evolve.

- The factor is present in most therapies. It is not necessary for the factor to be present in all therapeutic modalities, but it can be broadly defined in the categories of psychodynamic, behavioral, cognitive behavior, and humanistic orientations. Researcher consensus, as found in past and current literature, points to the factor being present and to what degree.

- A factor must be present at a theoretical level. Proponents of a therapeutic orientation may describe the factor, though not necessarily using the same terms or the same level of emphasis as in other modalities.

- A factor needs to be present on the level of actual practice; that is, the factor must reflect what therapists from differing therapeutic modalities actually do.

- The factor can be conceptualized to allow for variability and flexibility in its application to interventions. In other words, multiple techniques within a single modality or techniques from different modalities may address the same overarching change principle. Rather than avoiding potential overlap in the name of distinctness and specificity, a CF therapist would pragmatically seek multiple ways to address the same factor or change principle.

- The factor can be described with transtheoretical language.

- The factor can be operationalized both for demonstration in a treatment manual and for empirical research. CF therapy can be taught, and CF therapists can use deliberate practice principles to improve their application for their clients' benefit. Researchers can use operational definitions to examine its effectiveness.

Change principles may, however, be excluded from the CF therapy overarching framework based on the following exclusion criteria:

- There is a lack of persuasive research evidence that a proposed factor is related to outcome.

- The factor is exclusive to one therapeutic orientation, such that it is not present in any form in at least two different modalities.

- The factor is redundant with another factor already determined to be present. Parsimony can be best achieved with a superordinate concept, with related concepts subsumed beneath the overarching concept.

One can see several tensions within these criteria. The tension represents the bringing together of strange bedfellows, ideas that one might expect to be in different piles, driving in different lanes, or orbiting different planets. We embrace tension as this is consistent with the spirit of the CF hypothesis, and here we briefly mention each tension.

### The Tension Between Theory and Practice

Theoreticians in ivory towers may be criticized for not knowing what the practitioner experiences in the trenches. Pontificating about therapy through writing and discourse (e.g., writing this book) can be much different from sitting face-to-face with a client who is telling you their life story through tears, and you feel a strong desire to say the right thing to relieve their suffering. Theory as described in a manual can seem dogmatic, although every practicing therapist needs to act pragmatically when helping a client. Limited research has been conducted to study what techniques or interventions are common in practice across orientations. Pfammatter (2015) used experts to rate techniques according to common factors and identified four areas: (a) cognitive processing, (b) emotional processing, (c) coping, and (d) common factors fostering therapeutic alliance or therapy motivation. More research is needed on how the theory is used in live practice. We embrace the tension between theory and practice by focusing on change principles. These principles are described with theory and examples, but the therapist can focus on the overarching principle when in session.

We also recommend the use of deliberate practice to emphasize training in these change principles over time, taking the idea from esoteric concept to applied practice. Deliberate practice for therapists consists of identifying deficits in performance, getting input from a more expert coach or mentor, getting feedback on performance, and having focused solo practice for improvement (Ericsson et al., 1993, as cited in Rousmaniere et al., 2017). As developed by Rousmaniere (2016), deliberate practice for therapists can be a focused training practice for improvement. Accordingly, we have devoted space with each change principle for deliberate practice focused on learning and improving with specific therapeutic actions.

### The Tension Between Research and Practice

The gap between research and practice may seem similar to the tension between theory and practice. However, here we focus on the lag in the time it takes for the results of empirical studies to be put into practice by clinicians. Clinicians may be unaware of the current state of the field as studied empirically by researchers. Conversely, researchers often fail to take into account the realities of daily practice, with experiments using stringent criteria for selecting clients and strictly following treatment manuals that therapists may rarely use. The research–practice gap carries disadvantages in both directions (see Goldfried, 2019).

We embrace this tension by attempting to close the gap as suggested by Goldfried (2019). Rosen and Davison (2003) proposed that, to the field, empirically supported principles of change are more favorable than empirically supported treatments. CF therapy is consistent with this idea. The CF therapy approach focuses on change principles that are positively associated with outcome as a way to bring empirical research to clinicians in a format that is user-friendly. In addition, we recommend that CF therapy be a feedback-informed treatment; that is, therapists collect and use progress feedback from their clients (Lambert, 2015).

### The Tension of Differences in Language and Terminology

This is the Tower of Babel problem, as described by S. D. Miller et al. (1997), which shows how modalities may use different terminology and language to describe identical or at least similar concepts. As a result, as Castonguay et al. (2015) pointed out, a proponent of a therapeutic modality may falsely believe a common factor is unique to that modality, a "faux unique" variable. Defining common factors as change principles cutting across orientations will require overcoming semantic barriers by focusing on a unifying language that is less bound by a single therapeutic orientation. We hope to resolve this tension by offering our rationale around terms and decisions made, pushing for language that transcends any single particular modality.

### The Tension Between Global Concepts and Specific Concepts

A CF therapy is bound to run the risk of being too general. In our view, its historical and lingering position as metatheory is certainly too general to be of practical use. However, by giving specified components (both change principles and interventions associated with those principles), we run the risk of being so specific that we exclude some useful common factors. In addition, we believe there are likely factors that have yet to either be discovered or be articulated by researchers or theoreticians. We address this tension by emphasizing that the factors selected are not a closed canon. CF therapy may change, and different change principles may be highlighted in any future iteration of CF therapy.

One additional problem with being either too general or too specific is that CF therapy could miss the mark for therapists, that they would not find it useful in practice. A therapist could focus only on the change principles and interventions described in this book and refrain from enacting interventions that do not appear. Such a rigid view of adherence seems unlikely to be effective. Flexibility in applying change principles may instead look like a therapist choosing an intervention that is consistent with a change principle that may not be described in this guide or in any other manual. The change principles form the rubric for decision making in therapy, not rigid adherence. The change principle is the lens through which CF therapists can choose from the universe of interventions from any theoretical orientation (a "theory-verse" perhaps?) to enact interventions that actualize the change principle. A CF therapist needs to feel at liberty to adapt treatment in line with the change principles, possibly even shifting to another therapeutic modality. In this way, CF therapy may appear more eclectic than integrative (the difference to many readers may be purely academic), which we propose is consistent with the value of openness. In general, we hope that CF therapy can be a framework that is generative more than reductionistic, open to possibility rather than rigidly prescribed.

We expect that the treatment model, as it is based on change principles that have strong support in theoretical and empirical literature, will be as effective as most psychotherapies. Due to the extensive literature showing the relative equivalence of psychotherapy outcomes across orientations, we do not expect CF therapy to be more effective than other therapies. We do, however, propose it as a model of therapy that is both parsimonious and pragmatic. Therapists can use it as a practical framework for understanding clients and engaging in the work of therapy. In each subsequent chapter of this book, we describe each change principle. Our list of change principles shares much in common with Goldfried (2019), whose list shares much in common with Frank and Frank (1991) as well as other contributors to the field. We finalized our list based on the inclusion and exclusion criteria as described and then offered our overview of each principle with practical guidelines for a therapist to use. In Figure 1.3, we show the overall model including the following change principles we selected based on our criteria:

1. therapeutic relationship
2. motivation
3. corrective experiencing
4. insight
5. self-efficacy

## Rituals or Procedures

The interventions associated with each of the change principles are described in the remaining chapters of this book. We pause here to emphasize a point regarding common versus specific treatment choices, a point first addressed by Frank and Frank (1991).

**FIGURE 1.3. Common Factors (CF) Therapy Model**

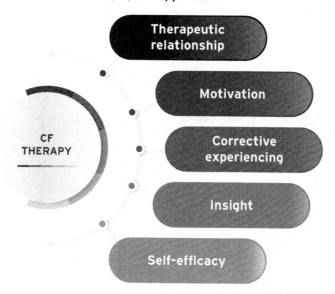

We have endeavored in this book to give specified components for CF therapy. However, these change principles are shared across therapeutic modalities and have been historically treated as nonspecific, incidental to treatments generally, or not in any way the basis of a bona fide treatment. As we describe these change principles and associated interventions, we recognize that the resulting focus on shared concepts may leave the door open for additions.

Some may see CF therapy as merely augmenting or maximizing the benefit of the common factors and not as a standalone therapy. We raise this point from Frank and Frank (1991), who compared two very different psychotherapies to two medications, "like penicillin and digitalis—totally different pharmacological agents suitable for totally different conditions" (p. 39). They continued, "On the other hand, the active therapeutic ingredient of both [therapies] could be the same, analogous to *two aspirin-containing compounds* [emphasis added] marketed under different names" (p. 39). They pointed to the aspirin-containing compounds as the more likely scenario and highlighted how aspirin is like the common factors, "nonspecific . . . [but] not inert. Its active pharmacological principle reduces fever and alleviates aches and pains regardless of the specific illnesses with which they are associated" (p. 39).

The key to the metaphor is that common factors share the qualities of aspirin. If the hundreds of existing psychotherapies are like aspirin-containing medications, the common factors are present in them just like aspirin is in the compounded medications. Where aspirin is present, it is not inert. Even so, the common factors are present and are active ingredients in therapy.

Carrying this metaphor a step further, one can imagine treatments that consist primarily of aspirin. Aspirin and other painkillers that also reduce fevers, such as ibuprofen and acetaminophen, are among the most common medications in our home medicine cabinets. Aspirin can be an effective medication for blood clots and angina. This medication, with its diffuse pharmacological effect, is everywhere. Aspirin can be a standalone treatment under a large number of circumstances, with Ittaman et al. (2014) noting that it is "the most widely used drug in medicine" (p. 147).

In like manner, CF therapy can be a standalone therapy by focusing on the shared active ingredients in therapy. CF therapy can be the aspirin of therapeutic orientations. Basing an entire therapy on common factors can broadly address the demoralization with which clients present for therapy. CF therapy can stand alone as a psychotherapy as long as it has specified, actionable components. We expect that the elements described in this book are already in use by most therapists. That is why they are common factors, after all.

# 2 THE THERAPEUTIC RELATIONSHIP, COMMON FACTOR 1

Relationships require participation from two individuals, and yet the relationship itself reflects another entity, almost a third party. The word "dyad" is often used to describe pairings such as a therapist and a client as if there are only two ingredients. However, the relationship between two individuals can be as varied as the individuals themselves. The relationship can be unique, warm, and unexpected on the one hand or predictable, static, and unhelpful on the other.

In the case of Pluto and Charon, two bodies that orbit one another billions of miles away from Earth, their relationship differs from the relationship between Earth and its moon in a key way. Because their masses are more similar to each other, Pluto and Charon rotate around a center of gravity, a barycenter, that is outside the mass of either body. The mutual attraction that governs their relationship is stable and dependent on the influence of each. Although Charon revolves around Pluto, both participate in the push and pull of the relationship that keeps them together (National Aeronautics and Space Administration, 2017). In a similar manner, the vehicle for change in therapy gains its force and energy from the relationship itself, the space

https://doi.org/10.1037/0000343-003
*Common Factors Therapy: A Principle-Based Treatment Framework*, by R. J. Bailey and B. M. Ogles

between the two individuals of the dyad of therapist and client. The center of gravity for a therapeutic relationship resides somewhere between the two bodies and is not centered within one or the other.

In this chapter, we explore the therapeutic relationship as a common factor, a center of gravity if you will, for all effective psychotherapy. We first provide an overview of the conceptual understanding of the therapeutic relationship before describing how it meets inclusion criteria as a common factor. We finish the introductory and conceptual portion of the chapter with our common factors (CF) therapy definition for the therapeutic relationship followed by an outline of ways to enact interventions consistent with the therapeutic relationship as a change principle. Figure 2.1 depicts the key features of our organizational framework for covering the therapeutic relationship as a CF principle with associated interventions.

In many ways, the therapeutic relationship is the guidepost for all successful therapy. From the first conversations with the client, even on the phone prior to the first appointment, the therapist is professional, kind, polite, and

**FIGURE 2.1. Common Factors (CF) Therapy Model With Therapeutic Relationship Interventions**

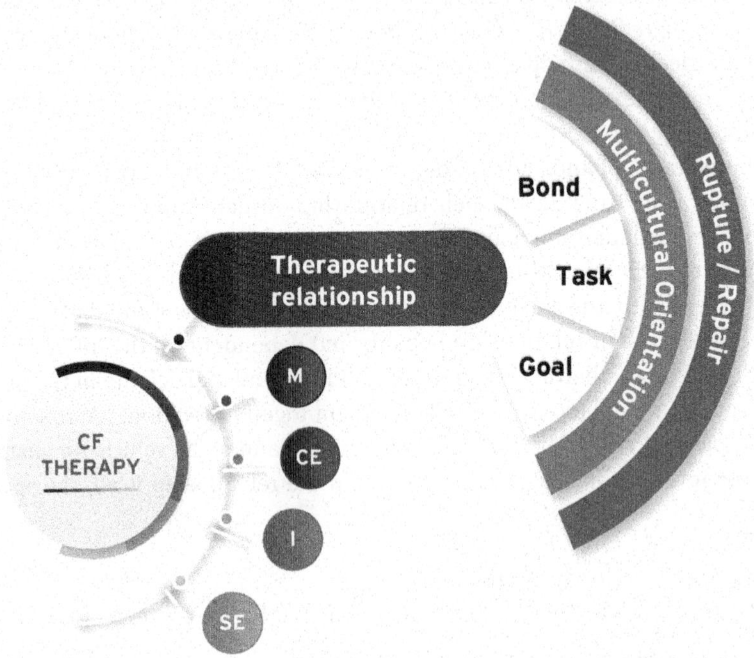

*Note.* M = motivation; CE = corrective experiencing; I = insight; SE = self-efficacy.

understanding so as to establish a relationship of trust, warmth, and confidence (bond; see Figure 2.1). Early sessions are often an opportunity for the client to learn how therapy works (task) and to establish goals for successful treatment (goal). In the context of a trusting and open working relationship with the therapist, clients can explore sensitive topics in an atmosphere of acceptance and confidentiality—what Frank referred to as the "emotionally-charged, confiding relationship" (Frank & Frank, 1991, p. 40). Sometimes the relationship becomes a central component of successful treatment and a therapeutic tool in and of itself, depending on the nature of the client's difficulties. Or, at the very least, the working relationship facilitates change through creating an environment where other avenues of change (e.g., corrective emotional experiencing, insight, and so on, which are covered in the succeeding chapters) can take center stage. So that the therapist can relate to clients in ways that are not undermined by unhealthy systems, a multicultural orientation (MCO) provides a necessary lens within the therapeutic relationship. Sometimes difficulties arise in the relationship. How these ruptures are handled becomes a vital element of successful treatment (rupture/repair). Finally, the end of treatment and the handling of the pending separation and loss of a relationship become a crucial part of therapy's closure. We organize the interventions within this chapter according to each of these elements of the therapeutic relationship with practical directives for CF therapists.

## OVERVIEW OF THE THERAPEUTIC RELATIONSHIP

Virtually every theoretical orientation sees a role for the therapeutic relationship in the effectiveness of psychotherapy. As a result, it was natural for Frank and Frank (1991) to include the "emotionally charged confiding relationship" (p. 40) as one of the key common factors in the contextual model of psychotherapy. Similarly, any discussion of common factors in psychotherapy typically begins with the therapeutic relationship as a central factor common across all theoretical positions (e.g., Lambert, 2013; Norcross & Lambert, 2019a).

Perhaps Carl Rogers (1959) was the first to emphasize the therapeutic relationship in both theory and research. He saw the therapeutic relationship as the essential ingredient for facilitating change in psychotherapy. His description of the necessary and sufficient conditions for change—accurate empathy, unconditional positive regard, and genuineness—strongly influenced current thinking about the relationship between therapist and client and its role in effective psychotherapy, but perhaps more important, also began the scientific exploration of the therapeutic relationship. Although views of the nature and role of the therapeutic relationship differ across orientations, the importance and necessity of a strong working relationship is common to all.

Later therapy researchers in the psychodynamic tradition developed definitions and measurements of the alliance both in general and with a healing perspective. For example, Luborsky (1984) proposed two types of helping alliance: Type I, which surfaced early in treatment as a client's sense that the therapist was supportive and that therapy would be helpful, and Type II, which represented the idea that the therapist and client were partnering or collaborating against a common enemy along with a client belief that the process of therapy would be successful.

For our purposes, the therapeutic relationship is the primary or foundational common factor for effective psychotherapy. It is clearly a core, common element across therapeutic orientations and modalities that facilitates change. The therapeutic relationship serves as both "the foundation upon which treatment is built and a mechanism of change" (Page & Stritzke, 2015, p. 12). Goldfried (2019) included it as the second of five transtheoretical and evidence-based principles of change—"establishing an optimal therapeutic alliance" (p. 488)—which he described using Bordin's conceptualization of the working alliance. Bordin (1979) suggested that the therapeutic relationship consisted of three elements: the therapeutic bond, agreement on therapeutic tasks, and agreement on therapeutic goals that reflects an interaction between therapist and client that is not centered on either individually but must include both.

The therapeutic relationship, as a common factor, is more than a series of steps. The appropriate attitude and interpersonal skills are necessary and can be improved through focusing on key principles. Importantly, two meta-analyses (Del Re et al., 2012, 2021) now also support the finding that "some therapists are better at developing the therapeutic alliance than others and that those therapist's patients tend to have better therapy outcomes" (Del Re et al., 2021, p. 5). Engaging with and forming a therapeutic relationship is critical to a CF approach as it underlies all other change-oriented interventions in successful therapy.

## THE THERAPEUTIC RELATIONSHIP AS A VEHICLE FOR CHANGE

From the perspective of many theoretical orientations along with the empirical research, a good therapy relationship is the foundation upon which change intervention strategies are built. In this respect, a warm, collaborative working relationship with an empathic, humble therapist makes it possible to take part in the activities or interventions that effect change. So, one element of a CF view of the therapeutic relationship is that a high-quality therapeutic relationship facilitates or makes it possible for the client to

- be exposed to and confront fears;

- discuss interpersonal relationships and gain insight about one's patterns of interaction, including emotional and behavioral responses;

- express intense, even traumatic, emotions about past events;

- engage in an emotionally intimate, personal relationship with the therapist that alters expected reactions and anticipated fears in other relationships; and

- create a safe space where the client can receive feedback about their thoughts, feelings, or behaviors.

We address some of these additional ingredients for change in a CF therapy framework in future chapters. Even when change elements such as insight or corrective emotional experiencing are the central avenue for healing, there is a continual monitoring and nurturing of the therapeutic relationship. In this way, the therapeutic relationship becomes the guidepost or weathervane for tracking effective intervention.

Though the therapeutic relationship is not the only CF therapy principle, it forms a basis for all of the others. Using the therapeutic relationship as a principle or guide, a CF therapist can then have the flexibility to apply other interventions. Consider this somewhat lengthy excerpt about the therapeutic relationship from celebrated cognitive therapy researcher Donald Meichenbaum (Fineman & Wiita, 2020) during an interview for the *Very Bad Therapy* podcast:

> The quality and nature of the therapeutic alliance is three to four times more important than any specific therapeutic procedures that we could use. . . .
>
> It's not only establishing and maintaining, but monitoring on a regular basis, the nature of the therapeutic alliance . . . [then] the degree to which you and the patient can agree on the treatment goals and the ways to get there. . . . And then, . . . tailoring the intervention or customize it, to where the client's theory is about what leads them to be there.
>
> So for example, if they don't see they have a problem, then you the therapist should be able to be competent in motivational interviewing, to get people to see that they have a problem, Once they see they have a problem, and you agree on that, then the next thing you have to do is nurture hope, that tomorrow in the future, they're going to be better. So, you're sort of highlighting the core task of what makes someone an effective therapist, establishing, maintaining,

monitoring the therapeutic alliance, and then doing a kind of psychoeducation and collaborative goal setting, and then checking in with them.

Now, where those manuals come into play is that you can ascertain that, in some instances, your clients may be lacking skills: that is, emotion regulation, distress tolerance skills, relapse prevention skills, avoiding victimization. And there are specific techniques or ways in which you, the therapist, being knowledgeable, can call upon in a selective way, and then as the client, as the degree to whether it fits when they're willing to try it, and how often we know it would work.

As you can see from this interview, Meichenbaum's idea is that the therapeutic alliance is the key element of change. The effective therapist establishes and monitors the alliance and then adds elements of empirically supported interventions as needed and permitted by the client in a collaborative process. In this process they agree on the direction and tasks of treatment using interventions required by the circumstance. This sequence of steps represents the essence of a CF therapy based in the therapeutic alliance.

Besides being the foundation of therapy, the therapeutic alliance can also become a healing ingredient of treatment in its own right. For example, establishing a relationship with a shy or introverted client who has extreme difficulties trusting others enough to share even the most basic information about themselves may be the essential healing element. Perhaps this example is simplistic, but it illustrates how the very act of engaging with the therapist enough to share personal thoughts and feelings can be prima facie evidence of progress, and the establishment of a relationship is a sign of behavioral, interpersonal change.

There are more complex examples of the therapeutic relationship serving as an agent of change. Consider a client who has disruptive relationship patterns from past experiences in family life and other relationships—what Luborsky (1984) might call a "core conflictual relationship theme" or Strupp and Binder (1984) might call the "cyclical maladaptive pattern"—that surface in the therapeutic process. This provides an opportunity for the therapist to help the client become aware of the influence of past experiences on their current interpersonal functioning in a safe environment that facilitates a new way of interacting.

Some might suppose that the use of the relationship as an agent of change is limited to interpersonal and psychodynamic therapies, but even early in the cognitive behavior therapy (CBT) literature, Persons (1989) discussed how a case formulation model of CBT could approach the therapeutic relationship by assuming that "the patient's behavior with the therapist is similar to [their] behavior with others and that interactions with both the therapist and with others are driven by the patient's central underlying problem" (p. 161). In this way, problems in the therapeutic relationship are viewed in the same way as any other problems the patient brings to therapy, and similar CBT strategies are used to help resolve them. As a result, the relationship becomes both a "route to understanding" and a "tool for change" (Persons, 1989, pp. 164–165). This type of change in the relationship, whether conceptualized more like a dysfunctional relationship pattern or a CBT presenting problem, moves in the direction of corrective experiencing, which we elaborate upon in Chapter 4 of this book.

## INCLUSION CRITERIA FOR THE THERAPEUTIC RELATIONSHIP

To be included in CF therapy, the therapeutic relationship as a change principle must meet our criteria for inclusion and exclusion as detailed in Chapter 1. We highlight some of the key evidence for including the therapeutic relationship in the next section.

### Research Evidence in Support of the Therapeutic Relationship

The therapeutic relationship or alliance is such a well-known, core ingredient for effective therapy that reviewing the empirical evidence for its role hardly seems warranted. Still, we provide a brief and general summary of the relationship between the therapeutic alliance and outcome. Recent work on the therapeutic alliance focuses on more narrow questions with subpopulations (e.g., therapeutic relationships with diverse clients), specific diagnoses (e.g., the role of the alliance in treatment for different disorders), various therapeutic orientations (e.g., impact of alliance on outcome within differing therapeutic orientations), or more nuanced questions (e.g., which comes first, symptom change or a positive therapeutic relationship?). We will not dip into this expansive literature.

The therapeutic relationship has been found to be a reliable predictor of therapy outcome in hundreds of studies and multiple meta-analyses (e.g., Flückiger et al., 2018; Horvath et al., 2011; Martin et al., 2000). Indeed, Crits-Christoph, Connolly Gibbons, and Mukherjee (2013) concluded that "in the past three decades, research findings have repeatedly demonstrated the therapeutic relationship as perhaps the most important common factor component to the therapeutic process" (p. 301). In the most recent of these meta-analyses, Flückiger et al. (2018) concluded,

> Based on over 300 studies, the positive relation of the alliance and outcome remains across assessor perspectives, alliance and outcome measures, treatment approaches, patient (intake-) characteristics, face-to-face and Internet-mediated therapies, and countries. (p. 360)

Past studies suggest that the client's point of view of the therapeutic relationship is most correlated with outcome (Horvath et al., 2011). However, the Flückiger et al. (2018) meta-analysis found similar relationships between outcome and alliance across raters of the relationship (therapist, observers, others, clients). Still, the client is typically the most accessible source of rating in clinical settings. As such we recommend relying primarily on client ratings of therapeutic alliance in clinical practice. Clients who report having a satisfactory bond with their therapist along with agreement on tasks and goals are more likely to benefit from treatment. Disruptions in the bond, tasks, or goals of treatment lead to a higher possibility of dropout and poorer outcomes. For a comprehensive review of the research evidence in support of the therapeutic relationship generally and with specific aspects in mind, please see *Psychotherapy Relationships That Work*, edited by Norcross and Lambert (2019b).

### The Therapeutic Relationship Is Conceptually Present in Most Therapies

As has been mentioned, the therapeutic relationship is present at a fundamental, theoretical level across theoretical orientations and has ready application in all therapies. Historically, psychodynamic and humanistic therapies emphasized the relationship in particular. For example, Langs (1981) indicated that one of the goals of the first hour in psychoanalytic psychotherapy is to establish the therapeutic alliance:

> Everything that the therapist does in this first session conveys [the therapist's] concern, competence, and interest in helping the patient. In this way [the therapist] offers the patient a therapeutic alliance, a partnership designed to resolve [the client's] emotional problems. (p. 81)

In Greenson's (1967) text on the practice of psychoanalysis, he suggested that providing an "analytic situation that will maximize the various transference reactions" and the "giving of insight by means of interpretation" is "not sufficient for producing lasting changes in the client" (pp. 190–191). From his point of view, a third factor, the working alliance—"the reasonable and purposeful part of the feelings the patient has for the analyst" (p. 192)—deserves to "be considered a full and equal partner" (p. 191). As has been mentioned, Carl Rogers (1959) centered the therapeutic relationship as the essential ingredient for facilitating change in psychotherapy. Empathy, unconditional positive regard, and genuineness are elements that many therapists emulate today.

Although they generally don't see the relationship as a central mechanism for change, cognitive behavior therapists recognize the beneficial and facilitating aspects of a warm, trusting therapeutic relationship. For example, A. T. Beck et al.'s (1979) manual describing CBT for depression includes a chapter on the therapeutic relationship in which therapist warmth, empathy, and genuineness are described as necessary general characteristics of the therapist. In addition, they address aspects of the relationship, including trust, rapport, and collaboration. Finally, they discuss therapist assumptions about the client and address negative interactions in a section about transference and countertransference. Other CBT books written for specific populations (people with anxiety, personality disorders, substance use disorders, and challenging problems) all provide similar descriptions of the importance or necessity of the therapeutic relationship as a foundation for implementing CBT interventions (A. T. Beck, 2005; A. T. Beck et al., 1993, 2005; A. T. Beck & Freeman, 1990).

## EXCLUSION CRITERIA FOR THE THERAPEUTIC RELATIONSHIP

In Chapter 1, we suggest three potential reasons to exclude a factor from CF therapy: (a) there is a lack of evidence connecting the factor to therapy outcome, (b) the factor is exclusive to a single therapeutic orientation, or (c) the factor is redundant to another factor. We have demonstrated in our inclusion criteria that the therapeutic relationship is positively associated with client outcome based on a mountain of empirical research. Similarly, the therapeutic relationship is not the sole province of any single theoretical orientation (i.e., no single school of thought has exclusive claim to the therapeutic relationship). Finally, regarding potential redundancy with other change principles, we use the term *therapeutic relationship* as an umbrella term inclusive of several key ideas: therapeutic alliance, working alliance, therapeutic bond, real relationship, alliance rupture and repair, and transference and countertransference. Historical uses of these terms can highlight nuances and shades of difference between them. However, using the transtheoretical term *relationship* conveys the umbrella term with the parsimony we are seeking in a CF therapy model.

## DEFINITION OF THE THERAPEUTIC RELATIONSHIP

An American Psychological Association task force on the therapeutic relationship used a concise and theoretically neutral definition from Gelso and Carter (1994) that we used as our starting point for a definition: "The *therapeutic relationship* is the feelings and attitudes that therapist and client have toward one another and the manner in which these are expressed" (Norcross & Lambert, 2019a, p. 3). Acknowledging "feelings and attitudes" reflects a central aspect of the relationship (i.e., that it highlights the "relating" aspect and that it is a relationship in which the persons focus on a particular attitude). However, the manner in which these are expressed seemed to us less actionable by the therapist, making it more difficult for a therapist to apply specific actions and interventions when addressing the relationship.

Bordin (1979) made significant effort toward a conceptual, CF-style integration by proposing a fusion of ideas that generalized the psychodynamic concept of working alliance. He noted three features that are important: "an agreement on goals, an assignment of task or a series of tasks, and the development of bonds" (p. 253). These elements represent the feelings and attitudes from our initial definition (*bond* in Bordin's parlance) as well as a focus for action (*task* and *goal* in Bordin's focusing the relationship for intervention that will be helpful to the client). Each of these three represent key elements of the therapeutic relationship that we address separately.

The task force noted that there was difficulty in capturing and describing all of the relational behaviors that mattered. They then offered a helpful metaphor to reflect the challenge in defining the therapeutic relationship: "In our deliberations, several members of the steering committee advanced a favorite analogy: the therapy relationship is like a diamond—a diamond composed of multiple, interconnected facets. The diamond is a complex and multidimensional entity" (Norcross & Lambert, 2019a, p. 4). The multifaceted nature of the therapeutic relationship is especially evident when one tries to define it, in that there are key pieces that would seem to be applicable and yet are not captured in *working alliance* or other past definitions of the therapeutic relationship. We found two key aspects of the alliance that are critical and may represent facets of the diamond, viewed best from an alternative angle. Rather than using the diamond, we present them as lenses through which the therapist can view the bond, task, and goal elements from Bordin's key elements (see Figure 2.1).

The first facet or lens is MCO. As has been shown by Owen et al. (2011), this orientation is not a specific treatment orientation but "a 'way of being' with the client, guided primarily by therapists' philosophy or values about the salience of cultural factors (e.g., racial/ethnic identity, client's cultural background) in the lives of therapists as well as clients" (p. 274). With this lens in place, a therapist can practice cultural humility to acknowledge that individual culturally or systemically based differences may impact the bond of the therapeutic relationship. The lens can inform the therapist as they work to address agreement on the goal of therapy, as differing cultural values lead to different goals. For example, a therapist may be accustomed to helping a client express emotion more actively (see Chapter 4, this volume, on corrective experiencing), but when culturally informed, they would take care to adjust their approach with a client who identifies with a culture that values being circumspect in the expression of emotions. The multicultural lens can also inform how a therapist and client collaborate and agree on the tasks of therapy—for example, acknowledging and adjusting for cultural differences in how people seek and offer help and how people view authority figures.

The second facet or lens is the potential for the therapeutic relationship to rupture, which requires therapists to address these concerns and work with their clients to repair any rupture. Safran and Muran (2000) laid the essential groundwork for understanding ruptures, though we also address other formulations later. They distinguished between withdrawal and confrontation ruptures and outlined principles for repair. As ruptures can influence the bond, task, and/or goal elements of the relationship, the potential for rupture requires ongoing monitoring by the therapist. They may use process feedback measures or frequent check-ins to address this with their clients, and for this reason, rupture/repair represents our second lens for the therapeutic relationship.

Finally, we wished to address an aspect of the therapeutic relationship that can be easily overlooked. As it is a special helping relationship, we tend to focus on the factors that help to begin or establish such a relationship. We may neglect, however, that the therapeutic relationship is designed to end. As Yalom (2000) wisely wrote, "My task as a therapist (not unlike that of a parent) is to make myself obsolete" (p. 234). Relationships such as this need to be ultimately empowering of clients in their lives, moving toward ending as therapy helps them to address the goals set during treatment. This would be consistent with the CF therapy theory of pathology: that demoralization is the primary target, and the desirable outcome is remoralization.

On the basis of the key elements we have described, we have arrived at the following CF therapy definition of the *therapeutic relationship*.

## COMMON FACTORS DEFINITION OF THE THERAPEUTIC RELATIONSHIP

A therapist relates to their client empathically to form a discernible bond and an attitude of working together on tasks to move toward agreed-upon goals that help the client remoralize. Therapists view this relationship through the humility of a multicultural lens and attend to potential ruptures with intention to repair.

## INTERVENTION CONCEPTS FOR THE THERAPEUTIC RELATIONSHIP

Translating the CF metatheory to specific interventions requires not merely that the therapeutic relationship be a change principle but that it be translated into specific, actionable interventions for use by CF therapists. As with the other change principles (motivation, corrective experiencing, insight, and self-efficacy), this intervention approach emphasizes attention to the change principle, as this is the lens of CF therapy. The CF therapist seeks to employ specific interventions to evoke this change principle with their client. In this section, we give an overview of therapeutic relationship interventions, followed by outlines of specific interventions to evoke this change principle with a client. The broad categories of therapeutic relationship interventions are bond, task, and goal, with these then seen through the lenses of MCO and rupture/repair. We also offer deliberate practice (DP) exercises for the aspiring CF therapist to hone their skills with the interventions.

### Bond

**PRINCIPLE 2.1**

Therapists orient to the client in order to work on a therapeutic bond by taking a stance of empathy, compassion, and acceptance, with the aims of understanding and of helping the client feel understood and supported in a true partnership.

We delineate approaches to conceptualize the initiation and maintenance of the bond in a therapeutic relationship (see Table 2.1 for a summary). The common focus of these differing perspectives centers on the mindset and attitudes of the therapist that allow the client to develop a warm, close, trusting relationship: the therapeutic bond. There are other descriptions of the key therapist characteristics and attitudes that help form the therapeutic relationship using different terms (e.g., those covered in separate chapters in Norcross and Lambert, 2019a, on empathy, positive regard and affirmation, congruence/genuineness, and so on), but we use Bordin's framework here. Bordin (1979) described the therapeutic bond as the element of the working alliance that reflects "the nature of the human relationship between therapist and patient" (p. 254). It consists of a basic level of trust that

**TABLE 2.1. Example Bond/Partnership Interventions**

| Intervention | Approaches | Resources |
|---|---|---|
| Reflective listening; empathy; acceptance; affirmations; summary statements | Client-centered therapy | Rogers (1975), "Empathic: An Unappreciated Way of Being" |
| | Counseling training | Hill (2020), *Helping Skills: Facilitating Exploration, Insight, and Action* (5th ed.) |
| | Motivational interviewing | W. R. Miller & Rollnick (2013), *Motivational Interviewing: Helping People Change* (3rd ed.) |
| | Common factors therapy | Chapter 4 (this volume), Reflective listening |
| Open-ended questions | Counseling training | Hill (2020), *Helping Skills: Facilitating Exploration, Insight, and Action* (5th ed.) |
| | | Chow (2018), *The First Kiss: Undoing the Intake Model and Igniting the First Sessions in Psychotherapy* |

blossoms into a deeper level of trust and attachment when "directed toward the more protected recesses of inner experience" (p. 254). In addition to trust and attachment, the bond in a therapy relationship also contains an element of accountability or personal responsibility. A therapy relationship, whether explicitly or implicitly, includes "a strong element of taking responsibility" (p. 255).

**Empathy and Acceptance**

Therapists from the very outset of interacting with a client take on a stance that orients toward the client with empathy. According to Rogers (1957/1992), the therapist adopts a facilitative attitude that includes the necessary and sufficient conditions for change: accurate empathy, unconditional positive regard, and genuineness. Empathy means trying to understand the client's inner, emotional world and to check to ensure whether one's understanding is accurate.

Although this attitude is paramount (according to Rogers, uniquely so), therapists can learn and improve skills to help them convey this attitude. As Hill (2020) wrote, "Skills are used to express a facilitative attitude, and a facilitative attitude is needed to express the skills well" (p. 97). Skills include reflective listening and open-ended questions, which help both to establish a bond and, for the therapist, to simultaneously explore and assess the client's concerns. We also highlight how motivational interviewing (MI; W. R. Miller & Rollnick, 2013) comprises a neat packaging of many of these principles and skills.

Empathy is an important feature of acceptance that has been the subject of many studies. Elliott et al. (2018) provided the most recent comprehensive meta-analysis on the subject. They found that the relationship between empathy and outcome over 80 studies and more than 6,000 clients was significant ($r = .28$). This finding was similar to earlier studies and points to the enduring relevance of therapist empathy. Training in empathy skills started with Rogers many years ago and evolved into microcounseling skills training. Current MI skills training, which we discuss later in this chapter, is an offshoot of these offerings. The current DP movement frequently includes opportunities for therapists to practice empathy (see, for example, the Sentio University website at https://sentio.org).

Consistent with Rogerian ideas and MI, the therapist cultivates an attitude of acceptance. The therapist accepts the client as they are without reservation. This is more than listening. The therapist believes that the client has the strength and ability to work through this partnership and determine the best path forward. According to Carl Rogers (1957/1992, 1959), this includes seeing a client's inherent absolute worth and potential, having accurate empathy to see their perspective, honoring their autonomy, and affirming their personal strengths and efforts. As stated in MI resources, the therapist "manifests acceptance of people as they are, which ironically frees them to change" (Steinberg & Miller, 2015, p. 13).

Empathy and acceptance are highly consistent with an attitude of compassion. Therapists cannot feign compassion and do their best to genuinely be themselves throughout their time with clients. From the perspective of W. R. Miller and Rollnick (2013), compassion is placing, promoting, and giving priority to the client's needs and welfare. The therapist is not in the relationship for their own personal gain and does not use the relationship in a manipulative or coercive way for their own benefit or to seek their own success or glory. The therapist puts the client's needs and goals first and acts in a way that facilitates their growth. As a result, therapists are helping the client to articulate their own desires, wants, needs, and reasons for change. The bond of the therapeutic relationship—consistent with Rogers and the spirit of MI—provides an atmosphere within which they can consider their motivations, and the evoking skills provide a way for them to hear and articulate their own vision for the future. We evoke, elicit, or activate their motivations for change (see Chapter 3, this volume, on motivation).

**Partnership**

Another element of the bond that extends beyond empathy and acceptance is the notion of partnership or collaboration between therapist and client. For example, J. S. Beck (2005) discussed several strategies for building the therapeutic alliance among which is actively collaborating with the client. Similarly, Weiner and Bornstein (2009) in their book on psychodynamic practice suggested that effective therapy is dependent on, among other characteristics, "whether the match between the patient and therapist facilitates their being able to collaborate in forming a strong working alliance" (p. 38). D. A. Langer et al. (2015) highlighted the importance of shared decision making and strategies for doing so. Partnership is also one of four key elements that W. R. Miller and Rollnick (2013) called the "four habits of the heart" (p. 15). Partnership by their estimation involves the therapist and client working together, as partners, to resolve the client's challenges. The therapist provides a relationship and structure to help guide the client's self-discovery in a collaborative, open, and inclusive way. Whereas the therapist is an expert about change, the client is an expert about themselves—their values, needs, emotions, thoughts, and aspirations. The therapist approaches the client in an attitude of profound respect. In a way, the practitioner is a privileged witness to change, and the conversation is a bit like "sitting together on a sofa while the person pages through a life photo album" (W. R. Miller & Rollnick, 2013, p. 16).

One challenge for many therapists involves the impulse to correct, instruct, or direct a client to change their behavior. W. R. Miller and Rollnick (2013) labeled this impulse the "righting reflex." Righting refers to the idea of righting a ship—restoring it to an upright position. Reflex suggests a spontaneous reaction or impulse. Taken together in therapy, the righting reflex refers to the urge to fix, repair, correct, counsel, advise, or lecture a client and implies that we somehow have all the answers or that we can simply motivate the client to change through sharing our expert wisdom. Although it is true that information or advice can at times be useful, in general, directing, lecturing, or counseling clients is more likely to be unhelpful. Prescriptive advice can undermine the change process and may even harden the client's position against change (W. R. Miller, 1983). Individuals who participate in finding the solutions and motivation to change within themselves are more likely to follow through with their commitments than are individuals for whom change is prescribed by someone else (W. R. Miller & Rollnick, 2002; Ryan & Deci, 2017, 2019).

Taken together, the ideas from this section combine to form a coherent picture of therapist therapy-related attitudes that facilitate the establishment of an effective therapeutic relationship and increase the probability of engaging the client. These features focus on the person of the therapist—their personal attitude and attributes, even before they enter the room, that contribute to relationship building. The humble therapist who is willing to learn from their client and work in partnership with them is open to conversations and opportunities to explore client values, goals, and needs and to accept their differences and respect their autonomy. The therapist sees the client as an equal who brings strengths, talents, and personal expertise to the relationship and is willing to prioritize the client's welfare over selfish needs. A therapist who is comfortable in their own skin can manage their own anxieties when having difficult or uncomfortable conversations and recognizes that clients have within themselves the strengths that are needed to change. This collection of features helps engage the client in a process that is emotionally charged, confidential, and potentially healing.

Importantly, empathy, acceptance, and partnership must be combined with basic attending and talking skills, or what are sometimes called microcounseling skills (see Hill, 2020). Many variations on therapist verbal response modes are available in the literature. We present a few core skills here while recognizing that many other options are available (e.g., Hill, 2020). In some ways, focusing on a few skills may be preferable to a longer list of potential therapist communication options both because they are easily understood and remembered and because studies suggest that intervening in a way that is consistent with these skills combined with the previously described attitudes independently contributes to client change (W. R. Miller & Rose, 2009).

### Reflective Listening

As Hill (2004) stated, "Reflection of feelings is probably the most important skill in the helper's repertoire. If beginning helpers could learn and use only one skill, reflection of feelings would be the one" (pp. 143–144). This intervention is closely related to Rogers's (1957/1992) idea of empathy, the focus of which is not merely reflecting feelings (Rogers disliked the term) but also checking whether one's understanding of the client's inner, emotional world is accurate (Rogers preferred terms such as *testing understandings* or *checking perceptions*; Rogers, 1986, as cited in Thorne, 1992, p. 51). The hope is not only for the therapist to understand the client's felt emotional experience but also for the client to feel from the therapist's communication that they are understood by the therapist. Accordingly, reflective listening interventions are questions and can be best offered tentatively, with wonder as to whether the therapist is accurately depicting the client's experience. The therapist's intentions here are to help the client openly express feelings and consequently deepen and explore feelings.

Methods for reflecting feelings can be conceptually straightforward (see Hill, 2020) but more challenging in practice, as doing so requires active attention and empathy by the therapist. In a simple reflection, the therapist repeats back to the client the basic content that the client just shared. In a complex reflection, the therapist communicates back (reflects) the meaning or emotion that was communicated by the client. In this way, the client begins to hear what the therapist understood from their statements. This is where the heart of accurate empathy exists: in a well-formed reflection. Reflections sometimes include interpretations of thoughts or emotions or connections between client reports. These complex reflections can move beyond attentive, reflective listening and potentially into the domain of other related common factor change agents (e.g., corrective experiencing or insight). The therapist attempts to be present with the felt meaning the client is communicating.

Hill (2004) recommended simple formatting for reflections, such as "You feel ____" or "You feel ____ because ____," and possibly adjusting the format over the course of a session with different forms of the same, such as "I wonder if you're feeling ____" or "You seem ____" (p. 151). Intonation is key here, with the therapist using a gentle tone and ending the reflective statement with a questioning inflection, as if to express "You feel ____, is that right?" When it is done gently and effectively, clients often respond to reflective listening by deepening their expression, including emoting. This can be very validating for the client, and clients often report this as helpful. Client disclosure, followed by therapist reflection of feeling, followed by more client disclosure and exploration, promotes corrective experiencing by the client. As seen in the insight chapter (Chapter 5, this volume), these moments of emotional experiencing can then be followed up with a cognitive loop or a step back to less emotional and more matter-of-fact discussion and solidifying of what the client experienced.

We have included a DP guide for learning and improving one's practice of reflective listening as a therapeutic strategy (see Table 2.2). In the early stage of therapy, we are focused on engaging to establish the therapeutic relationship, and the therapist's reflection is a way for the therapist to communicate that they are listening attentively, that they are concerned about the client's welfare, and that they hear and understand their concerns. As W. R. Miller and Rollnick (2013) suggested, because a reflection is a guess about the meaning of the client's statement, the therapist uses this strategy to communicate effort to not simply parrot back the client's statement but to consider it, weigh it, and provide an estimation of its meaning. A complex reflection that provides a guess also can lead to further grist for the mill through additional elaboration, exploration, and dialogue as the client and therapist work together to form a shared understanding.

**TABLE 2.2. Deliberate Practice Suggestions for Reflective Listening**

| Method | Descriptions |
|---|---|
| Video-assisted observation of your work | • Watch a video recording of one of your sessions, observing the client's verbal and nonverbal communication and practicing how you might respond to them.<br><br>– Practice saying out loud, "You feel ____," and supplying the emotion the client is expressing verbally and/or nonverbally.<br><br>– Practice pausing the video to give more time for you to pause and consider more fully what the client is feeling. Describe the felt meaning in detail, even if you would share only part of this with the client. Then practice abbreviating the reflection into fewer words. A reflection can be as brief as a single word, stated with warmth and inflection questioning whether it represents the client's felt experience.<br><br>– Practice reflections that help focus the client on important content. For example, it will be more helpful to the client to reflect what the client is feeling rather than reflecting a client's statement about what someone else (parent, partner, friend, etc.) is feeling. A reflection that helps the client focus on their treatment goal will be more helpful than one that focuses on a tangential story. Avoidance or resistance can also be included in a reflection to great effect, such as reflecting a client's sense of irritation or feeling stuck.<br><br>• Listen to your reflections, seeing how the client responds to them. Notice when the client goes deeper, contradicts your statement, or shuts down. Be careful to notice which reflections create any sense of expectation of the client on your part, and try to rework your reflections, avoiding "should"s or other expectations.<br><br>• As you practice reflective listening, notice your own emotional reactions. Pay particular attention to whether certain emotional presentations from your client leave you in discomfort or that leave you wanting to shy away.<br><br>• Identify key moments to share with a consultant, trying to identify and move through any defensiveness you may feel about sharing this. |
| Getting consultant feedback[a] | • Determine whether your relationship with your consultant is sufficiently supportive and safe for soliciting feedback openly. Consider working through defensive reactions with your consultant.<br><br>• Practice reflections with the consultant coaching you on what you may have missed from the client's expression or what could help the therapy move forward.<br><br>• Notice your own emotional reactions to particular client emotional content and request assistance in addressing them. If needed, work through them with a personal therapist. |

**TABLE 2.2. Deliberate Practice Suggestions for Reflective Listening (*Continued*)**

| Method | Descriptions |
|---|---|
| Setting small incremental goals | • Perhaps with a consultant's help, notice reflections that are at the boundary of your comfort level. For example, if anger is a difficult client presentation to respond to, pay attention to your comfort level during a role play with varying levels of anger expressed (your role-play partner could vary the intensity of anger through higher or lower volume, more or less expressive body language, or profanity). Find the level that is neither too easy (comfortable response) nor too difficult (overwhelmed response), and repeat. Set a goal on how to practice this on your own. |
| Solo deliberate practice | • Dedicate sufficient time to practice on your own. <br> • Use the session video or audio recordings of emotional client presentations or role plays to practice responding reflectively. <br> • Notice how comfortable/uncomfortable the practice is and adjust the practice as needed. |
| Feedback-informed treatment | • Use outcome measures at each session to determine how the client is progressing in treatment. If clients are signaling on outcome measures as not on track for a positive outcome, bring the feedback to the session to facilitate a discussion on what's working or not working. Be ready to reflect empathically on what the client is experiencing, including feelings of frustration or being stuck. Focus on wanting to understand what the client is experiencing, especially an increase in client distress. <br> • Use process measures to discuss what is happening in therapy: for example, "Looking at your survey results, I'm wondering about whether I'm really understanding what you're experiencing. Can we discuss what I don't understand yet about your experience?" <br> • Practice saying these interventions out loud, adjusting your language with the invitation as needed. |

[a]We use the word "consultant" in this and other deliberate practice tables for brevity. We mean this to refer to mentors, supervisors, trainers, colleagues, or other experts as appropriate to the skill being practiced.

## Open-Ended Questions

Open-ended questions represent a basic counseling skill that allows the client to tell their story. Closed-ended questions can be answered with yes, no, or very brief information and may be necessary sometimes. However, the client benefits from the act of telling their story, as they can feel more bonded to the therapist, can feel understood, and can thus engage in corrective experiencing (see Chapter 4). Therapists may feel they need to pepper the client with questions, as the insurance or clinical site may require the therapist to have certain information in hand at the end of a first visit. Open-ended questions can help a therapist still assess but build a relationship at the same time. Chow (2018) recommended using questions in order to listen rather than merely in order to question. This approach represents part of Chow's engagement model for the early sessions of therapy, with the focus on using questions as a way to relate to clients and help them engage right away. Having an accurate understanding of what the client is experiencing can be helpful for building a bond, for assessing the client's concerns, and for helping the client to feel understood by the therapist.

Open-ended questions are the invitation a therapist offers the client to provide information, explore thoughts and feelings, and engage in a give-and-take process that deepens understanding. Closed questions inadvertently stifle equal give-and-take and may even shut down engagement. Open-ended questions allow the client to choose the direction, amount, and content of their self-revelations. An open-ended question followed by attentive listening also communicates therapist interest in and concern for the client's point of view. The combination of good questions and an attitude of empathy, warmth, and engaged listening create the possibility of a thriving therapeutic relationship.

Although open-ended questions can be helpful in this way, too many questions may inadvertently result in the client assuming therapy is like a medical diagnostic and prescription process. That is, the client may believe that the expert therapist will ask enough questions to gather all the information necessary to formulate a diagnosis and then spout out a prescription that can solve the client's problems. Early in therapy it is important to both overtly and implicitly help the client to understand that therapy involves a process of self-exploration where the client often takes the lead.

Some common questions early in therapy that are often used to begin the therapeutic process and initiate the therapeutic relationship include the following: "What brings you to therapy?," "How may I help you today?," "What are you hoping to accomplish through this counseling relationship?," and "It sounds like you have been considering counseling for some time; what happened that you decided to enter treatment now?" Of course, there are many other, and perhaps better, possibilities for open-ended questions in treatment—you will be able to identify those that best suit your style. The key idea is to open the door for elaboration and exploration and to listen well to commence the therapeutic relationship. Table 2.3 lists suggested methods to monitor and improve delivery of open-ended questions using DP principles.

**TABLE 2.3. Deliberate Practice Suggestions for Open-Ended Questions**

| Method | Descriptions |
|---|---|
| Video-assisted observation of your work | • Watch an intake or early session, paying attention to the following moments:<br><br>  – Notice your inner experience while watching, describing out loud the emotions you notice while listening to your client and yourself.<br><br>  – Pause at each moment you speak. Notice if you are asking a question. What are the possible answers to the question?<br><br>  – Notice what information you may be missing at the moment in the session and how you could ask "how" questions or "tell me more about ____" questions to encourage open expression from the client. Do not restrict questions to the ever-present and often-parodied therapist question, "How does that make you feel?"<br><br>  – Pause at moments when the client offers one-word or very brief statements. Rewind to see what you said or asked just before, seeing if you can make it an open-ended question instead.<br><br>• Identify key moments to share with a consultant, trying to identify and move through any defensiveness you may feel about sharing this. |
| Getting consultant feedback | • Determine whether your relationship with your consultant is sufficiently supportive and safe for soliciting feedback openly. Consider working through defensive reactions with your consultant.<br><br>• Watch the session with your consultant, highlighting the questions you ask.<br><br>• Request assistance with open-ended questions in particular. Consider brainstorming possible questions to use in key moments of the session. |
| Setting small incremental goals | • Perhaps with your consultant's help, identify your current comfort level and competence with asking open-ended questions. Then, identify a behavior to practice on your own that stretches you just beyond this comfort level. Try to ensure that your practice is neither too overwhelming nor too easy. Be as specific as possible when describing what you are going to practice. |
| Solo deliberate practice | • Dedicate sufficient time to practice on your own.<br><br>• Use the session video to practice finding moments to ask open-ended questions and then speak them out loud.<br><br>• Notice how comfortable/uncomfortable the practice is and adjust the practice as needed. |
| Feedback-informed treatment | • Use outcome measures at each session to determine how the client is progressing in treatment. Open-ended questions can be very helpful to a discussion of client progress: for example, "How are things going as we work together?" or "I'm noticing that your scores are showing an increase in distress; can you tell me more how things are going for you?" |

## Affirmations

Having an optimistic attitude and recognizing client strengths is another important communication skill that helps to engage the client early in treatment and validates their participation later in treatment. The ability to recognize and affirm client traits is a technique that will strengthen the therapeutic relationship and help the client to engage in the treatment process. In other writing about MI (Ogles et al., 2021), we have considered several potential areas for affirmation when working with clients:

- Highlight and compliment client's positive attributes—their strengths: "You have a great deal of patience and courage."

- Notice and comment about the client's abilities: "Your ability to face adversity is inspiring."

- Express appreciation for the client: "Thank you for being willing to discuss our relationship. It is very helpful."

- Acknowledge action on the client's part: "Thanks for completing the homework. I can see you are making progress. That must be so satisfying."

In all cases, affirmations help communicate the helper's positive regard for the client while emphasizing their attention to and observation of client strengths.

## Summary Statements

Like its sister, the reflection, a summary statement is an opportunity for the therapist to communicate to the client what they have heard and understood over a time in the interview. For example, a therapist may stop the client to catch up and make sure they are hearing correctly using a summary such as "Let me see if I'm capturing the essence of your message," then provide key details of what they heard over the past minutes. Whereas a reflection typically refers to the most recent proximal statement, a summary may reach back over several minutes, over an entire therapy session, or even over the breadth of treatment. A summary is often an invitation to stop and reflect to review a time period and search for shared meaning about the connections over time. Summary statements can serve as collectors gathering a series of ideas or facts over time, such as "As I understand it, there are four main reasons why you came in to therapy at this point in your life. [The therapist then briefly summarizes the four key points.]"

Summary statements may also serve as connectors by pointing out the interweaving and interlocking ideas, emotions, and behaviors of multiple statements or events—for example, "As we look at the relationship struggles you have been talking about today, there seem to be some common themes emerging related to your sense that each person is critical of your success."

A summary statement by a therapist also communicates a very basic message about the therapist: They engaged in attentive listening over a sustained duration that they are now reviewing with the client to check understanding. Here is an example: "What seems very clear is that your repeated attempts to gain attention and affection from your partner almost always lead to disappointment through ignoring, absence, or rejection."

## Goal

**PRINCIPLE 2.2**

Therapists work to understand their client's desires for change, conceptualize their client's demoralization, and facilitate conversation about the goals they will work on together to address to bring about remoralization.

A Norwegian proverb, sometimes decoratively painted on a shoehorn, states, "Den vet best hvor skoen trykker, som har den på" (roughly translated, "The person wearing the shoe knows best where it hurts"). In fact, "it is the client who knows what hurts, what directions to go, what problems are crucial, what experiences have been deeply buried" (Rogers, 1961, p. 11). Bordin (1979) referred to this element of the working alliance through two ideas: agreement on the tasks of treatment and agreement on the goals of treatment. Following the client's lead to work toward mutually agreed goals in therapy can be essential, even as the therapist works to understand how best to be helpful to the client and plan treatment. Goal consensus has been shown in meta-analysis to be associated with outcome, with medium-sized effects (Tryon et al., 2019). Here, we address how therapists can work with clients to establish goals for treatment (see also Table 2.4).

Sometimes the focus of therapy is obvious, say when a client enters treatment with a very specific goal in mind. For example, a client once entered treatment with one of us (BMO) several years after having been involved in a serious car accident. The client had a long physical and emotional recovery period and had not driven a car since the accident. Fortunately, their work circumstances permitted them to continue making a living even without driving because they lived close to and could walk to work. In the months prior to entering treatment, however, they had been promoted to a new job

**TABLE 2.4. Example Goal Interventions**

| Intervention | Approaches | Resources |
|---|---|---|
| Problem list | Cognitive behavior therapy | Persons (1989), *Cognitive Therapy in Practice: A Case Formulation Approach* |
| Case conceptualization | Integration model | Sperry & Sperry (2012), *Case Conceptualization: Mastering This Competency With Ease and Confidence* |
| Workability | Acceptance and commitment therapy (ACT) | Harris (2013), *Getting Unstuck in ACT: A Clinician's Guide to Overcoming Common Obstacles in Acceptance and Commitment Therapy* |

that would require them to do some modest regional travel, and they were entering treatment with a very specific goal: to overcome their fears and be able to drive again so they could function in this new work role. In this case, the agreement on goals was evident from the first few minutes of the therapy. In the early sessions, agreement on the treatment tasks or path (which primarily involved graded exposure) to that goal was negotiated.

In other cases, the client may have multiple potential starting points, and the therapist and client work together to identify the primary goal and the path forward. The goals may shift over time as the client and therapist collaborate on the best current focus. In some ways, this is like a multiple-choice exam in which the therapist and client choose together from among the potential alternatives the order and priority for therapeutic work.

Finally, in some cases the client is uncertain or unclear about their preferences or the needed direction. They may be unintentionally vague about their purpose for entering treatment and are hopeful that the therapist can help them to clarify the origins of their distress. These cases involve more exploration, collaboration, and consultation as the client and therapist gradually feel their way forward (W. R. Miller & Rollnick, 2013).

Regardless of the client's goal clarity upon entering treatment, the collaborative process for settling on the goals of treatment is beneficial to outcome (Tryon et al., 2019) and is important for client continuation in therapy (e.g., Lingiardi et al., 2005). In general, agreement on goals is more important to clients than to therapists, and because goal consensus is related to outcome, Tryon et al. (2019) recommended that therapists "need to be trained to collaborate with patients to discuss treatment goals and the ways they will work to achieve them" (p. 195).

In many treatment settings, government or insurance regulations require a treatment plan that is developed by the therapist in consultation with, and signed by, the client. This provides an opportunity to specifically identify target problems, client strengths, and treatment goals. Often these forms also provide opportunities to document steps to achieve the goals, which may involve multimodal or combined therapies such as medication or case management in addition to individual therapy. Goal attainment scaling was also developed many years ago as a way for the client and therapist to jointly determine and measure progress toward individualized goals. These and other strategies may help the therapist as they begin establishing collaborative goals with the client in early sessions.

Persons (1989) recommended using a problem list to prioritize targets for clinical intervention as an overall case formulation approach to treatment. This approach includes, but does not rely exclusively on, diagnosis to set goals for treatment. The process needs to be collaborative, working with the client to determine the priorities for treatment. In this way, the goals inform the tasks and can be brought up at each session to check whether the therapeutic relationship continues to be helpful for the client.

Demoralization may represent a useful concept for engaging in conceptualization for planning treatment. Case conceptualization represents "a method and clinical strategy for obtaining and organizing information about a client, understanding and explaining the client's situation and maladaptive patterns, guiding and focusing treatment, anticipating challenges and roadblocks, and preparing for successful termination" (Sperry & Sperry, 2012, p. 4; see their book or Eells, 2022, for a complete treatment of an integrative approach to case conceptualization). With demoralization as the target for CF therapy, we repeat our definition of *pathology* from Chapter 1: Psychological, social, behavioral, emotional, cognitive, and biological factors combine to create disruptions in a person's life and associated demoralization. As a therapist gains understanding of the client's distress, they may consider how different factors fit together to contribute to said distress. From a CF therapy perspective, a therapist need not be tightly wedded to one theoretical orientation but instead may consider explanations from a variety of perspectives. These topics are treated in other chapters in this book, but in short the therapist can ask themselves what factors (psychological, social, behavioral, emotional, cognitive, and/or biological) impinge on the client to contribute to demoralization. The therapist can then build on client motivation and the therapeutic relationship through a focus on insight or corrective experiencing.

As the CF therapist listens and deepens their understanding of the client's demoralization, they may ask the client about their priorities for therapy. The client and therapist work together in a negotiation of these goals. On the therapist's side, they must consider whether the requested goal is workable for the client and whether they are competent to help them move in the direction of the goal. As is emphasized in acceptance and commitment therapy, they may see the client's goal as an avoidance (movement away) goal rather than a movement toward (see Polk & Schoendorff, 2014). Therapists can help the client by negotiating toward a workable goal (see Harris, 2013). For the therapist to agree to work toward a goal that they feel unable to assist with can be disingenuous and contraindicated based on ethical principles of competence and informed consent. However, the therapist needs to be sure that they have correctly understood the client's desires, respect the client's autonomy, and strive to work through possible conflicts (see the Ruptures/Repair section of this chapter).

Finally, agreement on therapy goals also has significant implications for what will constitute the end of therapy. As a client reaches their stated goals, therapy can move toward termination. The therapist and client can revisit and reconfigure therapy goals, of course. However, the therapeutic relationship is not intended to replace long-term relationships in the client's life. As treatment goals are met, the client moves toward self-efficacy and remoralization.

Through interrogating demoralization for the purposes of case conceptualization, collaboratively discussing goals with clients, and ensuring the workability of the treatment goals, CF therapists can help their clients move toward remoralization.

## Task

**PRINCIPLE 2.3**

Therapists facilitate client engagement by clarifying how therapist and client work together and focusing their in-session attention on agreed-upon content that will lead to change.

In this section, we describe approaches for attending to tasks in the therapeutic relationship (see Table 2.5 for a summary). As a therapist establishes a human relationship with the client, a relationship of trust and attachment, the therapist is simultaneously working on determining the direction and goals of treatment. Lack of agreement on tasks and goals may result in a meandering therapy reminiscent of Alice in Wonderland:

> "Would you tell me, please, which way I ought to go from here?" [Alice said.]
> "That depends a good deal on where you want to get to," said the Cat.
> "I don't much care where——" said Alice.

**TABLE 2.5. Example Task Interventions**

| Intervention | Approaches | Resources |
|---|---|---|
| Focusing | Client-centered therapy<br>Motivational interviewing | W. R. Miller & Rollnick (2013), *Motivational Interviewing: Helping People Change* (3rd ed.) |
| Agenda-setting | Interpersonal therapy | Weissman et al. (2017), *The Guide to Interpersonal Psychotherapy: Updated and Expanded Edition* |
| | Cognitive behavior therapy | J. S. Beck (2021), *Cognitive Behavior Therapy: Basics and Beyond* (3rd ed.) |

"Then it doesn't much matter which way you go," said the Cat.
"—— so long as I get *somewhere*," Alice added as an explanation.
"Oh, you're sure to do that," said the Cat, "if only you walk long enough."
(Carroll, 1865/2020)

As a result, either explicitly or implicitly the therapist and client jointly determine both direction and a strategy to get there. The focus can evolve from a conversation between therapist and client and may be suggested by the client, the context, or the therapist. Similarly, the style for engaging with the focus may be more directive, collaborative, or nondirective depending on the circumstance and the therapist style (W. R. Miller & Rollnick, 2013). There is much flexibility about direction and method within a CF approach.

In more structured therapeutic approaches, the direction or focus of therapy is typically explicitly discussed and agreed upon in the early parts of therapy. Indeed, the therapist may even work closely with the client to outline an agenda for each session (e.g., J. S. Beck, 2011). In her book, J. S. Beck (2011) outlined a typical agenda, including a brief update on events of the week, followed by a mood check-in, then a bridge from the previous session. In some therapeutic orientations, the tasks of therapy are learned more implicitly through the therapeutic encounter, and to some extent, the ambiguous nature of the work in therapy serves as a form of projective assessment that provides important information to the therapist about the client's emotional, behavioral, and thinking style.

Another example of agreement on task comes from Klerman et al.'s (1984) manualized interpersonal psychotherapy of depression (IPT). They suggested that early in treatment as the depression diagnosis is evident and the appropriateness of IPT is confirmed, the therapist devote attention to establishing the treatment contract, including dealing with depressive symptoms, and identifying focal problem areas. The explanation of the contract includes several potential steps including reviewing depressive symptoms and giving the syndrome a name, explaining both depression and treatment for depression, and giving the patient the sick role along with evaluating the potential need for medication. Importantly for IPT, the therapist then relates the symptoms to the interpersonal context by relating the client's relationships to symptoms. This step includes identifying major relationship problem areas followed by outlining, and obtaining client agreement on, the interpersonal treatment goals and IPT procedures. Klerman et al. provided a variety of examples of brief explanations the therapist might provide during the initial sessions, but we provide only an example here that outlines the tasks of treatment. In that vein, the therapist might say something like the following excerpts to help clarify the roles of the client and therapist in treatment:

- "We will try to understand what stresses and relationships in your life may be contributing to depression." (p. 92)

- "I'd like to meet with you once a week for twelve to sixteen more times for about an hour each time, to try to understand with you the stresses in your life and how they relate to your depression." (p. 93)

- "From what you tell me your depression began with recent . . . [insert the relational problem area]. I'd like to discuss with you the critical areas you seem to describe as related to your depression. . . . [Insert more problem areas as needed]. Do these sound like the issues we should discuss?" (p. 93)

- "Now that we have some sense of where we are going, I think I should tell you how we will proceed. Your task will be to talk about the things that concern you, particularly the things that affect you emotionally. We have already identified specific areas where there is room for change, and we have agreed upon certain specific goals. Naturally, we will be discussing material relevant to these issues. However, as we work together, other important issues may emerge—and you should feel free to raise them. I will be interested not only in what happened but, even more important, in your *feelings* about these events. It will be your responsibility to select the topics which are most important to you. After all, it is you who are most in touch with the way you are feeling and the relationships that seem to present problems for you. There is no 'right' or 'wrong' thing to talk about, as long as it concerns you—is something that you have strong feelings about. This includes feelings about me, our relationship, or the therapy. Sometimes ideas or feelings will come to mind—ideas that don't make much sense to you or seem embarrassing. These are important to bring in and discuss. It is important that you talk about feelings that arise during the session or when you think about it later." (pp. 93–94)

As can be seen, the therapist gives clear context for the focus of the treatment on relationships along with describing the short-term duration, identifying the problem area, and instructing about the client's role in treatment. Note how agreement on goals (the next section in this chapter) informs the agreement on tasks. This early session work helps set the foundation for agreement on the tasks and goals of treatment, which, combined with a strong bond, provide the framework for effective IPT. In the excerpts above, taken from an interpersonal model of treatment, the focus is on relationships and their influence on the client's symptoms of depression, but the point we are making has to do with helping the client to know what is expected of them to achieve shared goals. In CF therapy, the therapist is engaged in a similar dialogue with the client to establish the goals and tasks of treatment. Those tasks may, like IPT, focus on the connection between symptoms and relationships, but they may also focus on other key change factors that are identified in the other chapters of this book. The guiding principles are that tasks and goals are shared and agreed upon between client and therapist.

CF therapists can check in with their clients around agreement on task by asking open-ended questions regarding how the client experienced the session. For example, they could make an observation such as "We talked a lot today about ____; how does this line up with what you want to work on in therapy?" or "I did a lot of listening today, hoping to understand your situation and make sure you get a chance to express what is going on for you. How did you experience that?" This can facilitate a clarifying discussion of how the client is expecting to be helped and how the therapist hopes to be helpful to their client, with both parties working to bring their respective roles into alignment.

From an MI perspective, the focusing principle (not to be confused with Gendlin's focusing for emotional expression discussed in Chapter 4, this volume) relates to how the conversation of therapy proceeds. W. R. Miller and Rollnick (2013) pointed out that being in conversation is not the same thing as being focused within it. Westra and Aviram (2015) pointed out that beginning therapists can mistakenly believe their role is to reflect everything the client says as though all is of equal importance. Instead, the role of the therapist is to watch for content that can help the therapist know how to direct the conversation and what to reflect and therefore deepen the discussion. On the basis of the agreed-upon goals, the therapist helps to guide the process of the session (the task) in helpful directions. During or at the end of the session, it can be helpful for the therapist to check in with the client regarding the task, as we have described. See our DP guide for task interventions (Table 2.6).

**TABLE 2.6. Deliberate Practice Suggestions for Task Interventions**

| Method | Descriptions |
| --- | --- |
| Video-assisted observation of your work | • Watch an intake or early session, paying attention to<br>  – Your inner experience while watching, describing out loud the emotions you notice while listening to your client and yourself.<br>  – As you watch, notice who is speaking (you or your client) and the content. Notice how much of what is being said relates to (or does not relate to) the client's main reasons for being in therapy.<br>  – Notice whether the client says things about "talking in circles" or expresses verbal or nonverbal signs of impatience or frustration.<br>  – Notice whether the client feels regret at the end of the session for missing some important content, for talking too much, etc.<br>  – Find moments when you could check in with the client about whether you are on the same page for the "how" of the session. Find the best agenda-setting moment at the beginning, for example. Find moments when the session goes off track. Find moments near the end when you could check in about the therapeutic relationship, including agreement on task.<br>• Identify key moments to share with a consultant, trying to identify and move through any defensiveness you may feel about sharing this. |
| Getting consultant feedback | • Determine whether your relationship with your consultant is sufficiently supportive and safe for soliciting feedback openly. Consider working through defensive reactions with your consultant.<br>• Watch the session with your consultant, highlighting moments when you could direct the session to stay on track with what the client hopes to address. Be careful to check with your consultant about whether this represents your desire for content to be addressed versus your client's desire for content to be addressed.<br>• Ask for help to find moments when the session goes off track, especially subtle signs from the client that there is disagreement on how the session is going. |
| Setting small incremental goals | • Perhaps with your consultant's help, identify your current comfort level and competence with addressing agreement on task with your clients. Then, identify a behavior to practice on your own that stretches you just beyond this comfort level. Try to ensure that your practice is neither too overwhelming nor too easy. Be as specific as possible when describing what you are going to practice. |

**TABLE 2.6. Deliberate Practice Suggestions for Task Interventions (*Continued*)**

| Method | Descriptions |
|---|---|
| Solo deliberate practice | • Dedicate sufficient time to practice on your own.<br>• Use the session video to practice finding moments to practice focusing (i.e., directing the conversation through reflections based on key content). Practice saying these reflections or redirections out loud.<br>• Notice how comfortable/uncomfortable the practice is and adjust the practice as needed. |
| Feedback-informed treatment | • Use outcome measures at each session to determine how the client is progressing in treatment. If client progress is off track, ask about whether you are working on the most helpful goals and in the most helpful way to address these goals.<br>• Use process measures so client can respond whether they are in agreement about how the sessions are addressing their treatment goals. Use this feedback to have clarifying conversations with clients around the task or process in therapy. |

## Multicultural Orientation

### PRINCIPLE 2.4

Therapists strive for cultural humility in order to recognize and comfortably address cultural opportunities in therapy, thus improving the treatment environment for the client.

To revisit our earlier metaphor, "the therapy relationship is like a diamond—a diamond composed of multiple, interconnected facets. The diamond is a complex and multidimensional entity" (Norcross & Lambert, 2019a, p. 4). An MCO (Owen, 2013) represents just such a perspective shift that can change one's view on every aspect of the therapeutic relationship—or any aspect of treatment for that matter. Bond, task, and goal can each benefit from a multicultural perspective. Not taking a different perspective on the "diamond" would be like risking not taking a multicultural perspective, which would default to centering a monocultural or dominant perspective (see Sue & Sue, 2008). Learning to work this way requires not only learning but also unlearning beliefs that have held sway in the dominant monoculture (see Lantz et al., 2018).

An orientation in the sense of an MCO refers not to the therapist's dominant theory for therapeutic intervention but rather to "a 'way of being' with the client, guided primarily by therapists' philosophy or values about the salience of cultural factors (e.g., racial/ethnic identity, client's cultural background) in the lives of therapists as well as clients" (Owen et al., 2011). Although the MCO framework was developed specifically to guide therapist interactions with clients having diverse identities, it is easy to see that the spirit of MCO fits with any client because all clients differ in one degree or another from the identity of the therapist. In other words, cultural considerations are always relevant; some even argue they serve as a common factor in and of themselves (Bathje et al., 2022). The humility to learn from, respect, and be attuned to the client is a stance that is helpful in any therapeutic encounter. Respect for autonomy is a hallmark of therapy, and taking an MCO can highlight systemic oppression to assist clients as they seek empowerment.

Empowering a client in the face of disempowering systems is a hallmark of feminist therapy and multicultural approaches to therapy. Social dominance theory represents one way of understanding power as it relates to the individual or a system, that a behavior can be hierarchy-enhancing versus hierarchy-attenuating (see Lantz et al., 2018). Social dominance can be seen in the therapeutic relationship as the therapist notices how cultural dynamics may play out in hierarchical ways. The goal of therapy itself, as well as the tasks and process of the therapist–client interaction, can be culturally bound. In an ongoing process of therapists unlearning dominant monocultural frames for therapy, they can learn an MCO approach to work with clients with cultural humility and competence.

The three pillars of an MCO are cultural humility, cultural opportunities, and cultural comfort. We recommend seeing each of these constructs as a lens through which to see the therapeutic relationship. We also acknowledge that a mere overview of these principles is no substitute for the therapist's ongoing internal work to sincerely engage the content (see Table 2.7).

## Cultural Humility

*Cultural humility* refers to one's ability to maintain an other-oriented interpersonal stance, even under the strain of cultural differences between the

**TABLE 2.7. Example Multicultural Orientation Interventions**

| Intervention | Approaches | Resources |
| --- | --- | --- |
| Cultural humility | Multicultural orientation | Hook et al. (2017), *Cultural Humility: Engaging Diverse Identities in Therapy* <br> https://www.multiculturalorientation.com/ <br> https://sentio.org/mcovideos |
| Counseling perspectives | Multicultural competence | Sue et al. (2019), *Counseling the Culturally Diverse: Theory and Practice* (8th ed.) |

client and counselor (Owen et al., 2011). This often requires both intro-spective and interpersonal work from the therapist to position themselves to act when there are cultural opportunities and to feel at ease when engaged in uncomfortable but culturally relevant conversations. As one experiences discomfort in such interactions, cultural humility suggests that a therapist works to recognize reactions for what they are, undermine the assumptions that undergird their reactions, and remain focused on the client's needs.

An MCO first involves a therapist's ability and willingness to examine their own values, biases, limitations, and strengths. It includes an openness to feedback from peers, supervisors, and especially clients. In fact, Hook et al. (2017) suggested that "the ability to incorporate this information in a non-defensive, open stance is the hallmark of intrapersonal humility" (p. 29). Therapists who are nondefensive and eager to learn will develop greater comfort and will naturally begin to see more opportunities for culturally rel-evant conversations. This type of work is an emotional journey (see Sue & Sue, 2008, p. 17).

The interpersonal aspect of cultural humility overlaps substantially with the MI habits of the heart. It represents an openness to the client, a respect for the client's autonomy and ideals, and a curiosity about their cultural background, beliefs, values, and differences. The interpersonal stance is also one of equality or partnership and not one of arrogance. It is the process or spirit with which the therapist approaches differences in the therapeutic environment. When using a monocultural perspective, a therapist can too easily minimize the experience of the client, delegitimizing their experience. The culturally humble attitude helps to respect the client's autonomy.

When combining the intrapersonal and interpersonal aspects of cultural humility, we find that "culturally humble therapists are able to have an accu-rate perception of their own cultural values as well as maintain an other-oriented perspective that involves respect, lack of superiority, and attunement regarding their own cultural beliefs and values" (Hook et al., 2017, p. 29). Cultural humility then allows a therapist to build the courage needed to notice and take action when cultural opportunities arise.

## Cultural Opportunities

Therapists who can develop cultural humility recognize moments in the therapy where the client's cultural identity, including attitudes, beliefs, and values, can be explored. Unfortunately, many opportunities to explore the client's culture are missed or are not thoroughly explored and integrated into the therapy (Hook et al., 2017). The tendency to take advantage of and not miss cultural opportunities is associated with higher cultural humility and better overall therapy outcomes.

Cultural opportunities occur when the content of the therapy session includes relevance to the client's identity or cultural background. Sometimes the opportunity arises because the client mentions something about their cultural heritage, and at other times, nuances of the process may hint at areas for further discussion and exploration. For example, a client who identifies as Native American and is a student at a predominantly White college may express a sense of social isolation with their peers. The cultural opportunity is present for the therapist to discuss the client's experience of being an Indigenous person in a majority White environment and how this relates to the sense of isolation.

At times, the therapist's cultural comfort may be an obstacle to more open conversation about the client's cultural identity. Therapists with cultural humility notice and respond to opportunities to explore client differences. This provides opportunities to be more other-focused, clarify and deepen the therapeutic bond, and provide care and support (Hook et al., 2017). Therapists working from an MCO perspective can work to expand their repertoire of helping responses based on differences.

Therapists can recognize cultural opportunities early in therapy and often throughout the course of therapy. Addressing an opportunity in an initial session or as early as possible sends a message to the client that culturally relevant content can be openly discussed in therapy. To improve their ability at recognizing opportunities, a therapist could notice ways they differ from their clients. A simple exercise could be for a therapist to list their own demographic descriptors next to the descriptors that the client identifies with, noticing differences where the therapist may be likely to miss cultural opportunities. As recommended by Sue and Sue (2008), a therapist could pay attention to differences in communication styles, both verbal and nonverbal, such as proximity of speakers and kinesics or body language.

In a conference keynote attended by one author (RJB), Dr. Karen Tao (2015) described cultural opportunities as similar to cultural courage. A therapist decides to address the opportunity with a client by speaking up, saying things such as "This sounds important" or "I wonder since I'm different if I'm missing things you say." Noticing the opportunities, then speaking up with humility allows the client to choose to address this or not.

### Cultural Comfort

The third, and final, pillar of the MCO is an emotional comfort with conversations about cultural identity. Cultural comfort may be especially notable for both client and therapist when they are quite different from each other. Therapists who have difficulty developing cultural humility and openness may be uncomfortable having conversations about values, attitudes, and beliefs that are different from their own. As a result, they may avoid certain topics or exude nervousness that influences the therapeutic process (especially client openness).

*Cultural comfort* refers to a degree of emotional security and a sense of calmness. Hook et al. (2017) suggested that "the emotional states of feeling at ease, open, calm, and relaxed are hallmarks of cultural comfort" (p. 37). Therapists who develop cultural humility are not afraid to be wrong or to receive feedback so they are more likely to engage in conversations when they have the opportunity because they can monitor and manage their anxieties within the moment for comfortable conversations with clients about their cultural background and heritage.

Please note that building cultural comfort requires significant effort on the part of the therapist. You may be unaware of how you contribute to rejection of your client, are not inclusive, or blame the client for something that has been brought about by an unjust society rather than individual pathology. Knowledge may help, such as learning identity development models and how oppression features in these models, learning interventions to address specific concerns, and taking time to appreciate cultural differences in one's daily life.

We point out that tensions may exist and that embracing those tensions is highly consistent with the CF therapy model. Many of the interventions and concepts in this book come from a Western tradition and may need to be interrogated, reexamined, and refined to move away from cultural bias as therapists seek to intervene with clients of many backgrounds. To acknowledge that one does not know everything, does not hold an omniscient perspective, seems obvious when it is written out on paper but can be challenging to acknowledge when one expects themselves to be the "expert therapist" face-to-face with a client. As Tao (2015) emphasized, cultural comfort reflects authenticity when discussing cultural identities, including saying, "I know that I don't know and it's okay to talk about it."

MCO reflects an essential lens for the therapeutic relationship, as cultural differences can impact the bond experienced between therapist and client. The goals of therapy can differ from this perspective, as cultural factors impact the explanations and conceptualizations offered to our client. The tasks of therapy can differ, based on different cultural norms for speaking, sharing information, or deference to authority figures. Noticing these differences can be invaluable for effective therapy. Please see https://sentio.org/mcovideos for more practices to improve one's skills related to MCO, as well as Table 2.8 for our outline of DP strategies for practice.

**TABLE 2.8. Deliberate Practice Suggestions for Multicultural Orientation**

| Method | Descriptions |
|---|---|
| Video-assisted observation of your work | • Watch an intake or early session, paying attention to<br><br>– Your inner experience while watching, describing out loud the emotions you notice while listening to your client and yourself. Notice in particular how you feel about addressing cultural opportunities with this client. Is there any discomfort you feel? What biases do you already recognize within yourself that may play out with this client?<br><br>– Watch for culturally relevant content, verbal and nonverbal. Notice the length of each speaking turn, the content that is openly shared versus unacknowledged, the physical proximity that is comfortable for you and the client, and the body language, such as hand motions. Interrogate whether any of these have some cultural relevance.<br><br>– Notice what information you may be missing to understand the client's experience. Cultural humility means acknowledging what you do not know and how you may be limited.<br><br>– Pause at any cultural opportunities you find and practice acknowledging these aloud with a statement or question that will help your client explore or address the opportunity.<br><br>• Identify key moments to share with a consultant, trying to identify and move through any defensiveness you may feel about sharing this. |
| Getting consultant feedback | • Determine whether your relationship with your consultant is sufficiently supportive and safe for soliciting feedback openly. Consider working through defensive reactions with your consultant.<br><br>• Work with your consultant to acknowledge your biases, asking for help to see blind spots you may have.<br><br>• Watch the session with your consultant, highlighting the cultural opportunities you have identified. Your consultant may help identify moments you may have missed. Discuss ways to engage with these opportunities. |
| Setting small incremental goals | • Perhaps with your consultant's help, identify your current comfort level and competence with multicultural orientation. Then, identify a behavior to practice on your own that stretches you just beyond this comfort level. Try to ensure that your practice is neither too overwhelming nor too easy. Be as specific as possible when describing what you are going to practice. |
| Solo deliberate practice | • Dedicate sufficient time to practice on your own.<br><br>• Use the session video to practice noticing your internal experience, approaching this with cultural humility, and engaging with cultural opportunities.<br><br>• Notice whether your cultural comfort is increasing as you do this. Adjust the practice as needed. |

**TABLE 2.8. Deliberate Practice Suggestions for Multicultural Orientation (*Continued*)**

| Method | Descriptions |
| --- | --- |
| Feedback-informed treatment | • Use outcome measures at each session to determine how the client is progressing in treatment. Notice how these assessments may be approached differently by your client based on cultural differences. A discussion of feedback may help with negotiating or renegotiating the goals and tasks of therapy to meet your client's needs. |

## Ruptures/Repair

### PRINCIPLE 2.5

Therapists strive to notice the inevitable miscues or ruptures that arise in the therapeutic relationship and nondefensively work for repairs for the client's benefit.

The therapeutic relationship can falter. Therapists would do well to expect moments of disconnect, when clients and therapists are misaligned on their goals and tasks or when there is interpersonal distancing, tension, or conflict. The potential for ruptures represents another key facet of the "diamond" of the therapeutic relationship (see also Figure 2.1), a lens through which an alternative perspective of the therapeutic relationship can be helpful when working with clients.

Ruptures in the therapeutic relationship can occur with regard to the bond, the task, or the goal. As discussed in the previous section, ruptures can occur due to cultural differences. Davis et al. (2016) pointed out how microaggressions are a subset of alliance ruptures in which clients attribute the offense to an aspect of their identity. Different therapeutic orientations have acknowledged ruptures with or without the use of the term *rupture*, and multiple strategies can be used to address or repair these ruptures. In this section, we review key themes from the literature in more detail.

Safran and Muran (2000) spawned an incredibly productive line of therapy research that examined ruptures in the therapeutic alliance and their repair over a 25-year period. Their notion of an alliance rupture was not a severe breakdown but rather subtle miscues that resulted in a distancing of client and therapist. The literature on ruptures has expanded rapidly and has now generated several conclusions. First, ruptures in the alliance are relatively common. In one study, 37% of clients and 56% of therapists reported a rupture in 6 weeks of treatment. Second, unrepaired ruptures increase the likelihood of client dropout. Third, alliance repair is associated with positive outcome of treatment.

In their book on negotiating the therapeutic alliance, Safran and Muran (2000) discussed two types of ruptures in particular: withdrawal ruptures and confrontation ruptures. In a later publication (Safran et al., 2011), they conceptualized ruptures in the alliance around Bordin's three components of the working alliance "consisting of (1) disagreements about the tasks of therapy, (2) disagreement about the treatment goals, or (3) strains in the patient-therapist bond" (p. 81). More recent work, such as a special issue of the *Journal of Clinical Psychology* (Muran et al., 2021), maintained a similar perspective on these key categories: withdrawal and confrontation in relation to bond, tasks, and goals.

There are two main categories of alliance rupture: withdrawal and confrontation. In some ways the withdrawal rupture is more difficult because the therapist may miss signs of the client stepping back from the relationship or cooperating in treatment even when they have some negative emotion about the bond, tasks, or goals. For example, a client may agree in-session to participate in homework all while silently thinking that the assignment will not be helpful. In the follow-up session, they may simply report that they did not have time to do it when in fact they have concerns about the assignment. Indeed, there may even be a risk that they drop out of treatment related to this disagreement about the tasks of therapy. Markers for withdrawal include signs that the client is moving away from the therapist or moving away from some aspect of themselves (Muran et al., 2021). Importantly, the withdrawal might occur because of issues with the bond, tasks, or goals of therapy, and in some cases the client may withdraw in an effort to preserve the relationship, as in denying their disagreement to preserve the peace. As a result, the first step in alliance rupture–repair is to become aware of the rupture.

Confrontation ruptures are more easily identified because the client is typically overt about their misgivings. These ruptures are identified by signals that the client is moving against the therapist and include such things as criticism, anger, or manipulation. In both the withdrawal ruptures and confrontation ruptures, it is important to remember that a rupture involves client and therapist. As Muran et al. (2021) explained, "They are co-constructed. It takes at least two to rupture" (p. 363). Similarly, the repair takes at least two to resolve the rift.

With recognition of a potential rupture, whether confrontational or withdrawal, the therapist invites the client to join with them and engage in the metacommunicative task of considering the rupture together. This process is like the couples therapy literature where therapists ask couples to consider their patterns of interaction together as if the pattern were external to them (see Jacobson & Christensen's, 1996, discussion of "unified detachment," for example). As the therapist and client step back from the ongoing work, they can observe and discuss the withdrawal or confrontation together and explore the circumstances and emotions that led to the rupture.

The stage process for identification and acknowledgement of the rupture is followed by an invitation by the therapist to curiously explore the rupture in a joint venture with the client. In withdrawal ruptures the process typically involves creating an environment and sufficient separation from the ongoing moment so that the client can express their negative emotions in a more assertive way without fear of damaging the relationship. In confrontation ruptures, the process typically involves exploration such that the client can express disappointment in a more vulnerable way. The exploration process might include the therapist working with the client to clarify, understand, and validate their feelings; renegotiate therapeutic tasks or goals; or explore the rupture experience (Muran et al., 2021, p. 364).

The strategies for repair were identified through intensive task analysis, which resulted in a description of three common pathways for alliance repair (Muran et al., 2021):

- a return to engagement and alliance building through explaining, clarifying, or motivating the client to participate in the tasks and goals of therapy while exploring any misunderstandings and validating the client's emotions concerning treatment;

- directly adjusting the tasks or goals in collaboration with the client based on their withdrawal (or feedback) through the exploration process; and

- an expressive process for exploring the rupture using the processes identified in the previous paragraph.

As can be seen, therapist attitudes and characteristics, such as empathy, humility, and compassion, are as important in the rupture repair process as they are for initial engagement in therapy.

Alliance ruptures cannot be repaired if they are not identified, acknowledged, and explored with the client. Therapists need to be attuned to events in the therapy that may indicate alliance ruptures such as withdrawal, criticism, avoidance, defensiveness, or discord. An early signal may be emotions that the therapist experiences that can indicate a change or shift in the relationship between client and therapist. Regularly providing the client opportunities to report on the experience of therapy is another way the therapist can monitor the state of the relationship. Finally, noting in-session or between-session events and following up with curious queries provides an opportunity for the therapist to receive feedback from the client about their experience of the relationship.

According to the Safran and Muran (2000) perspective, one potential avenue for recognizing alliance ruptures is related to therapist self-awareness and ability to tune in to their emotions and reactions so that they recognize the mutual influence that client and therapist have on one another and the emotional experiences that may help the therapist understand the current relationship.

From a CBT perspective (note that ruptures are not limited to more relationally oriented forms of therapy), Burns (1999) first discussed the importance of empathy for successful therapy and described a variety of circumstances that can lead to a "failure of empathy" (p. 639), such as being late for a session, charging for a missed visit, a comment that comes across as sarcastic, an intervention that comes across as not being genuine, problem solving too quickly without adequately hearing their concerns, or other events in the therapy process that lead the client to feel as if the therapist were not listening or that "rubbed them the wrong way" (p. 639). Burns recommended that when a rupture in the alliance is recognized or identified that the therapist first break from the CBT agenda and address the relationship by inviting a conversation and exploration of the difference. He, too, like Safran and Muran (2000), suggested that clients are often reluctant to express their feelings, so it is important to provide opportunities for them to disclose differences and to monitor the sessions for any signs of problems in the relationship.

From an MI perspective, W. R. Miller and Rollnick (2013) suggested that the therapist should "tune [their] ear to hear signals of dissonance and recognize them as important" (p. 204). They defined *discord* as "signals of disharmony in your collaborative relationship" (p. 204) and used the metaphor of smoke alarms to help therapists attend to and recognize potential discord in the relationship. They described several signs of discord including clients defending themselves, squaring off, interrupting, or disengaging and reminded the therapist to be mindful of the cultural nature of signals, which may significantly vary across clients.

As we discussed in the Bond section, the therapist's attitudes, therapeutic stance, and way of being in therapy are crucial for setting the foundation to an environment where therapeutic ruptures can be explored. If the therapist is defensive and caught up in their own emotions, it is difficult for them to create a therapeutic milieu that allows for safe exploration of the client's thoughts and feelings about therapy and the therapist. As a result, therapists can work on their self-care and personal improvement as a way of maintaining their humility, patience, and curiosity such that their personal stance in therapy sets the tone for explorations of the relationship.

When appropriate, therapists should acknowledge their role in alliance ruptures and apologize when they have contributed to client disengagement or defensiveness through their own missteps. Even when we do our very best to engage and facilitate change, events inside or outside of therapy can be disruptive to our working relationship with the client. A therapist might have a bad day that affects their ability to be attentive to the client's words. An emergency might result in the therapist arriving late to a session with a client who perceives the delay as a signal of therapist disdain for them. The heavy load of clients may result in the therapist forgetting details about the client from session to session, which weakens the client's sense of trust when they are required to repeat the information. An intervention may not go as planned or a client may not like or complete assigned homework, leading to tension in the session. Any number of actual or imagined slights might influence the quality of the therapeutic alliance and threaten the effectiveness of treatment. In these situations, the therapist's ability to respond to and repair alliance ruptures is key to maintaining the relationship and continuing the work of therapy. In all these situations, the therapist's ability to return to the original characteristics and attitudes required for engaging in therapy is essential. Perhaps the key ingredient is humility—an ability to learn from the client, apologize when necessary, reconnect, and move forward. Muran et al. (2021) discussed several therapist attitudes that facilitate rupture repairs, including humility, compassion, curiosity, and patience.

One way that Burns (1999) recommended to stay attuned to potential lack of empathy is to regularly ask clients for positive and negative feedback. He suggested asking, "I'd like to hear your positive and negative feelings about the therapy so far. Let's start with the negatives first" (p. 639). In this way, the client gets used to the idea of thinking about the therapy and expressing their feelings on a routine basis. If the client seems reluctant or hesitant to express negative feelings, Burns suggested following up and creating a more open dialogue that permits discussion of the concerns. He also suggested administering an empathy questionnaire after each session to assess in a more standardized and less interpersonally direct way if the client has concerns.

From an MI perspective, W. R. Miller and Rollnick (2013) also noted that discord can occur as a result of the therapist's contribution to the process. A therapist who is tired or stressed may not listen as well as usual. In truth, when the therapist gets caught up in their own internal thoughts and feelings, they probably aren't listening well. Discord can arise in any of the four processes of MI: engaging, focusing, evoking, and planning. Difficulties in engaging and focusing seem to be very similar to the notions of rupture in bond (engaging) or agreement on tasks and goals (focusing). Discord in evoking and planning seems similar to Burns's notion of failure of technique when the therapist pushes forward despite the client's lack of motivation or disagreement on the pathway forward.

Empathic exploration of the client's reactions in therapy provides an opportunity for them to express concerns that might otherwise remain under the surface. As therapists provide regular opportunities for feedback and monitor subtle changes in the relationship followed by querying regarding the client's experience, ruptures can be identified and thoroughly explored. The essential element of rupture repair is a collaborative stepping back from the therapeutic process to engage in metacommunication about the relationship (a unified detachment). This exploration provides an opportunity to reengage, renegotiate expectations, or disrupt expected interpersonal patterns.

According to Burns (1999), in addition to failures in empathy, the other path to difficulties in the relationship involves technical failures: a need to negotiate goals or develop a collaborative agenda (what Bordin, 1979, might call agreement on goals), a need to settle on a strategy for resolving problems (what Bordin might call agreement on tasks), or low client motivation. Burns provided some ideas for reestablishing rapport that are based in either technique or relationship.

The key ingredient from the therapist's perspective is empathy with the client's emotional response and a focus on reducing the client's anger, dissatisfaction, or withdrawal by validating their feelings (or criticism), responding with empathy (using accurate reflections), and taking at least partial responsibility for the disruption in the relationship. Burns (1999) suggested three specific techniques: (a) disarming through finding some truth in the client's reaction, (b) empathy through paraphrasing and trying to understand their concerns (both thoughts and feelings), or (c) inquiry through using gentle questions to understand and validate their concerns. Importantly, Burns suggested practicing this pattern repeatedly through reviewing client interactions after the sessions by recording the original responses, developing alternative responses (with feedback from colleagues when possible), and then trying again in future sessions. Role playing difficult situations is also a path for learning skills to deal with therapy interruptions.

MI strategies for responding to discord also sound and look similar to our previous descriptions: The key element is empathic listening with the reflection as the therapist core communicative skill for expressing understanding and demonstrating that they are attentive to the client's concerns.

W. R. Miller and Rollnick (2013) also suggested that the therapists learn to apologize when they have "stepped on someone's toes" (p. 209). They continued, "This costs you nothing and immediately acknowledges that this is a collaborative relationship" (p. 209). Other techniques for responding to discord include respectfully affirming the client's perspective or shifting away from the sore spot that resulted in pushback rather than focusing on it and potentially fanning the flame.

Although discord may be unpleasant for the therapist, responding to it is important for successful treatment. As a result, W. R. Miller and Rollnick (2013) suggested that the therapist treat discord as an opportunity. As clients respond with disengagement or defensiveness, they are probably repeating a response to the possibility of change from earlier in their lives and expect (consciously or unconsciously) the therapist to repeat an expected role in that exchange. If the therapist can alter the script and respond with empathy, understanding, and exploration, the client's pattern can be disrupted and altered, paving the way for reengagement and change.

The path to repairing the rupture varies by the client's presentation, the nature of the relationship, and other factors, but the principles that govern appropriate exploration typically include some form of client expression, therapist empathic understanding, therapist humility and acknowledgement of a role in the dyadic relationship, and efforts to renew the bond, tasks, and goals of therapy.

To respond flexibly and nondefensively, therapists do better when they use facilitative interpersonal skills (FIS; Anderson et al., 2020). This body of research literature from Anderson and colleagues is highly applicable to alliance ruptures. Anderson developed a method of assessing therapist FIS by using difficult situations drawn from therapy in the Vanderbilt II study (Strupp, 1993). The situations were specifically selected because they represented various alliance rupture scenarios. Indeed, some of the situations were very similar to situations presented by Burns (1999). With actors playing the roles of the clients, the eight situations were presented to the therapists, and the therapists recorded their verbal responses to the situation. Therapist responses were then rated by trained judges on several dimensions (verbal fluency, emotional expression, persuasiveness, warmth/positive regard, hopefulness, empathy, alliance bond capacity, and alliance rupture–repair responsiveness) that were combined to create an index of FIS.

Anderson and his colleagues (Anderson, Crowley, et al., 2016; Anderson, McClintock, et al., 2016; Anderson et al., 2009) have found in both retrospective and prospective studies that therapists with higher FIS have better client outcomes. This finding led to additional studies in which FIS are practiced using modeling and video simulations, with the focus of the training on developing warmth and empathy. Although the training did not include any didactic component or even an explanation of the modeled skills, the presentation of good and poor examples of responses to rupture events provided sufficient information for the therapists to improve their responses to subsequent client video presentations (Anderson et al., 2020).

As we have shown, recognizing ruptures requires awareness and humility. Recognizing and repairing ruptures can lead to therapeutic benefits for the client. Therapists can practice recognizing and repairing ruptures in many ways; see https://sentio.org/dpprompts for several DP examples. Please see also our suggestions for DP to address ruptures and repair in Table 2.9.

**TABLE 2.9. Deliberate Practice Suggestions for Ruptures and Repair Interventions**

| Method | Descriptions |
| --- | --- |
| Video-assisted observation of your work | • Watch a video of a session, paying attention to the following moments: <br>   – Identify your client's verbal and nonverbal signals of withdrawal. These may be especially subtle and require close attention. <br>   – Identify your client's verbal and nonverbal signals of confrontation. Watch for moments when the client may challenge the content of your statements or express irritation. <br>   – Check in regarding bond, task, and goal with this client. Is your alignment with your client strong in each area? Check in with multicultural orientation. How is your understanding of your relationship altered from this perspective? <br>   – Notice your own internal reactions. Notice defensiveness arising, often the signal for irritation or annoyance. Try to work through your own defensiveness, acknowledging the thwarted expectations that may be at their root. <br>   – Identify moments that may be especially challenging due to the intensity of conflict, such as expressions of anger by you or by the client. Notice your internal reactions to these moments with curiosity. <br> • Identify key moments to share with a consultant, trying to identify and move through any defensiveness you may feel about sharing this with your consultant. |
| Getting consultant feedback | • Determine whether your relationship with your consultant is sufficiently supportive and safe for soliciting feedback openly. Consider working through defensive reactions with your consultant. <br> • Show your consultant the moments in the session that seem to be ruptures and practice responding with more humility and flexibility. Discuss how these moments could be of therapeutic benefit to your client. |

TABLE 2.9. Deliberate Practice Suggestions for Ruptures and Repair Interventions (*Continued*)

| Method | Descriptions |
|---|---|
| | • Role play or practice addressing moments of more intense conflict with your consultant.<br>• Watch the session with your consultant, seeing whether your consultant notices the same rupture moments that you did. |
| Setting small incremental goals | • Perhaps with your consultant's help, identify your current comfort level and competence with noticing ruptures and responding with repairs. Then, identify a behavior to practice on your own that stretches you just beyond this comfort level. Try to ensure that your practice is neither too overwhelming nor too easy. Be as specific as possible when describing what you are going to practice. |
| Solo deliberate practice | • Dedicate sufficient time to practice on your own.<br>• Use the session video to practice noticing ruptures based on your own observations and your consultant's feedback. Practice responding out loud to each rupture.<br>• Notice your comfort level as you do this. Adjust the practice as needed. |
| Feedback-informed treatment | • Use outcome measures at each session to determine how the client is progressing in treatment. A client's signaling as "not on track" can be a particularly important moment to address the therapeutic relationship and whether there is alignment on bond, task, and goal. A discussion of feedback may help with negotiating or renegotiating the goals and tasks of therapy to meet your client's needs. |

## ENDING THERAPY

Unlike with other areas of practice discussed in this chapter, not much empirically based research is available to guide a discussion of the therapeutic alliance at the end of treatment (Bhatia & Gelso, 2017). Because a good therapeutic relationship facilitates client engagement, prevents attrition, and leads to better outcomes, most of the literature focuses on developing the relationship early in treatment, using the relationship as an agent of change, or maintaining the relationship after inevitable miscues. The ending of that relationship is important and relevant even with less empirical data at our disposal. Indeed, Weiner and Bornstein (2009) suggested that the "final phase of psychotherapy is exceeded only by the initial phase in its importance for determining the degree to which treatment has a positive and lasting impact" (p. 277).

The end of therapy is especially of theoretical and practical importance in psychodynamic and interpersonal therapies where the relationship loss associated with the end of therapy is considered in detail by some writers (e.g., Strupp & Binder, 1984). Late therapy from other perspectives takes on a more practical point of view by focusing on solidifying treatment gains, attributing progress to the client, anticipating future challenges, and reviewing tools learned through participation in therapy (e.g., J. S. Beck, 2011). As Rotter (1954) wrote, "It is the purpose of therapy not to solve all of the patient's problems, but rather to increase the patient's ability to solve [their] own problems" (p. 342). Of course, many of the preparations for treatment's end begin early in therapy and continue throughout the treatment. For example, by agreeing on treatment goals, the therapist and client are already collaborating on the terms for treatment ending. As the therapy progresses, the therapist and client can review that progress together and discuss the reasons for the progress (attributions to client), the tools that have been learned (now lifelong aids for living), and any setbacks (setting realistic expectations for change both during therapy and after therapy).

The ideal end for treatment might proceed like this:

1. The client and therapist collaboratively identify treatment goals early in treatment.

2. Throughout treatment, the client and therapist periodically review progress toward treatment goals and adjust the goals as needed.

3. The therapist also conducts the therapy in a way that facilitates progress maintenance through helping the client to identify the knowledge and skills they have accumulated and to help them properly attribute treatment gains to their growth.

4. As the client approaches a point of satisfactory resolution of issues or goal accomplishment, raised first by the client or the therapist, they consider and discuss ending treatment along with contemplating posttherapy continued growth and ways to handle any challenges or setbacks.

5. As needed, the therapist may begin to stagger sessions or plan periodic booster sessions to help review and remember knowledge and skills and to address concerns that arise.

Of course, therapy often ends in other ways. Indeed, the modal number of therapy sessions is one. As a result, many therapists see clients one session, and they simply do not come back for a second session. Although they might benefit from additional sessions, there are a variety of reasons why a client may unilaterally decide that they will not return for a second session, such as practical problems with the schedule, transportation, or finances; feeling they accomplished what they needed to in the first session; the therapy or therapist did not meet their expectations; deciding they didn't want to participate; poor match with the therapist or a bad experience in the session; or attending the session only because of external pressure. Similarly, after a few sessions or more, clients may simply decide not to return without any further communication for any of these reasons or for other reasons. As a result, it is important for therapists to be taking advantage of helpful moments along the way and anticipating potential termination at unexpected times.

When therapy does proceed through all phases of therapy, the termination process can be approached from a collaborative point of view. For example, Goode et al. (2017) described a collaborative approach to termination that begins with establishing termination expectations in the initial sessions. They suggested that this collaborative process begins by having the client share their expectations and preferences followed by the therapist sharing their knowledge and experience, after which they come to a joint decision. An important part of the process involves therapist empathic listening and helping the client to have realistic expectations for treatment. Periodically throughout treatment, the client and therapist revisit the expectations, including the review of routine outcome measurement, which may lead to additional discussion about the client's progress.

The strategies for termination in the final session are facilitated by good preparation initially and throughout therapy. Collaboration in the final session according to Goode et al. (2017) involves several strategies:

- Help the client take ownership for gains and recognize their role in change (and that it can continue beyond therapy).

- Review what was helpful (or not) during treatment from both client and therapist perspective; this may include the therapist sharing mistakes they made as an equalizing measure.

- Develop a plan for client future growth including responding to setbacks, defining success, and considering the possibility of future sessions as needed.

- Close with a final goodbye by having the client and therapist discuss the personal impact that the therapy had on each of them and by processing the feelings associated with ending therapy.

As the therapist and client collaborate on the ending of therapy, they can discuss both the feelings of accomplishment that accompany successfully achieving desired goals and the feelings of sadness at the ending of the therapeutic relationship. A collaborative approach that facilitates the client transformation and separation can consolidate gains and prepare the client for the inevitable challenges that they are likely to encounter in the future. The relationship loss can be very much like the simultaneous taste of sweet and sour, bittersweet chocolate, or salty caramel where the combination produces an ultimately pleasurable and satisfying experience.

## SUMMARY

In this chapter, we have focused on the central common factor in successful psychotherapy: the therapeutic relationship. The therapeutic relationship has been repeatedly demonstrated to be correlated with the outcomes of therapy across therapeutic orientations, and therapists who are more effective at forming therapeutic relationships have better outcomes. We framed our discussion of the relationship on the transtheoretical formulation of Bordin (1979), which includes the bond, agreement on tasks, and agreement on goals. Engaging the client early in treatment involves establishing that bond and implicitly or explicitly establishing the work and focus of therapy, including the goals and negotiation of tasks or processes. This alliance then forms a foundation for incorporating other mechanisms of change as described in the following chapters, or, in some cases, the relationship becomes an instrument of change in and of itself. MCO forms an essential lens to view the therapeutic relationship with cultural humility. Importantly, miscues and misinterpretations or other circumstances may, rather frequently, disrupt the therapeutic relationship at times. The therapist's ability to heal or repair these ruptures is critical to the success of both the relationship and ultimately therapy. Finally, a collaborative approach to ending treatment helps to maintain and sustain treatment gains while bringing the relationship to a satisfactory closure.

For CF therapy, the change principle of the therapeutic relationship is the lens that guides decisions. As CF therapists consider their relating with their client, they may consider the main ideas from this chapter along with the specific interventions and suggestions. Bond, task, and goal form the initial focus, with an MCO and attention to ruptures and repair as key facets of the relationship to consider.

# 3

## MOTIVATION, COMMON FACTOR 2

If you have ever set an ambitious goal and tried to keep it, you are familiar with the complexity of human motivation and getting ourselves to make desired changes. Humans, across the epochs of time and through daily challenges, have adapted by solving problems. We solve problems by making changes in our lives, with various and sundry reasons for making those changes. When we lack compelling reasons, we are less likely to make difficult changes and may default to easier, more convenient solutions. Without intending to, sometimes the solutions interfere and end up causing more problems and requiring more adaptations and solutions. Problems in our lives often reflect our attempts at solutions gone awry. It can be overly simplistic to suggest that just because a person wants to make a change in their lives, the solution is always simple and requires only effort and willpower. This is illustrated by the well-worn joke, "How many psychologists does it take to change a light bulb? Just one, but the light bulb must want to change." In fact, change is more difficult than simply wanting. Sometimes a change is hard to make because of internal or external obstacles. Due to complex motivations, a stated desire to change may not be carried out in reality. A decision to change may not actually result in making a change.

https://doi.org/10.1037/0000343-004
*Common Factors Therapy: A Principle-Based Treatment Framework*, by R. J. Bailey and B. M. Ogles

This can be easily seen when we think of the things that we really, truly want in our lives, and yet we find it difficult to take the necessary steps to pursue them. I want to run a marathon, but I also want to enjoy my early morning sleep, and my body tells me that shorter runs would be preferred. I want a healthier romantic relationship, but I also want to enjoy my personal preferences that irritate my romantic partner. I want to work hard, but I also want to enjoy leisure (for example, while I am attempting to write this chapter, distractions beckon and sometimes the writing is neglected. Alas).

Our motivations for any behavior can be complex, and reducing them to a single idea can be misleading. Consider the last film or show you watched and whether any of the characters did something that was surprising or unpredictable. In the film *Good Will Hunting*, the protagonist Will Hunting has interviews for prestigious jobs but is intentionally rude and absurd with interviewers, even sending his best friend to the interview in his place (to comedic effect). In addition to tanking the interviews, Will sabotages what appears to be a meaningful romantic relationship. Will's academic mentor (and the audience) is baffled by his behavior. As his therapy progresses over the course of the movie, Will's motivations become clearer. Both his reluctance to be vulnerable and his distrust of others making decisions for him become understandable, and to the viewer, his behaviors make much more sense. In fact, by his actions Will is showing what is important to him, namely, self-protection and autonomy. He needs to be his own person, secure in his decisions based on his own emotional needs. We humans have complex motivations, even if our behaviors do not initially make sense to those around us.

It can be overly simplistic and even insulting to suggest that a client is not making changes because they do not want to change. You may be familiar with a comedy sketch by Bob Newhart in which he plays a therapist whose only therapeutic approach is to tell his client, "Stop it!" Granted, it is comedy, but if this were to occur in real life, it would be insulting and ineffectual. If only it were so easy to make radical life changes!

Not only do we want to change, but often we are unaware of how our attempted solutions may be inadvertently contributing to our challenges. Our motives for our behaviors may be implicit, not totally unknown to us but needing the process of dialogue for the motives to be made fully explicit. Psychological theories have a long history of highlighting such factors, whether as unconscious drives, a reinforcement history, self-actualization, or other explanations. Often these implicit factors represent barriers to making change.

Clients would not seek out therapy or continue to participate in therapy without some expectation of help from the therapist to see how to change. And yet, often the changes clients need to make require discomfort and effort that they would rather not endure. In order to endure the discomfort of such change, they may need to marshal personal resources, courage, or intestinal fortitude. They, and we when we want to change, need to be able to see why change is needed and important. This is where therapy can be especially helpful. Therapy can be a vehicle for exploring not only the whats and hows of change, but also the whys, the reasons that feel compelling enough to help clients move toward change.

In this chapter, we consider the work of the therapist that enhances motivation and creates the conditions in which change can occur. We first provide an overview of motivation as a common factor with its conceptual underpinnings, followed by reviewing the research and theoretical evidence for motivation as a common factor. Before moving on to practical common factors (CF) interventions, we provide a CF definition of motivation that evolves out of our theoretical discussion. Our CF definition then leads into a description of interventions for enhancing motivation divided into three broad categories: attuning to expectations, evoking change talk, and planning change (see Figure 3.1).

Motivation and the therapeutic relationship of Chapter 2 (this volume) represent the foundational common factors for interventions that come later.

**FIGURE 3.1. Common Factors (CF) Therapy Model With Motivation Interventions**

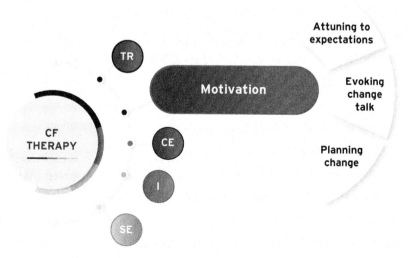

*Note.* TR = therapeutic relationship; CE = corrective experiencing; I = insight; SE = self-efficacy.

A healing relationship and the expectancy and motion toward change represent essential elements, usually in place before therapists focus their intentions more specifically on corrective experiencing, insight, and self-efficacy (Chapters 4–6). Now on to our discussion of motivation as a common factor.

## OVERVIEW OF MOTIVATION

Complex motivations lead clients to participate in therapy. They may enter treatment because they experience distress and expect that treatment may be helpful for relieving distress. On the other hand, there are often factors that must be weighed against commencing or continuing treatment—for example, the financial costs or perceived stigma associated with mental health concerns. As clients engage in the work of therapy, they may vary in the degree to which they are willing to accede to, succumb to, or submit to what treatment entails. For example, a client may find talking about their personal life to be intimidating, and therefore they dread the potential moment when a therapist encourages them to open up. Their self-perceived ability to make the changes required can have a significant impact for or against change. If change seems impossible, this can be further demoralizing and self-defeating. The factors motivating entering therapy and participating in therapy are valenced (in favor of therapy/engaging in therapy or against therapy/engaging in therapy) and are potentially infinite in number.

Given these complex motivations, it is clear that ambivalence toward change, even change that is openly desired, is a normal human experience. *Ambivalence* literally refers to the state of having mixed feelings on a subject—in this case, mixed feelings about making change through therapy. If a client is in a state of ambivalence, they may argue against the therapist's recommendations for change, even when those recommendations are sound. Ambivalence has little to do with the merit of the argument and much more to do with how ready a client may feel for making a change. CF therapists focusing on motivation to change may recognize this ambivalence and intentionally make motivation an active topic in therapy.

Addressing motivation in therapy involves recognizing complex motivations as well as maximizing the potential for positively valenced change. As Frank and Frank (1991) described in the contextual model, it matters that the client believes in the treatment, more than what the particulars of the treatment may be. In writing about common factors related to this, Goldfried (2019) described a key change principle in this way: "promoting client expectation and motivation that therapy can help" (p. 488). From this description, motivation includes multiple ideas. The therapist may attune to motivations (as discussed in the opening paragraphs of this chapter) as well as what the client expects, maximizing positive expectancy from the client. In other words, working to help clients recognize and resolve ambivalence about change is one part of motivation while the other part is instilling hope and positive expectations for change.

## Placebo Effect

Another term for positive expectation for change is *placebo*, or "I shall please." This much maligned aspect of treatments (literally seen as a nontreatment or a sham treatment by the field of medicine generally) received more positive treatment by Frank and Frank (1991). Historically, placebo referred to a sugar pill, a faux intervention with no therapeutic value, against which to compare other treatments and by which these other treatments could be seen as legitimate.

The historical perspective—often the dominant perspective, even in contemporary science—misses a powerful, salutary, and active effect. The placebo effect, contrary to naysayers, shows significant effect for the client and shows much promise for future research (see Colloca et al., 2015, for how the placebo effect may inform brain–body research). Participation in treatment of any form in a treatment setting with a healer tends to activate the participant's expectation that it will help. Frank and Frank's (1991) argument was that the key elements of what would later be called the contextual model (i.e., the treatment setting, myth, and ritual) combined to promote hope for relief of demoralization. According to a thorough review of the available evidence regarding therapist actions to address expectancy, Weinberger and Eig (1999) pointed to evidence for "therapist friendly and caring behavior; enthusiasm; provision of a credible, scientifically based rationale; and assignment of doable homework" (p. 370). They also reviewed placebo-compared studies to conclude that psychotherapy is superior to placebo treatment, but "placebo treatments are effective in their own right" (p. 370). These sources give evidence for placebo medication, placebo therapy, and even placebo surgeries that have shown to be effective.

Inspired by Frank and Frank (1991) and their contextual model, Fish (1973) described placebo therapy along similar principles. Among the initial goals of a therapist beginning treatment is not to undermine the client's expectation that it will help but rather to "inspire faith" (p. 8). Fish continued:

> Thus, the therapeutic transaction can be seen as taking place between two believers, the healer and the one to be healed, in something like the following form. Patient: "I'm sick." Therapist: "Participate in this healing ritual with me and you'll be well." (The patient then free associates or expresses affect or

whatever he is supposed to.) Patient: "I'm well." . . . Effective placebo therapy involves both the therapist's recognition of the context of therapy—the patient's "faith"—and his consequent choice of a ritual in which the patient can believe. (pp. 8–9)

## Expectations

Placebo effects may work by maximizing a client's expectancy, a positive-valenced view of the process and outcome of the treatment. Rotter's (1954) social learning theory first used the term *locus of control* to describe how the belief of an individual in their behavior could lead to a desired outcome (a person generalizes their expectancies for reinforcement, and they adjust their behavior to enact control over the reinforcement they receive). In a related vein, Bandura's (1989) social cognitive theory emphasized self-efficacy to show how a person expects or believes that they can perform some behavior in the future. Remoralization, as we discuss and explore in Chapter 2, seems highly related to these ideas. In other words, as a person benefits from therapy, they tend to feel more confident in their ability to maintain changes they have made.

These more positive expectations are highly associated with outcome, as we show later in this chapter. Therapist attunement to these expectations for therapy can be especially important, given that sometimes clients may be unsure what to expect. As Frank and Frank (1991) wrote,

The expectations that patients bring to therapy are often quite vague and at variance with the actual therapeutic experience. A patient will probably not remain in therapy or profit from it unless his or her expectations are soon brought into line with what actually transpires. (p. 148)

In many—perhaps most—cases, clients often show some defenses, resistance, or ambivalence about therapy and making changes in therapy (see Coyne et al., 2021). Because motivation can only be within the locus of control of the client, the question remains as to how therapists work with client motivation when it is resistant or ambivalent.

## Resistance

Inadequate levels of motivation to make a desired change, including everything from ambivalence to resistance to opposition, requires our attention. Psychotherapists have long been interested in defenses and resistance as a key element of therapy. In a primer on psychodynamic therapy, Kaner and

Prelinger (2005) highlighted how resistance manifests as difficulty expressing certain topics and tends to be motivated by anxiety: "Anxiety then motivates resistance to change, the patient seeking safety by remaining in his current state of adaptation" (p. 176). They recommend collaboration with the client to undermine the sources of anxiety.

In his psychoanalytic work, Messer (2002) emphasized the importance of resistance because it is both inevitable and defensive, writing, "We would no more expect clients to present themselves to us as exposed, bleeding wounds, vulnerable and defenseless—that is, without resistances—than would a physician want or expect a patient to be without an immune system" (p. 158). Resistance to sharing feelings with the therapist, resistance to sharing feelings about the therapist, clients showing their self-sufficiency, clients not changing behavior outside the therapy room, or a failure of empathy on the therapist's part all represent Messer's functions of resistance. In these cases, Messer recommended responding based on the needs of the client rather than on the countertransference reactions of the therapist.

Inadequate motivation may also hinder a client's ability to make desired changes. Beutler et al. (2002) explored different theoretical perspectives on resistance and reviewed evidence for how different therapies address it. They cited how many theoretical orientations may see resistance as avoidance, countertherapeutic, or even a "moral pejorative" (Kirmayer, 1990, as cited in Beutler et al., 2002). From such a viewpoint, which can be a tempting trap for therapists to fall into, the therapist believes that they are somehow morally superior to their clients when they do not change as expected. However, clients see themselves not as lacking in motivation but as lacking in personal control. Far better, perhaps, to expect defenses and resistance. Beutler et al. (2002) noted how from a family therapy perspective therapists expect resistance to change as inevitable in a family system because any change may disrupt the homeostasis of the system.

Therapists would do better to attune to the client's current level of motivation and adapt rather than blame the client. As is shown more in the Intervention Concepts section of this chapter, the motivational interviewing (MI) perspective recommends "rolling with the resistance." Rather than pushing back against a client's defenses, this allows for exploration of ambivalence and is far more likely to lead to a client pursuing change. On the basis of a review of 20 studies, Beutler et al. (2002) found that the effects of resistance in treatment can be successfully counteracted through the use of nondirective or self-directed interventions. They found that more directive therapies tend to be more helpful when clients are highly motivated and less resistant.

## Stages of Change

In keeping with therapists attuning and adapting, Prochaska and DiClemente (1984) posited a transtheoretical model for how clients move through various levels of motivation for change. Guided by ideas around psychotherapy integration, they conceptualized a synthesis model for how clients approach change in therapy. A more recent summary from Norcross et al. (2011) described these stages of change according to the transtheoretical model that highlights motivation and different motivation-focused interventions dependent on the stage of the client:

> *Precontemplation* is the stage in which there is no intention to change behavior in the foreseeable future. Most patients in this stage are unaware or under-aware of their problems. Families, friends, neighbors or employees, however, are often well aware that the precontemplators suffer from the problems.
>
> *Contemplation* is the stage in which patients are aware that a problem exists and are seriously thinking about overcoming it but have not yet made a commitment to take action. Contemplators struggle with their positive evaluations of their dysfunctional behavior and the amount of effort, energy, and loss it will cost to overcome it.
>
> *Preparation* is the stage in which individuals are intending to take action in the next month and are reporting some small behavioral changes ("baby steps"). Although they have made some reductions in their problem behaviors, patients in the preparation stage have not yet reached a criterion for effective action.
>
> *Action* is the stage in which individuals modify their behavior, experiences, and/or environment to overcome their problems. Action involves the most overt behavioral changes and requires considerable commitment of time and energy. Individuals are classified in the action stage if they have successfully altered the dysfunctional behavior for a period from 1 day to 6 months.
>
> *Maintenance* is the stage in which people work to prevent relapse and consolidate the gains attained during action. This stage extends from 6 months to an indeterminate period past the initial action. Remaining free of the problem and/or consistently engaging in a new incompatible behavior for more than 6 months are the criteria for the maintenance stage. (p. 144)

Please note how motivation can be seen as complex and dynamic based on this model. However, critics of the model, such as Littell and Girvin (2002), noted how these stages may be more like a heuristic because the stages suggest discrete differences that may not reflect client experience. Littell and Girvin found the stages to be neither mutually exclusive nor sequential for clients' movement through them. As Beutler et al. (2002) raised the issue with motivation (also known as resistance or reactance) generally, it seems unclear whether motivation is dichotomous (i.e., either present or absent) or a range. In the face of these critiques it seems helpful to consider the range of motivation, if not the discrete stages as proposed by the trans-theoretical model.

On the basis of this transtheoretical theory, the rationale is that there are also transtheoretical processes of change. Different therapeutic approaches (e.g., more directive therapies vs. less directive therapies) are needed at different stages of change:

> In sum, the psychotherapist's relational stance at different stages can be characterized as follows: With patients in precontemplation, often the role is like that of a *nurturing parent*, who joins with a resistant and defensive youngster who is both drawn to and repelled by the prospects of becoming more independent. With clients in contemplation, the role is akin to a *Socratic teacher*, who encourages clients to achieve their own insights into their condition. With clients who are in the preparation stage, the stance is more like that of an *experienced coach*, who has been through many crucial matches and can provide a fine game plan or can review the participant's own plan. With clients who are progressing into action and maintenance, the psychotherapist becomes more of a *consultant*, who is available to provide expert advice and support when action is not progressing smoothly. As termination approaches in lengthier treatment, the therapist is consulted less and less often as the client experiences greater autonomy and ability to live free from previously disabling problems. (Norcross et al., 2011, p. 145)

Note how therapists can adapt in response to a client's presentation of motivation or ambivalence, whatever the case may be. Although the stages may reflect a heuristic more than discrete stages (see Littell & Girvin, 2002), the main point is that therapist attunement and adaptation to client expectation and motivation can promote movement toward change. MI shares much content with the transtheoretical model, including the evolving change talk of a client and the focus on ambivalence; however, they are also distinct (see W. R. Miller & Rollnick, 2013, p. 35). In our CF therapy motivation interventions, you will notice some similar progression from attuning to the expectations and motivation of a client to evoking change talk with MI interventions to planning changes with a client.

For therapists, it takes intention and effort to recognize moments when motivation needs to be addressed with a client. Therapists may notice their internal reactions of skepticism ("My client wants to do *that*? Impossible!"), conflict ("My client does not know what they are talking about!"), values divergence ("My client thinks this will help them, but that's not the way to go about it."), or frustration ("I wish my client would just do [fill in the blank] because it would make their life so much better!"). The temptation in these moments is to blame the client for being insufficiently motivated or skilled in some way. What we present here represents a nonpejorative, nonblaming, and more effective alternative. The therapist's response to these states—once the therapist notices them—can be to attune to the client's motivation, what matters to them, and their reasons for wanting what they want. Rather than blame the client, try to understand the client and their desires so the therapeutic work honors the autonomy and self-determination of the client. The results of such practice can be clarifying and yes, even motivating.

In summary, a client's expectations about therapy, as well as beliefs and motivations about change, matter. Therapy goes best when a client has positive expectancy about being helped. Therapists would do well to attune to what a client expects from therapy. Motivation for treatment can be varied and complex, and ambivalence about making changes can be considered a normal aspect of treatment. Therapists who attune to their clients' motivation are more likely to notice ambivalence and be responsive in ways that are less reactive and more promoting of change. Expectancy and motivation can be thought of as aspects of a common change principle (i.e., motivation for change in therapy). CF therapists can consider their clients' motivation for change to support them in making desired changes in their lives.

## INCLUSION CRITERIA FOR MOTIVATION

To be included in CF therapy, motivation as a principle of change must meet our established criteria. Here we take each criterion in turn to show how motivation aligns with our requirements.

### Research Evidence in Support of Motivation

Significant empirical evidence lends support for expectancy (frequently referred to as *outcome expectation*), for attunement to client expectation, and for other interventions that increase client readiness or motivation to change (e.g., MI). We review the evidence here for these factors as reflective generally of motivation for change in therapy and therapeutic interventions to address motivation.

One area of early empirical work on expectation setting comes under the heading of client role preparation or role induction. For example, Orlinsky and Howard (1978) in their chapter on process and outcome in psychotherapy reviewed nine studies completed by that time with "very promising results" (p. 309), especially for brief therapy and for orienting both therapists and clients to their roles in therapy. When the participants know what to expect, especially before beginning treatment, then treatment may be able to proceed with greater chances at progress for the client. They also reviewed early evidence for attunement or a consensus on roles and expectations (Orlinsky & Howard, 1978). As we noted in Chapter 2 (this volume), role induction as a CF therapy intervention could have easily been incorporated into the chapter on therapeutic relationships as an element of agreement on tasks within the Bordin (1979) model. Though it could fit there equally well, we elected to include it here as an element of enhancing motivation or readiness for treatment. As you read this section, please consider how it may also apply to the establishment of the therapeutic relationship. In addition, we hope that the very fact that we discuss this overlap of role induction and expectation setting as relevant to both this chapter (on motivation) and Chapter 2 (on the therapeutic relationship) is evidence of the relevance of a CF approach.

Not all expectation setting happens before treatment through separate, pretherapy role preparation programs, which are not commonly discussed in current literature. Regarding outcome expectations in particular, Sotsky et al. (1991) found that outcome expectations were related to outcome across the four treatments in the National Institute of Mental Health Treatment of Depression Collaborative Research Program. Because the therapist can help to address expectations and introduce the client to the work of therapy, an in-session approach may be more easily adopted—thus a potential reason that role induction strategies are rarely included in practice. Constantino, Vîslă, et al. (2019), in a comprehensive meta-analysis of outcome expectations prior to or early in treatment in relationship to therapy outcome, found that outcome expectations (in early treatment) are indeed related to outcome with a small, positive effect, $r = .18$, over 81 studies.

Attuning or paying attention to clients' expectations can be an effective practice in its own right. Coyne et al. (2021) found in a study of different treatments with a generalized anxiety disorder population that in general, therapists tended to underestimate patients' outcome expectations, but then as therapy progressed, the therapist's perception began to match the client's perception of the expectations. They also found that the more accurate the therapist attunement, the better the outcome.

Expectancy has demonstrated persuasive evidence of its association with outcome. On the basis of their comprehensive review of meta-analyses by the task force, Norcross and Lambert (2019a) noted that the body of evidence indicates that cultivating positive expectations is probably effective. Other effective elements of the relationship they cite as important include collaboration and goal consensus. Similarly, promoting treatment credibility (Constantino, Coyne, et al., 2019) is also considered a common factor that encourages successful treatment.

Motivation to engage with the therapist or to engage with the treatment itself contributes to outcome. Motivation to engage in treatment may reflect confidence in the therapist as well as confidence in the treatment (see Finsrud et al., 2022). Sijercic et al. (2016) distinguished between counterchange talk that was opposed to the therapist or therapy (*resistance*) versus counterchange talk that reflected opposition to change itself (*ambivalence*). Resistance as they defined it—statements in opposition to change, which were demonstrated as opposition either to the therapist or to the therapy itself—was a "substantive and consistent predictor of lower homework compliance and poorer outcomes" (p. 13). This finding is highly suggestive that alliance ruptures (see Chapter 2, this volume) may differ from ambivalence per se and may require different interventions. Agreement on task and goal (which we also discuss in Chapter 2) may be more helpful for addressing resistance, whereas motivation work may be more helpful for addressing ambivalence. As already noted, collaboration and goal consensus, as reported by the task force, show evidence for being probably effective (see Tryon et al., 2019).

Reviewing the evidence for the Stages of Change and outcome, Norcross et al. (2011) showed through meta-analysis that the body of evidence is stronger for behavioral health (e.g., substance abuse treatment, behavioral medicine) compared with psychotherapy. Littell and Girvin (2002) cataloged methodological problems with the stage model of the Stages of Change, noting overlap between the stages. They refrained from total dismissal of the theory, however, instead noting that the field can focus on the "stage model's contributions—emphasis on cognitive precursors and correlates of behavioral change, the concept of readiness, and nonlinear movement—[which] can be retained without a stage theory" (p. 255). They also noted that even without the stages (and consequently without the stage-based choices of interventions), the practice of W. R. Miller and Tonigan (1997) could be appropriate (i.e., giving feedback to clients on their Stages of Change assessment results to start a conversation about their motivation).

Ambivalence could be considered the major target for MI, through the vehicle of rolling with resistance and evoking change talk. The evidence for MI's effectiveness is very strong, though the effect sizes tend to be small. In a meta-analysis of 25 years' worth of studies with 119 studies included on MI, Lundahl et al. (2010) found a small but robust and positive effect across multiple domains (average $g$ of 0.28). MI significantly increased clients' engagement in treatment and their intention to change, the two variables most closely linked to motivation to change. MI certainly gives therapists interventions to meet clients where they are, enhance client change intentions and treatment engagement, and boost their confidence in their ability to change.

## Motivation Is Conceptually Present in Most Therapies

Motivation, hope, and expectancy have a long history of being considered as common factors across theoretical orientations. Frank and Frank (1991) considered the installation of hope and positive expectations to be a key common factor in therapy that directly addresses the client's demoralization. Similarly, Howard et al. (1986, 1993), in their phase model of psychotherapy, suggested that the first phase of psychotherapy change is related to a hopefulness, which is then followed by symptom change and later life functioning changes (e.g., work, social relationships). Goldfried's (2019) first transtheoretical and empirically supported principle of change is "promoting client expectation and motivation that therapy can help" (p. 488).

Motivation may often reflect a theory in practice rather than an explicit, articulated aspect of the therapy. For example, Weinberger and Eig (1999) pointed out that expectancy is not emphasized by any major school of therapy. Although not often integrated into treatment, there is also a body of early psychotherapy literature that supports the notion of setting expectations and introducing the client to their work in therapy. Role induction reflects the idea of preparing a client with what to expect in therapy either just before their initial session or at the outset of treatment. This preparation of a client while still early in treatment reflects the CF therapy theory of pathology directly, that expectations promote positive change and remoralization.

Motivation, seen in this light, suffers the same conceptual problem of abstraction that CF therapy as a whole faces. In other words, motivation is often discussed as metatheory, as embedded in all therapies. Previous efforts to make motivation a specific change principle include the transtheoretical model, with the concept of stages of change. If motivation is to be a change principle within CF therapy, we must take care to avoid some of the conceptual pitfalls of the Stages of Change. To accomplish this, motivation remains as a heuristic, a change principle that can provide the paradigm for enacting motivation-related interventions. As with other change principles, the CF therapist sees their work with a client through the lens of the change principle and then chooses interventions from the broad world of orientations that actualize the change principle.

We return to the inclusion criterion, that motivation needs to be included conceptually in most therapies. If the construct under consideration is a generally expanded idea of motivation—or, perhaps with the single qualifier, motivation *for therapy*—there are a host of ways that the construct is addressed in theoretical orientations. Indeed, as R. P. Greenberg et al. (2006) argued, expectancy is already embedded in therapies: "The reshaping of patient expectations (or assumptions) appears to be at the foundation of virtually every major model of therapy" (p. 670). They pointed to cognitive therapies working to directly modify clients' expectations, behavioral exposure working by thwarting clients' expectations, and psychodynamic working through of a transference relationship as revising of clients' expectations. From a CF therapy perspective there is overlap in their conceptualization, in that the corrective experience idea (see Chapter 4, this volume) is thought of as an expectations-altering idea.

Motivation theories abound in the history of psychology. Consider Freud's drive theories, with the tripartite division each having motivations and motivations told through the story of psychosexual development. Consider behaviorist ideas over the past century or more, describing the law of effect and how reinforcement and incentives shape motivation. Humanistic theories such as Rogers's organismic enhancement and Maslow's hierarchy of needs are essentially motivation theories focused on human drive toward actualization. Behaviorist ideas were criticized by proponents of a more humanistic self-determination theory because of behaviorists' focus on external factors rather than the self (see Ryan & Deci, 2019). Self-determination theory as specifically a motivation theory appears more aligned with humanistic perspectives and focuses on autonomy and supporting a client's autonomy. Cognitive approaches to motivation focused on things like social learning (Bandura, 1989) and in so doing reemphasized internal factors in the face of intellectual disputes about free will, agency, and determinism.

With regard to addressing low motivation, ambivalence, or resistance in therapy, all major theories address this but in slightly different ways. Psychodynamic therapy highlights how clients present with defenses and how these are essential in understanding and working with clients. Recall Messer's (2002) psychoanalytic perspective on the functions of resistance, including resistance to sharing feelings with the therapist, resistance to sharing feelings about the therapist, clients showing their self-sufficiency, and clients not changing behavior outside the therapy room. Psychodynamic lists of defense mechanisms (inspired by Anna Freud) show how clients are motivated to reduce anxiety by defending ego. Repression, avoidance, projection, somatization, denial, and so on reflect defenses, and where there is smoke, there is fire. From the psychodynamic perspective, where there is resistance, there is anxiety yet to be named and explored (Kaner & Prelinger, 2005, p. 172). The work of therapy illuminates anxiety as well as key desires and motivations for the client. Resistance is grist for the mill of therapy.

Behavioral therapists focus on determinants of behavior (i.e., the variables and conditions and principles that control behavior). Learning principles help to explain reinforcement for behavior and by doing so help to explain motivation (see Wilson, 2008). Though strict behaviorists may avoid considering cognitive aspects of these motivations, second- and third-wave theorists highlight social cognitive learning, appraisal of learning, the dialectic between acceptance and change, and the roles of language and avoidance in maintaining behavior. By focusing on factors that control behavior, at their core these theories are motivational theories and therapies that address not only change but client motivations for (and against) making changes. Cognitive behavior therapy (CBT) proponents Barlow and colleagues (2010) included motivational enhancement via MI strategies as part of the unified protocol for transdiagnostic treatment of emotional disorders. This protocol can be considered a CBT adaptation or an assimilative integration of MI (see Boswell et al., 2017).

Humanistic therapies focus on motivation as intrinsic, inherent to the human experience. Rogers emphasized this inherent tendency, that humans are moving toward "greater order, complexity, and interrelatedness" (Raskin et al., 2008, p. 142). Because motivation is inherent from this perspective, therapists focus on recognizing and respecting a client's perspective and right to self-determination. The recognition of this fact inspired a novel and similar approach but with slightly different emphases.

MI, as an approach to working on client's motivations for change, is deeply rooted in client-centered therapy, though it is in many ways its own orientation (W. R. Miller & Rollnick, 2013, p. 17). Acceptance as grounded in Rogers's ideas is the root of MI, focused on supporting the client's autonomy and recognizing their absolute worth. MI has been associated with the transtheoretical model of change, but W. R. Miller and Rollnick (2013) pointed out that they are related but not essential parts of one another. In other words, one can use MI without ascribing fully to the concept of Stages of Change. Rather than use the Stages of Change whole-cloth, W. R. Miller and Rollnick emphasized generalities and evolving client change talk, with ambivalence being the key target (see pp. 163–164). The highlighting of competing motivations and change inside and outside of therapy (see Prochaska & Norcross, 2018, p. 417) can be helpful aspects of the Stages of Change, which MI appears to embrace.

In summary, preparatory discussions of expectations in therapy and presentation of a treatment rationale (whether by role induction or not) is a general principle considered as common. Motivation concerns are central to psychodynamic, behavioral, cognitive behavior, and humanistic approaches to therapy. MI relies heavily on Rogerian client-centered therapy. However, its transtheoretical use across orientations makes it especially useful. Overall, therapists can maximize expectancy and work with client motivation by discussing expectations, attuning to their client's motivation, rolling with resistance, and promoting change talk by discussing ambivalence.

## EXCLUSION CRITERIA FOR MOTIVATION

Our main inclusion criteria regarding empirical evidence and the common conceptual nature of the principle have been met. Parsimony is needed with this change principle. Though expectancy and motivation for change can be considered as conceptually distinct, combining them could reduce redundancy. Goldfried (2019) combined these concepts in his articulation of key change principles. Both concepts involve expectations for change, mobilizing these expectations for change, and attuning to the client's motivation to harness their resources and move toward change.

Motivation certainly shows some overlap with the therapeutic relationship, particularly the task and goal aspects of the relationship. Agreement on task and goals is essentially a quality of a working relationship, but what is distinct with motivation may be the work by the therapist and client when agreement is unclear or absent. Indeed, many MI interventions are included in our therapeutic relationship chapter (see Chapter 2). However, motivation must be considered not as an aspect of the therapist–client dyad but as a client factor. The client experiences their expectations and motivations, and the therapist attunes to them. This difference is the primary distinction between the concepts and the primary reason the two are not redundant concepts.

Motivation influences one's engagement in treatment and therefore likely impacts corrective experiencing and insight. While working on motivation, one could certainly gain insight or engage in corrective experiencing. Motivation represents the expectations and willingness to engage that reside in the client, rather than the actions taken or the emotions or cognitions experienced.

Other terms used in the field include expectancy, outcome expectations, goal consensus, collaboration, ambivalence, resistance, defense mechanisms, or defensiveness. Motivation represents an overarching umbrella term and therefore reflects a more parsimonious approach for CF therapy.

## DEFINITION OF MOTIVATION

Defining *motivation* as a change principle for CF therapy requires several elements, not the least of which is using transtheoretical language to describe it. The existence of a transtheoretical model of change (Prochaska

& DiClemente, 1984) may introduce some confusion, which we seek to dispel. The CF therapy definition will need to be distinct but also transtheoretical in the use of language it describes. The CF therapy definition may reflect elements of the stages of change, but it is intended primarily as a lens for the CF therapist to use when focusing on their client's motivation for engaging in treatment.

Consistent with the work of Frank and Frank (1991), our definition requires an acknowledgement of expectancy in therapy. Clients present for therapy with demoralization and expect to get better, hoping for remoralization. These expectations appear to contribute to treatment responses that have been described as placebo, which is nowise meant pejoratively. CF therapists may seek to capitalize on and even maximize these expectations. According to Constantino, Vîslă, et al. (2019), remoralization is the same as their term *outcome expectation*, defined as "a patient's belief about the mental health consequences of participating in treatment" (p. 461). Our definition needs elements regarding a client's expectations or beliefs about treatment.

Expectations and motivation are typically valenced. The more positive terms—expectancy and placebo—can be counterbalanced with negative expectancy and a lack of motivation to engage in treatment or make important changes in treatment. CF therapy needs to account for the negative valence of motivation. Resistance in treatment has a rich history, though unfortunately it sometimes has a disparaging tone, as if the client is to blame somehow by resisting the therapist. MI work on rolling with the resistance is especially helpful for therapists to collaborate with the client rather than blame and induce defensive responses from a client. W. R. Miller and Rollnick's (2013) use of the term *ambivalence* reflects this attitude toward client motivation. They described it as part of human nature: "Ambivalence is simultaneously wanting and not wanting something or wanting both of two incompatible things" (p. 6).

Unlike the therapeutic relationship, which is defined as residing in the dyad of the relationship, motivation resides in the client. As W. R. Miller and Rollnick (2013) wrote, "Arguments both for and against change already reside within the ambivalent person" (p. 7). Psychodynamic descriptions of resistance sometimes even emphasize the phenomenon as a trait of the person (see Beutler et al., 2002). An emphasis on traits may not be a necessary aspect of the definition in that it may contribute to blame of the client. Rather, it is important to recognize that although the therapist may not be able to generate the motivation, they have the capability to intervene to address the client's motivation in helpful ways.

The CF definition of *motivation* can imply that the therapist has the capacity to intervene while honoring the autonomy of the client. Humanistic therapies and self-determination theory emphasize this aspect, which is well-encapsulated by MI's description of the heart of MI. W. R. Miller and Rollnick (2013) described the core conditions that form the heart of MI and summarized thus:

> Taken together, these four person-centered conditions convey what we mean by "acceptance." One honors each person's *absolute worth* and potential as a human being, recognizes and supports the person's irrevocable *autonomy* to choose his or her own way, seeks through *accurate empathy* to understand the other's perspective, and *affirms* the person's strengths and efforts. (p. 19)

To ensure that therapists do not view these interventions as a formula to induce change, like a sales technique or manipulation, W. R. Miller and Rollnick (2013) added the element of compassion to their description. They emphasized how with compassion, the therapist can have their "heart in the right place" (p. 20).

The interventions to reflect in the definition include focusing on expectancy by attuning to the client's expectations (see Coyne et al., 2021). Role induction will also be addressed in a similar light. Evoking change talk with ambivalent clients using MI is essential, so we offer the definition of MI as well:

> Motivational interviewing is a collaborative, goal-oriented style of communication with particular attention to the language of change. It is designed to strengthen personal motivation for and commitment to a specific goal by eliciting and exploring the *person's own reasons* [emphasis added] for change within an atmosphere of acceptance and compassion. (W. R. Miller & Rollnick, 2013, p. 29)

Bringing all of these elements together, we offer the following as our working CF therapy definition of *motivation*. The two-part definition acknowledges the locus of motivation as being in the client, while the therapist's role is supportive and collaborative.

---

**COMMON FACTORS DEFINITION OF MOTIVATION**

Clients enter and engage in treatment with varying and complex expectations, including ambivalence regarding taking steps toward remoralization. Therapists can accept this by attuning to their clients' expectations, supporting their autonomy, exploring their clients' ambivalent reasons for change, and supporting planned steps toward change.

## INTERVENTION CONCEPTS FOR MOTIVATION

Translating the CF metatheory to specific interventions requires that motivation not merely be a change principle but also be translated into specific, actionable interventions for use by CF therapists. As with the other change principles (therapeutic relationship, corrective experiencing, insight, and self-efficacy), this intervention approach emphasizes attention to the change principle as the lens of CF therapy. The CF therapist seeks to employ specific interventions to evoke this change principle with their client. In this section we give an overview of motivation intervention, followed by outlines of specific interventions to evoke this change principle with a client. The broad categories of motivation interventions include attuning to expectations, evoking change talk, and planning change. We also offer deliberate practice exercises for the aspiring CF therapist to hone their skills with the interventions.

As the authors of MI emphasize, the heart of MI is essential as a foundation for working with clients on their motivation for treatment. Blaming and pathologizing a client's defenses are likely to contribute to a client's doubling down on ambivalence and reasons not to change. Compassion and acceptance go hand in hand through these interventions, with the therapeutic relationship forming the foundation for working on motivation. Too often intervention is thought of with the therapist as the subject of a sentence and the client as the object. Collaboration is key, as is respect for the client's autonomy. CF therapists need to remember that the motivation resides within the client. With this perspective, the interventions from this book do not control the client; they are meant to merely help the therapist to collaborate with the client. The descriptions of intervention are meant to reflect this reality, such that when therapists recognize their client's motivation and when their client seems to resist intervention, the therapist can approach them with curiosity and openness.

Therapists can use motivation, as with any of the guiding change principles of CF therapy, as a heuristic (see Lazarus & Wachtel, 2018). Think of heuristics as practical mental shortcuts to more complex ideas, like a general guideline. When therapists work with clients, the change principles can readily come to mind to guide intervention decisions. As clients progress in therapy (and therapists use routine outcome monitoring to continuously assess progress), therapists can use the rubric of CF therapy change principles to determine how to apply interventions.

We offer several questions to guide therapists in the use of the heuristic of motivation:

- How is my client hoping that therapy will be helpful to them?
- How can I support that hope and encourage positive expectations?

- How did my client arrive at the decision to seek therapy? Did someone else recommend it or insist on their participation in therapy?
- What hesitations might my client have about therapy and making changes through therapy?
- What conflicting feelings may be present for my client with regard to the changes they want? Do I have a sense of both sides of their ambivalence?
- When my client expresses a desire to make a change, how can I support them to enact the change?

These questions can help a therapist maintain the big-picture view of motivation in CF therapy. What follows is a general outline, which is admittedly an incomplete picture of interventions that focus on motivation. It is consistent with CF therapy to seek out interventions from multiple theoretical orientations, guided by the lens of the CF therapy change principle of motivation. To emphasize this point by carrying it forward, we strongly recommend a review of the volume *Motivational Interviewing: Helping People Change* by William R. Miller and Stephen Rollnick, currently in its third edition (2013). The overview of attitudes of MI, as well as the delineation of specific interventions and examples, is invaluable.

For the remainder of this chapter, we emphasize MI principles but bring together intervention concepts from across the spectrum of therapeutic orientations. These principles are attuning to expectations, evoking change talk, and planning change.

## Attuning to Expectations

**PRINCIPLE 3.1**

Therapists focus on becoming aware of the client's expectations and motivations for therapy, seeking to meet their clients at their current readiness rather than impose expectations for change.

Clients enter therapy and engage in therapy for varied and complex reasons and generally hope for improvements to their demoralized state. The CF therapist can begin to maximize expectancy by focusing on the perspective offered by Frank and Frank (1991) for how therapy (or any treatment, for that matter) typically begins to work to remoralize. The elements we review in Chapter 1 (this volume) are as follows:

- "an emotionally charged, confiding relationship with a helping person" (Frank & Frank, 1991, p. 40);

- "a healing setting" (p. 41);

- "a rationale, conceptual scheme, or myth that provides a plausible explanation for the patient's symptoms and prescribes a ritual or procedure for resolving them" (p. 42); and

- "a ritual or procedure that requires the active participation of both patient and therapist and that is believed by both to be the means of restoring the patient's health" (p. 43).

The first element can be reflected in our content from Chapter 2 on the therapeutic relationship. The second and third elements, including the healing setting and the myth, can directly relate to motivation and can be amplified by the CF therapist in specific ways to maximize the expectancy for improvement. For example, Weinberger and Eig (1999) pointed to evidence for expectancy improving outcome and cited several very general interventions, including "therapist friendly and caring behavior; enthusiasm; provision of a credible, scientifically based rationale; and assignment of doable homework" (p. 370). We review these and other interventions in this section (see Table 3.1 for an outline).

Therapist friendliness and enthusiasm seem too simple to be considered interventions. However, these may be significant for a client whose previous experience in therapy included a less friendly therapist, one who greeted the client with a vacant expression, who was disengaged throughout, who

**TABLE 3.1. Example Interventions for Attuning to Expectations**

| Intervention | Broad theoretical categories | Specific theoretical approaches | Additional resources |
|---|---|---|---|
| Focusing | Transtheoretical | Motivational interviewing | W. R. Miller & Rollnick (2013), *Motivational Interviewing: Helping People Change* (3rd ed.) |
| | | Common factors therapy | Chapter 2 (this volume), Task and Goal sections |
| Fostering expectancy | Transtheoretical | Contextual model | Frank & Frank (1991), *Persuasion and Healing: A Comparative Study of Psychotherapy* (3rd ed.) |
| Defenses | Psychodynamic | Contemporary Freudian psychoanalytic psychotherapy | Wolitzky (2020) chapter from *Essential Psychotherapies* (4th ed.) |

was emotionally overworked and burned out, who worked in a drab or disorderly office, or who seemed pessimistic about chances for improvement. How different is it when a therapist presents as engaged, works in an inviting office, and expresses optimism about the likelihood of finding relief through the work of therapy? For many clients these simple interventions could be significant in their communication that remoralization is possible. CF therapists who recall that demoralization is the common state for which most of us enter therapy are more likely to be able to attune to their client's demoralization.

Taking expectancy even further, Constantino, Vîslă, et al. (2019) suggested that clinical training should incorporate systematic strategies for fostering outcome expectancies. Importantly, many of the more specific clinical strategies that they provide in their chapter line up with empathic attunement and reflective listening that is accompanied by regularly checking in on client expectancies and helping clients to adjust as needed, especially early in treatment. Historically, role induction has shown evidence of being effective. Whether in a pretherapy session or during an initial session, CF therapists can meet the client where they are, not merely tell their client, "This is what I expect from you." Rather, the conversation includes questions from the therapist to the client to explore what the client expects or hopes to gain from therapy. MI techniques called *focusing* can be especially relevant here, helping the client to identify the actual change they hope to make. As with the Goal section from Chapter 2 of this book, the therapist works toward consensus with the client on the goal of therapy and then works collaboratively toward it (see Tryon et al., 2019, for evidence.)

Attuning to client expectations can be facilitated by the therapist checking to ensure that they have been addressed. During the session, the therapist can privately ask themselves about the client's expectations and motivations. W. R. Miller and Rollnick (2013) recommended therapists ask themselves questions such as "What goals for change does this person really have?," "Do I have different aspirations for change than this person?," and "Are we working together for a common purpose?" If there is a lack of clarity or a lack of agreement, therapist and client continue to work together to attune on the change goal of therapy.

Building hope that therapy will be effective is one major purpose of these early attuning interventions. R. P. Greenberg et al. (2006), for example, encouraged therapists to make "hope-inducing statements" early in therapy, highlighting that their diagnosis is treatable. Therapists could cite outcome research about how most people get better with therapy and include specific information if possible, based on a diagnosis. MI points to strengthening confidence as an intentional intervention, including soliciting confidence talk with open-ended questions that clients can answer with such talk and then using reflective listening to support the client's confidence as it is evoked. A therapist could use a "confidence ruler" (rating confidence on a 1 to 10 scale) to work with this, helping them notice and build confidence (see Chapter 16 of W. R. Miller & Rollnick, 2013).

Several sources, including Frank and Frank (1991), have pointed to the need to offer a credible rationale for treatment. In light of the fact that CF therapy is focused not on diagnosis but on change principles, this framing needs to reflect the distinction. Because CF therapy is not couched in a more conventional, singular, and siloed theoretical orientation, the rationale needs to reflect the principles on which CF therapy is based. We offer potential language to use for CF therapy. In this example, we highlight all five common factors (see the bracketed elements). However, it is not essential to include all five factors when providing a rationale for treatment; instead, the therapist can tailor this based on the clinical situation in which they find themselves:

> You may be wondering how therapy can help, possibly in particular how I approach therapy or how common factors therapy can help. You are coming to therapy to address several concerns that are causing you distress, and therapy is designed to help alleviate that distress and contribute to improvement in several key ways. Common factors therapy focuses on the ways that help that are common to all or most therapies, that are associated with research-based principles of change. For example, our working relationship is key [therapeutic relationship], so I'm hoping we can continue to discuss how we work together to help you. Your reasons for wanting change [motivation] matter, and we can explore those. New experiences in the way you feel [corrective experiencing] and the way you think [insight] can also help you improve and have confidence to implement or apply these improvements [self-efficacy], so as we continue to work together, we will land on specific ways to do this. What questions do you have about this process?

Clients may respond to this with wanting more specific details, and therapists can work with them to determine what specific next steps can be. Many therapists believe it most helpful to resist clients' requests to be specific about steps to take, as this constitutes prescriptive advice-giving that improperly gives the therapist authority to dictate the client's life. Therapists can rightly hesitate to make suggestions that presume a level of knowledge of the client's life that they do not have. Therapists have the luxury of being removed from the consequences from the decisions of others, which makes it tempting to overstep and be overly prescriptive.

However, therapists can collaborate with their clients to arrive on steps that are consistent with both the change principles and the client's request and leave room for the step to be more specific as the work of therapy unfolds over multiple sessions. For example, when a client is presenting the therapist with their distress over a dilemma over a romantic relationship, they may ask, "But what do I do? Do I break up or do I keep trying to make it work?" The therapist may respond with an intervention such as this:

> It seems like you are genuinely at a loss for what to do next and wanting a clear decision one way or another. This is distressing for you! While I can't make a decision for you, I hope we can figure out the next step for you to get closer to making your decision.

The therapist can then help with potential concrete next steps such as writing about the potential consequences of the decision, making a pros and cons list, making a communication plan to discuss this with the romantic partner, and deciding on how to manage the anxiety of making a decision.

In addition to helping the client to develop positive expectancies and hope with regard to the therapist and the treatment, the therapist can also intervene in ways that help the client to have faith in themselves. For example, Swift and Derthick (2013) suggested that the therapist can express confidence in their clients through acknowledgement of client strengths or through noting their fit with the selected treatment approach. Noticing and emphasizing strengths and resilience can help the client to see needed resources that will help them in their journey. Importantly, these kinds of interventions can begin very early in treatment, as soon as the initial phone call or first meeting.

Tailoring treatment to what the client needs requires the therapist to be ready to be responsive and adaptive. Volume 2 of *Psychotherapy Relationships That Work*, edited by Norcross and Wampold (2019), is devoted to tailoring treatment to clients, with emphasis on several elements that could fall under the umbrella of motivation as we have described here:[1] preferences, reactance, and stages of change. Tailoring to the client's preferences was associated with lower dropout and improved outcome (Swift et al., 2019). As has been reviewed already, current client levels of motivation (reactance and lower levels of stages of change) are associated with outcome (Edwards et al., 2019; Krebs et al., 2019). Attuning to these elements allows a therapist to be responsive and adaptive, as we see especially in the next section on evoking change talk.

CF therapists can expect their clients to show defenses. A classical understanding of defenses may be useful here by considering psychoanalytic

---

[1]As with our earlier discussion, these elements could also be included in the chapter on the therapeutic relationship, where they could also be useful for establishing the goals and tasks of treatment.

concepts of ego defense mechanisms. For reference, see Wolitzky's (2020, pp. 38–39) summary of the major defense mechanisms, including repression, denial, projection, displacement, intellectualization, isolation of affect, reaction formation, undoing, regression, splitting, rationalization, and sublimation. When a client describes behavior or demonstrates behavior in-session that exemplifies defenses, the CF therapist has several options. The therapist may ask questions to clarify the client's intent, they may gently challenge the defense in order to clarify, or they may simply make a mental note of what content the client appears to be defending against. This may become important in motivation work as the treatment progresses.

Therapists are often tempted to correct their clients or to immediately and directively challenge the client's defenses in order to undermine them. As W. R. Miller and Rollnick (2013) described, the righting reflex is often a natural response by helpers when they see changes, but it tends to create an oppositional conversation. The therapist who follows the righting reflex argues for change using the logic that the client already knows but has not been able to use to persuade themselves. People feel bad when being told what to do in this way, which tends to undermine their changing (see W. R. Miller & Rollnick, 2013, p. 7). The MI approach is much different, as W. R. Miller and Rollnick (2013) wrote: "If you are arguing for change and your client is arguing against it, you've got it exactly backward" (p. 9). Rather than being either a following approach to the conversation or a directing approach to conversation, MI offers a guiding approach.

Notice in the following overview of the MI approach with ambivalent clients how the process shifts focus to attuning to expectations and not the therapist setting the expectations. W. R. Miller and Rollnick (2013) offered a description of the process as follows:

1. "Why would you want to make this change?"
2. "How might you go about it in order to succeed?"
3. "What are the three best reasons for you to do it?"
4. "How important is it for you to make this change, and why?"

Your friend listens patiently, and then gives you back a short summary of what you have said: why you want to change, why it's important, what the best reasons are, and how you could do it in order to succeed. Then your friend asks one more question, and again simply listens as you reply:

5. "So what do you think you'll do?" (p. 11)

The emphasis with this approach to motivation is with attuning and clarifying expectations, not undermining defenses but rolling with any resistance the client may demonstrate. We recommend several ways to practice attuning to expectations using deliberate practice in Table 3.2.

**TABLE 3.2. Deliberate Practice Suggestions for Attuning to Expectations**

| Method | Descriptions |
| --- | --- |
| Video-assisted observation of your work | • Watch an intake session, paying attention to the following:<br>  – Notice how your client describes changes they want to make. Watch for defenses they may show, what they may be avoiding, and how they go about avoiding it.<br>  – Notice how your client talks about reasons for making changes. Distress is often motivating but can also be the result of changes that the client may feel reluctant to make.<br>  – Identify discussions about the rationale for how therapy can help. How hopeful is the client about the changes that can come through therapy?<br>  – Identify discussions about goals of therapy. How clear are the goals? How clearly do you understand what the client wants and expects?<br>  – Notice resistance. Watch for moments when the client appears to give reasons against changing. What is your reaction? How does your righting reflex feel? What are some ways to practice rolling with the resistance? Practice out loud.<br>• Identify key moments to share with a consultant, trying to identify and move through any defensiveness you may feel about sharing this. |
| Getting consultant feedback[a] | • Determine whether your relationship with your consultant is sufficiently supportive and safe for soliciting feedback openly. Consider working through defensive reactions with your consultant.<br>• Watch the session with your consultant, asking for assistance to notice whether you are accurately attuning to your client's expectations.<br>• Request assistance with noticing defenses and resistance that may have eluded your notice. Pay particular attention to moments when you experience the righting reflex and get help to see whether your responses roll with the resistance.<br>• Discuss the goals you collaboratively made with your client, whether these are sufficiently clear and whether there is agreement and attunement. |
| Setting small incremental goals | • Perhaps with your consultant's help, identify your current comfort level and competence with attuning and arriving at clear goals. Then, identify a behavior to practice on your own that stretches you just beyond this comfort level. Try to ensure that your practice is neither too overwhelming nor too easy. Be as specific as possible when describing what you are going to practice. |

**TABLE 3.2. Deliberate Practice Suggestions for Attuning to Expectations (Continued)**

| Method | Descriptions |
|---|---|
| Solo deliberate practice | • Dedicate sufficient time to practice on your own.<br>• Use the session video to practice responding to your client's defenses, rolling with resistance, and clearly attuning to their expectations and goals.<br>• Notice how comfortable/uncomfortable the practice is and adjust the practice as needed. |
| Feedback-informed treatment | • Use outcome measures at each session to determine how the client is progressing in treatment. When progress feedback shows the client as not on track, checking in around motivation for change can be especially helpful. Exploring ambivalence, rolling with resistance during such a discussion, and clarifying treatment goals can be practiced. |

ªWe use the word "consultant" in this and other deliberate practice tables for brevity. We mean this to refer to mentors, supervisors, trainers, colleagues, or other experts as appropriate to the skill being practiced.

Concrete steps, such as homework assignments, are often requested by clients. Homework may be much more common in CBT than in psychodynamic or humanistic therapy. From a CF therapy perspective, when clients want to begin to make changes and there is close attunement and agreement between therapist and client about the changes to be made, it would make sense to offer and collaborate on concrete next steps in alignment with the therapy goal. However, when the client is more ambivalent or well-defended in opposition to change or there is a lack of attunement or agreement, then motivation work needs to take place first. CF therapists can be specific in their descriptions of steps, offering options while still remaining open to the client accepting or dismissing these options. Recall that the motivation, the locus of control, remains within the client.

### Evoking Change Talk

**PRINCIPLE 3.2**

Therapists evoke change talk by noticing their client's ambivalence, resisting the righting reflex, and using reflection to promote more discussion around change.

In light of the fact that ambivalence is a frequent state of affairs, working with a client on their motivation often requires specific attention. Evoking change talk as an intervention reflects less of an action done to a client and more something in line with synonyms such as summoning, stirring up, wakening, eliciting, drawing forth, or rallying a client's motivation for change. Rather than confronting or demanding change—as the righting reflex would naturally incline a therapist to do in the face of defenses or ambivalence—the therapist works to align with the client, roll with resistance, and promote talk and action in the direction of change. We review several interventions in this section for encouraging change talk (see Table 3.3 for a summary).

Recall the classic TV character Columbo, played by Peter Falk, who as a master detective would interview suspects while appearing uninformed, uncertain, awkward, and confused. By taking this somewhat naive position with sincerity, not only did he put the interviewees off their guard, but they began to helpfully offer more information to the detective. A similar strategy from a therapist leaves the door open for the client to fill the space with their descriptions of reasons to enact change. In a therapeutic sense, as described by Kanfer and Schefft (1988), a Columbo strategy moves clients' statements beyond their face value, such as an initial denial (p. 141). Fraser and Solovey (2007) noted how this keeps therapists in a one-down position, emphasizing that the therapist does not have the power to change the client. Fisch et al. (1982) described therapist maneuverability as this one-down

**TABLE 3.3. Example Interventions for Evoking Change Talk**

| Intervention | Broad theoretical categories | Specific theoretical approaches | Additional resources |
|---|---|---|---|
| Evoking | Transtheoretical | Motivational interviewing | W. R. Miller & Rollnick (2013), *Motivational Interviewing: Helping People Change* (3rd ed.) |
| Reflect change talk | Cognitive behavior therapy | | |
| Open-ended questions | | | |
| Affirmations | | | |
| Consider the past | | | Barlow et al. (2010), *Unified Protocol for Transdiagnostic Treatment of Emotional Disorders: Workbook* |
| Looking forward | | | |
| Consider values/goals | | | |
| Double-sided reflections | | | |
| Instill discrepancy | | | |
| Reflective listening | Humanistic | Client-centered therapy | Rogers (1975), "Empathic: An Unappreciated Way of Being" |

position. Being tentative in understanding the client's experience allows the client to be specific about what they want and how they want to proceed. The client feels in control, their autonomy feels respected (a cornerstone of motivation work), and the Columbo therapist provides space for the client to engage in change talk.

W. R. Miller and Rollnick (2013) stated the underlying idea regarding evocation this way: "The spirit of MI starts from a very different strengths-focused premise, that people already have within them much of what is needed, and your task is to evoke it, to call it forth" (p. 21). This perspective is consistent with the notion that those who are ambivalent about change see value in both sticking with the status quo and turning over a new leaf. This may overstate the cognitive element of ambivalence because habit (including motivations about which the client lacks conscious awareness), emotion, and external factors also play a role, yet the idea still stands that the therapist is helping the client to engage with the part of them that desires change. Evocation entails helping the client connect with one side of that argument—the one that says change should or could occur—and through that focus helping to draw out and activate an inner desire to move forward.

Though based in Rogerian client-centered therapy, MI's use of evoking is somewhat distinct in delineating specific intervention strategies. Focusing and engaging, as described in the Bond and Goal sections of Chapter 2 of this book, are foundational MI principles that precede evoking. The spirit of MI that focuses on warmth and collaboration is vital in making the evoking efforts fruitful. Theoretical ideas around motivation can still be used to conceptualize and work with client motivation; however, MI provides a transtheoretical enhancement of motivation-based strategies.

To understand evoking change talk, several key MI ideas can provide support. Ambivalence has already been discussed, but it may be helpful to note whether the client is demonstrating ambivalence based in approach dilemmas (e.g., an approach–approach dilemma in which a person must decide between two desirable paths) or avoidance dilemmas (e.g., fears about making a change and wanting to avoid perceived negative outcomes on the path). When we engage in change talk, we are discussing the preparation to make a change or how to mobilize ourselves in the direction of change. Preparatory change talk (MI describes it as uphill change talk) includes talk of desires to change, ability to change, reasons for a change, and needs for a change. Mobilizing change talk (which MI describes as downhill change talk) involves stating a commitment for change, describing action, and taking steps. MI interventions seek to promote change talk and minimize unproductive interventions that would promote *sustain talk* and maintain the status quo.

Change talk may occur spontaneously as the client discusses their goals for therapy, but often the therapist aims to evoke more change talk with evocative questions. These are open-ended questions that focus on change talk, especially preparatory change talk. Therapists can ask specific but open-ended questions about their client's desires to change, ability to change, reasons for a change, and needs for a change (MI uses DARN as an acronym for desires, ability, reasons, and need). See our Bond section in Chapter 2 for more general discussion of open-ended questions. As clients engage in change talk (with or without the therapist's prompting), MI proponents recommend using reflective listening to align with the client, which supports or strengthens the increase in change talk. To some degree, therapists can selectively reflect the change talk (giving less attention to sustain talk) and highlight with their reflections the change talk in contrast to the sustain talk.

At its core, MI-style evoking is about noticing ambivalence, resisting the righting reflex, and instead using reflection to promote change talk. This may sound simple, but it requires effort and practice to enact effectively with clients. In the moment of a client giving reasons not to change, a kind-hearted therapist may feel inclined to contradict and persuade. These strategies contain demand elements, which will not promote change talk. Reflecting, affirming, and other MI interventions will allow clients to talk through their reasons not to change and enable them to engage in more change talk. Fortunately, evidence suggests that deliberate practice can help trainees get better at MI and evoking change talk, beyond merely learning about the strategies (Westra et al., 2021).

Another key MI example is to ask about the importance of the focused, agreed-upon goal. The therapist uses language such as "How important is it to you to ____, with 1 being not important at all and 10 being the most important thing for you right now?" (adapted from W. R. Miller & Rollnick, 2013, p. 174). The answer to the question not only helps the therapist attune to their client's motivation but also brings grist to the therapeutic mill. The therapist can follow up with a question such as "What would it take for you to go from a (current number) to a (higher number)?" (see W. R. Miller & Rollnick, 2013, p. 175). Visual examples such as a seesaw or a number line can be used to help the client conceptualize not just the change they want but also their contradictory, ambivalent emotions regarding making the change. Even while a client is expressing ambivalence, such a discussion promotes change talk.

Amplifying the change talk can take place with greater nuance as one learns specific MI evoking interventions. For example, one can use evocative questions to encourage ambivalent clients to consider their past (thinking of where they've been to develop contrast), look forward (imagining how changes could improve their lives), and consider their values and goals. Double-sided reflections can be especially helpful by joining sustain talk from a client with the word "and" to include the counterbalanced change talk. For example, a client may state something like "I am so sick of checking my blood sugar! If my family didn't care I would just stop!" Then the therapist may reflect back, "It's so painful and exhausting to check your blood sugar, and you're trying to ensure your long-term well-being for your family as you've mentioned." This serves to reflect and join the client while emphasizing the change talk and promoting the client's motivation.

Instilling discrepancy represents another key MI strategy. When clients notice a discrepancy between their deeply held personal values and their behavior, this can promote change talk. One approaches this only carefully (too large a discrepancy can undermine our motivation as we feel guilty about the difference between our goal and our status quo) and by creating space for clients to talk about it themselves. Open-ended questions can lead to an exchange of information on a topic: for example, "What have you learned about smoking and health?" Open-ended questions can bring in content from concerned others: for example, "Your partner noted concern about how depression impacts your work; what have you noticed?" Exploring deeply held personal values can also help to instill discrepancy. W. R. Miller and Rollnick (2013) emphasized how the therapist needs to maintain neutrality around the client's desired changes. They wrote how this neutrality is so fundamental that it trumps adherence to their model:

> In a way it doesn't matter whether it's MI if it's the right thing to do. Certainly our recommendations here about how to counsel with neutrality arose from what we have learned through MI research regarding guiding and the psycholinguistics of conversations about change. From the earliest description (W. R. Miller, 1983) MI has been about strategically evoking the client's own arguments for change, usually with a conscious goal of steering toward a particular outcome. The intended outcome when counseling with neutrality is to help the person make a difficult decision without influencing the direction of choice. The direction is toward making a decision. (p. 241)

Note how emphasizing autonomy and personal choice is essential while developing discrepancy, and this emphasis can help clients to make choices that are consistent with internal values.

Sustain talk differs from discord in MI. In the past, sustain talk could have been somewhat pathologized when it was called "resistance," but W. R. Miller and Rollnick (2013) pointed out that sustain talk is really the other side of ambivalence. The target change is still the topic of conversation, but the client is describing their ambivalence about making the change. Discord, however, is about the relationship with the client and requires different sorts of attention. Conflict in the relationship (i.e., not just about the target change) usually reflects a rupture. See our Chapter 2 section on ruptures and repairs to explore how to address the relationship in these situations.

Practicing evoking can occur with deliberate practice. Please see our deliberate practice suggestions in Table 3.4 for improving skills with evoking change talk. Again, we recommend W. R. Miller and Rollnick's (2013) full text and MI workshops for more information and for improving proficiency. MI represents an example of a transtheoretical enhancement of a common factor. CF therapy, as we are describing it, can be thought of as an approach that enhances all of the identified common factors through a transtheoretical lens. Motivation work can be implemented at any stage of the process of therapy, whenever ambivalence is noticed by the therapist, and evoking interventions can occur.

## Planning Change

### PRINCIPLE 3.3

Therapists assist their clients with anticipating how change can be enacted in practice.

Once a person feels motivated to change, translating this into action becomes easier. There are no guarantees, however, that a statement of intent will be followed by a carrying out of the intended action. Planning action steps, with support for those action steps, increases the likelihood of follow-through. Therapists may engage in setting homework for their client to complete, a practice that tends to be more common in behavioral and cognitive behavior therapies even though it is not exclusive to these frames. Mausbach et al. (2010) found a modest but significant ($r = .26$) effect size between homework compliance and treatment outcome in CBT. Gollwitzer (1999) noted that intentions account for about 20% to 30% of the variance in behavior. Rather than dismissing good intentions as paving the way to hell, Gollwitzer instead recommended methods to help establish implementation intentions. Essentially involving self-regulatory strategies, planning helps us to anticipate situations in which our intentions will be difficult to carry out and specify how we will behave to carry our intentions forward. Table 3.5 provides a list of interventions that can be used in planning.

For the CF therapist, when clients express their intention to change (possibly as change talk that has been evoked), this is the opportunity to support

**TABLE 3.4. Deliberate Practice Suggestions for Evoking Change Talk**

| Method | Descriptions |
|---|---|
| Video-assisted observation of your work | • Watch an intake or an early session, paying attention to the following:<br>  – Notice ambivalence about a target change related to the therapy goals. Look for change talk (preparatory, mobilizing) and sustain talk with regard to a target change.<br>  – Notice how your client responds to reflections, based on whether your reflections capture your client's change talk.<br>  – Notice the righting reflex arising in response to ambivalence. See how reflections and affirmations can play out instead. Practice reflections and affirmations directly related to the ambivalence and change talk, joining the client rather than demanding change.<br>  – Notice moments with opportunities for open-ended questions. Practice jumping in with open-ended questions regarding your client's desires for change, ability to make change, reasons for making change, and needs related to making change.<br>  – Notice opportunities to practice other evoking interventions, including<br>    ○ Questions about the importance of change (e.g., when a client focuses primarily on sustain talk)<br>    ○ Double-sided reflections (e.g., when a client is expressing both sustain and change talk in the same expression and you are hoping to emphasize change talk)<br>    ○ With caution, instilling discrepancy. Ensure that you have a neutral stance toward changes in the client's life before attempting. Practice exchanging relevant information, bringing in content from concerned others, and exploring core values.<br>• Identify key moments to share with a consultant, trying to identify and move through any defensiveness you may feel about sharing this. |
| Getting consultant feedback | • Determine whether your relationship with your consultant is sufficiently supportive and safe for soliciting feedback openly. Consider working through defensive reactions with your consultant.<br>• Watch the session with your consultant, asking for assistance to notice whether your identified moments reflect client ambivalence, change talk, sustain talk, etc.<br>• Request assistance with noticing opportunities to reflect and evoke change talk. Practice together ways of responding to ambivalent moments.<br>• With your consultant, use a role play to practice interventions out loud using different phrasing and verbal inflections. Get feedback from the consultant and continue practicing. Focus saying the words you would actually say to a client, not just talking about what you might say to a client.<br>• Request assistance with discerning between sustain talk and discord. |

*(continues)*

**TABLE 3.4. Deliberate Practice Suggestions for Evoking Change Talk (Continued)**

| Method | Descriptions |
|---|---|
| Setting small incremental goals | • Perhaps with your consultant's help, identify your current comfort level and competence with evoking change talk. Then, identify a behavior to practice on your own that stretches you just beyond this comfort level. Try to ensure that your practice is neither too overwhelming nor too easy. Be as specific as possible when describing what you are going to practice. |
| Solo deliberate practice | • Dedicate sufficient time to practice on your own.<br>• Use the session video to practice responding to ambivalence, reflecting change talk as much as possible. Vary these practices as you get comfortable, increasing your repertoire of possible responses that evoke change talk.<br>• Notice how comfortable/uncomfortable the practice is and adjust the practice as needed. |
| Feedback-informed treatment | • Use outcome measures at each session to determine how the client is progressing in treatment. When progress feedback shows the client as not on track, checking in around motivation for change can be especially helpful. Exploring ambivalence, rolling with resistance during such a discussion, and clarifying treatment goals can be practiced. |

the client in enacting the change. Mobilizing change talk may help indicate readiness for this shift, honoring the client's readiness with identifying specific action steps. Watch especially for commitment talk, that the client indicates a stronger sense of intention to enact the change. The therapist recognizes their role as primarily supportive because it is the client who will take the action. Clients may test the water and make small steps toward change, which can give the therapist an opportunity to reinforce this movement (see W. R. Miller & Rollnick, 2013).

One may consider planning a change as essentially a self-regulation strategy. Planning is a strategy for committing to a change and anticipating how the self will behave in the future in response to contingencies that may interfere with the change. Turn to learning theories and cognitive theories (Burnette et al., 2013) as well as neuroscience theories (Heatherton, 2011) for descriptions of self-regulation as a core human strategy for meeting important goals. Popular ideas such as growth mindset and grit may have merit for clients who are trying to engage with a specific change.

At times the target of the motivation work, spoken of as the *target change*, is the therapy itself. Working through the ambivalence about attending therapy through evoking change talk can be helpful, especially when followed up with discussion of the commitment to participate in therapy. Therapeutic

**TABLE 3.5. Example Planning Interventions**

| Intervention | Broad theoretical categories | Specific theoretical approaches | Additional resources |
|---|---|---|---|
| Implementation intentions | General psychology | Self-regulation strategies | Gollwitzer (1999), "Implementation Intentions: Strong Effects of Simple Plans" |
| Encourage specific goals<br>Address ambivalence<br>Take small steps<br>Offer a menu of options<br>Create contingency plans | Transtheoretical | Motivational interviewing | W. R. Miller & Rollnick (2013), *Motivational Interviewing: Helping People Change* (3rd ed.) |
| Homework | Behavioral<br>Cognitive behavior | Workbooks, tracking, bibliotherapy, or other interventions | Riggenbach (2012), *The CBT Toolbox: A Workbook for Clients and Clinicians* |
| Relapse prevention | Substance abuse treatment | Substance abuse treatment | Marlatt & Donovan (2005), *Relapse Prevention: Maintenance Strategies in the Treatment of Addictive Behaviors* (2nd ed.) |

interventions that bring corrective experiencing (see Chapter 4) and insight (see Chapter 5) often require significant effort and motivation. The change talk around therapy participation can be followed up with specific homework tasks, such as self-monitoring practice or journaling or breathing practice. The actions that take place in the therapy room (e.g., exposure interventions) can be intimidating and can be the subject of a client's ambivalence. Motivation work is helpful here too. For specific ways motivation work can be combined with therapy such as CBT, see Westra et al. (2016) and Naar and Safren (2017).

Clients will often be making the target change outside of the therapy session, in between therapy sessions. Recall the importance of client factors—previously also called extratherapeutic factors, referring to how experiences in the client's life external to the events of therapy—which contribute or explain 40% of overall change in therapy (Lambert, 2013). Therapists working on a plan with a client are helping them to apply self-regulation in their lives outside of therapy. In this way, motivation work helping outside of therapy can build self-efficacy (see Chapter 6).

Certainly, there are differences between a cognitive behavior therapist's assigning of homework and the client-driven commitment to a change that MI proponents describe. However, the common threads appear to be addressing motivation through the mechanism of planning to increase the likelihood that the client can self-regulate as they hope to do. These elements can be seen in the many intervention strategies described by W. R. Miller and Rollnick (2013) and captured in adapted form in the list that follows. These are not a bag of tricks but rather ways to meet one's client where they are when they are committed to making a change, supporting them as they enact change. The key question to begin such a discussion may be something like "So what do you think you'll do?" (W. R. Miller & Rollnick, 2013, p. 265). They offer several ideas to guide the planning of concrete steps:

- Help the client to be specific. "Get a better relationship with my partner" leaves much to be desired in specificity. "Express affection with my partner every evening when we're together" is much more specific. Specificity can greatly help with anticipating potential difficulties as they plan to self-regulate.

- Throughout the process, be ready to address ambivalence and the need to continue reinforcing preparatory change talk.

- Take small steps. See how to break larger actions down into smaller increments to make it less overwhelming and more practical.

- Match the difficulty of change steps to the client's readiness for change with easier steps coming before more challenging steps.

- Offer a menu of options to the client, especially if they are at a loss for how to proceed in spite of feeling committed.

- Summarize the plan to the client. This can increase clarity and prevent miscommunication and confusion when the therapist follows up with the client.

- Troubleshoot any foreseeable problems. Barriers will arise, and the plan can include contingency plans to address barriers.

As the plan takes shape, therapists can continue to support the client in strengthening their commitment to the change. Rather than asking "Are you committed?" W. R. Miller and Rollnick (2013) recommended asking questions such as "What steps are you willing to take this week?" (p. 287).

Continuing effort to make change can be supported by the therapist following up with the client in subsequent sessions. A therapist neglecting to follow up on a target or homework assignment with a client sends the message tacitly that the target did not matter after all. It can be very rewarding to celebrate a client's successes with them. However, a therapist must take care to not include demand characteristics when following up with a client who has not enacted the change they had intended, such as expressing disappointment in the client or delivering shame-inducing messages. Rather, the therapist aims to normalize failure and backsliding (in substance abuse treatment and the transtheoretical model of change, this is typically conceptualized as relapse prevention; Prochaska & Norcross, 2018).

The motivational work continues as the therapist expresses curiosity and collaboration with the client. Barriers to change are identified and explored. The therapist can wonder with the client whether the target represented what they really wanted, modifying if necessary. If avoidance was the main explanation for the inaction, the therapist can explore motivations for avoidance rather than using avoidance as an accusation against the client.

In short, the motivation elements of attuning, evoking, and planning can be thought of as an iterative process to be repeated. Whenever progress in therapy stalls at any stage of the treatment, motivation interventions can serve to refocus the client on changes they want to make and their reasons for doing so. In this way, motivation work can be implemented at any point in therapy, with a therapist remaining attuned to a client's potential for ambivalence regarding potential changes. Therapists can remind themselves that motivation resides in the client and situate themselves in a collaborative and supportive role. Note our suggestions for deliberate practice with planning interventions in Table 3.6.

## SUMMARY

A key element in CF therapy, motivation encompasses the expectations a client brings with them to treatment as well as the often mixed, ambivalent desires for moving toward change. Often the expectations themselves promote hope and healing, as illustrated with placebo effects and reviewed expertly by Frank and Frank (1991). These expectations are associated with outcome, especially when the therapist attunes to these expectations. We brought particular attention to ambivalence, when clients have mixed feelings about participating in therapy or enacting the changes discussed in therapy. Motivation for change resides within the client, and therapists respect the autonomy of their client, taking a supportive and collaborative stance.

**TABLE 3.6. Deliberate Practice Suggestions for Planning Change**

| Method | Descriptions |
|---|---|
| Video-assisted observation of your work | • Watch a session in which there is change talk that is mobilizing, including a discussion of feeling committed to therapy or an action the client intends to take. Watch for the following:<br>  – Identify how the mobilizing change talk can include discussions of the client's commitment, activation, and taking steps.<br>  – Identify what action steps are discussed. Note ways that they can be made more specific or clarified in any other way.<br>  – Identify what barriers or obstacles are anticipated. Self-regulation can involve taking action based on contingencies when obstacles arise.<br>  – Notice how committed the client is to the action. Do they express feeling both capable of and willing to take the action?<br>• Watch a session in which you are following up with a client about an intended action. Watch for the following:<br>  – Identify opportunities to follow through. Do you remember to follow up?<br>  – Notice how the client responds to you. Do they express guilt or shame or in some way that they fear they have disappointed you? Do they recognize this as part of change?<br>  – Identify opportunities to be curious and collaborative. Recapitulate attuning to expectations and evoking change talk.<br>• Identify key moments to share with a consultant, trying to identify and move through any defensiveness you may feel about sharing this. |
| Getting consultant feedback | • Determine whether your relationship with your consultant is sufficiently supportive and safe for soliciting feedback openly. Consider working through defensive reactions with your consultant.<br>• Watch the session with your consultant, asking for assistance to notice how the planning discussion proceeds. Ask for help to ensure you are respecting autonomy. Ask for help to ensure that you are also focusing on action steps that are specific enough to be helpful to the client.<br>• Request assistance with noticing moments when mobilizing change talk is present and planning is encouraged.<br>• With your consultant, use a role play to practice planning interventions out loud using different phrasing and verbal inflections. Get feedback from the consultant and continue practicing. Focus saying the words you would actually say to a client, not just talking about what you might say to a client. |

**TABLE 3.6. Deliberate Practice Suggestions for Planning Change (*Continued*)**

| Method | Descriptions |
|---|---|
| Setting small incremental goals | • Perhaps with your consultant's help, identify your current comfort level and competence with discussions that include planning change. Then, identify a behavior to practice on your own that stretches you just beyond this comfort level. Try to ensure that your practice is neither too overwhelming nor too easy. Be as specific as possible when describing what you are going to practice. |
| Solo deliberate practice | • Dedicate sufficient time to practice on your own.<br>• Use the session video to practice noticing mobilizing change talk and supporting the client with planning action steps. Practice verbalizing these questions and statements aloud as if you are speaking to the client.<br>• Notice how comfortable/uncomfortable the practice is and adjust the practice as needed. |
| Feedback-informed treatment | • Use outcome measures at each session to determine how the client is progressing in treatment. When progress feedback shows client as not on track, checking in around actions taken outside of therapy can be helpful. Repeat attuning to client expectations and evoking change talk as needed. Renegotiate treatment goals as needed. |

CF therapists can intentionally address these expectations by attuning to them with open-ended questions and focusing on treatment goals. MI interventions are especially helpful with resisting the righting reflex and instead evoking change talk with open-ended questions and reflections, among other interventions. Although conceptually simple, this approach to client motivation requires intention, effort, and practice on the therapist's part. As a client feels more committed to the actions discussed in therapy (including therapy itself), they can be further supported by the therapist in planning change.

This chapter and the previous one (Chapter 2, on the therapeutic relationship) represent common change principles to promote a therapeutic environment. They can be thought of as the conditions required for change. The therapist's role is to facilitate the creation of conditions that support changes the client is working toward for remoralization. The next chapters (4–6) focus more on active ingredients in the therapy, beyond the conditions for change. They describe the hows of change from a CF therapy perspective, actualizing the change that the foundational conditions promote. The change principles of CF therapy present a lens for guiding the therapist in making treatment decisions with their client, moving from the conditions of therapy to action principles.

# 4 CORRECTIVE EXPERIENCING, COMMON FACTOR 3

Our initial definition of *corrective experiencing* refers to when a client engages with their felt emotions in a novel approach that contrasts with their expectations and contributes to remoralization. We elaborate later in our usual order after further discussion of the conceptual underpinnings of this common factor. First, let's begin to unpack the idea of corrective experiencing with two stories—one fictional and one factual, but with some common threads. Story number one was first used by the original users of the term *corrective emotional experience* in 1946, psychoanalysts Alexander and French. They told the story of the well-known protagonist Jean Valjean from Victor Hugo's novel *Les Misérables* but highlighted a lesser-known story element that did not make it into the Broadway musical adaptation.

Let's review the well-known elements: Jean Valjean had stolen bread to feed his starving family members and had been caught, convicted, and sentenced to prison, eventually serving 19 years after multiple escape attempts. He is now paroled but soon steals valuables from Bishop Myriel of Digne. When the gendarmes bring him to face Myriel, the bishop feigns that he willingly

https://doi.org/10.1037/0000343-005
*Common Factors Therapy: A Principle-Based Treatment Framework*, by R. J. Bailey and B. M. Ogles

gave him the treasures, adding candlesticks to the haul to ensure his freedom, then telling Valjean privately that he has redeemed his soul for God.

In the lesser-known details that follow, Valjean wanders about in confusion and bewilderment to a small village and encounters a 10-year-old boy named Gervais, who apparently plays the hurdy-gurdy (a musical instrument) for coins. While playing with his coins, Gervais loses one of the coins, which rolls toward a hidden Valjean, who then steps on the coin. In his bewildered state, Valjean learns the boy's name but does not move his foot off the coin, and the frightened Gervais gives up and leaves. After a time, Valjean realizes that he has robbed the boy, runs in the direction that he left, does not find him, but tries to recompense for his actions by giving money (many times the value of the coin that was stolen) to a priest. Then comes Valjean's anguish and Hugo's description of his being overcome with complex emotions. These emotions relate to his experience with Bishop Myriel but also to his having wronged Gervais and the two potential paths for him to be an angel like Myriel or monstrous (as seen through his actions against Gervais) and to seek vengeance on his oppressors. Hugo wrote,

> Then his heart burst, and he began to cry. It was the first time that he had wept in nineteen years. . . . Jean Valjean wept for a long time. He wept burning tears. . . . As he wept, daylight penetrated more and more clearly into his soul; an extraordinary light; a light at once ravishing and terrible. His past life, his first fault, his long expiation, his external brutishness, his internal hardness, his dismissal to liberty, rejoicing in manifold plans of vengeance, what had happened to him at the Bishop's, the last thing that he had done, that theft of forty sous from a child, a crime all the more cowardly, and all the more monstrous since it had come after the Bishop's pardon,—all this recurred to his mind and appeared clearly to him, but with a clearness which he had never hitherto witnessed. (Hugo, 1887/2021)

This moment leads to Valjean's transformation, and throughout the remainder of the novel he is an agent of compassion and mercy.

Several elements from this story were first related to psychotherapy by Alexander and French (1946). We pause to note our own lessons for the purpose of this chapter. Notice several contrasts in Valjean's experience: the clemency of the bishop in contrast to the rage and desire for vengeance he felt for the injustices reaped on him; Valjean's robbing of Gervais in contrast to the mercy of the bishop; and the contrast of his trying to pay the first priest he finds. The contrast elicits powerful emotions, breaking through the hardness of 19 years, and he commits his life to a path consistent with what he values. The experiencing was emotional, contrasting, and corrective in that it led to remoralization for Valjean.

Now story number two, this one a recollection posted by Jackie on a blog hosted by the International OCD (obsessive–compulsive disorder) Foundation (Sommers, 2013):[1]

> After 20 years of suffering, countless hours of talk therapy, loads of failed prescriptions (and their accompanying side effects), and one utterly exhausted psychiatrist, I was referred to an OCD specialist in the Twin Cities who broached the topic of cognitive-behavioral therapy (CBT) with me.
> He didn't mince words: "It will be hell," he said.
> But I knew I was ready for it: the daily hell of living with my OCD had become so much for me that I was willing to endure a short-term dose that had a glimmer of hope on the other side.

At first blush, her therapist's words hardly seem a strong endorsement for the treatment typically seen as the gold-standard treatment for OCD. Isn't therapy supposed to be warm and fuzzy? What followed, however, showed the therapist's words to be accurate for Jackie.

> My therapist outlined the measurable goals of my initial treatment plan: a fifty-percent reduction in distress when focused on upsetting stimuli and six consecutive weeks of no avoidance or rituals. The next few months of therapy were starting to sound like a long, long time.
> Since my obsessions were primarily religious-based (most often tied to blasphemy and a fear of hell and condemnation, a type of OCD sometimes called scrupulosity), my exposures needed to be imaginative (since, obviously, there was no way to literally expose me to hell). So my therapist began to write a story, and my homework was to finish it. It was the story of the worst day I could possibly imagine—pretty rough indeed as I ended up literally in hell in my version of the story!
> My therapist recorded my story (along with his own additions to it) digitally, and I was sent home with an 18-minute recording from the pit of hell. My job was to listen to it four times a day—two times through, twice a day—every day and record my anxiety levels when prompted. And I needed to do this consistently until my anxiety levels reduced by 50% from what I'd recorded on the initial exposure. Oh, and I couldn't perform my compulsions (repetitive prayer and seeking reassurance) to make myself feel better.
> It. Was. Awful.

No doubt only persons who have experienced OCD for themselves can truly understand how overwhelming the daily fear of hell from scrupulosity-focused OCD can be. Contradicting obsessions with exposure practices can be terrifying, inducing high levels of anxiety. It may seem to the person

---

[1]From *My Journey to Hell and Back, a Personal Experience With CBT and ERP*, by J. L. Sommers, 2013, International OCD Foundation (https://iocdf.org/blog/2013/08/27/my-journey-to-hell-and-back-a-personal-experience-with-cbt-and-erp). Copyright 2013 by International OCD Foundation (IOCDF). Reprinted with permission.

experiencing it as unnecessary, that surely simply continuing to surrender to the obsession will lead to less misery. This was Jackie's experience:

> I won't lie to you, listening to that recording—that exposure—was like torture. It was being triggered left and right and not being allowed to do anything to ease my anxiety.
>
> I hated it. It made me sick to my stomach, made my heart race, made me terrified. I tried to listen to the recording right away in the morning, in order to get half of my required exposures out of the way early in the day, but eventually, I couldn't do it that way anymore—the weight of beginning my morning in such misery made it hard to get out of bed, and I had to push it all back later in the day just so that I wouldn't dread waking up.
>
> It felt like needless torture, and I honestly wanted to quit at about week 8 or 9 when my anxiety levels weren't dropping.

The emotional labor of exposure therapy was intense, and you may question if this was worth it. It turned out to be very much worth it for Jackie:

> I was frustrated with my therapist and was certain that I couldn't accomplish all that he wanted. It was when I was at this lowest point, and felt like I couldn't go on, that my therapist introduced me to a tool to side-step my way into the exposure. Instead of thinking the blasphemous thoughts directly, he suggested that I think, "My OCD wants me to think X." It was just the tool I needed.
>
> Within a week of implementing this side-step, things just clicked. One day I was listening to the recording—this device of torture and grief—and instead of feeling terror, I thought, *This is so annoying*. And then I smiled and thought, *FINALLY*.
>
> This, of course, is just a brief description of my experience. I could tell you so many more things—about how hard it was, about what other exposures look like for other types of OCD, about the tools my therapist gave me for success.
>
> It was one of the hardest things I have ever had to do—but not as hard as living for 20 OCD-riddled years without help. I hated to go through ERP [exposure and response prevention], but I love that I have gone through it. It rescued me and that period of ERP is a defining period of my life.

Clearly, the experience of exposure had an impact, though it was not the only tool used by Jackie or by her therapist in helping Jackie. Just like Valjean, she experienced intense emotional distress, based on an active attempt to act in a manner in contrast to her typical approach to her thoughts and behavior, with a helper suggesting a direction to move. However, story one occurred with a helper outside of therapy (obviously a different sort of helper, because 1862 preceded Freud by half a century), and story two included very specific elements of treatment based on a specific diagnosis. Clearly, the stories have more in common than strong emotion, but both stories involved contrasting experiences that led to significant corrective change and remoralization.

**FIGURE 4.1. Common Factors (CF) Therapy Model With Corrective Experiencing Interventions**

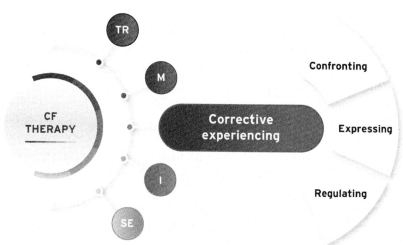

*Note.* TR = therapeutic relationship; M = motivation; I = insight; SE = self-efficacy.

In this chapter, we expand on this beginning through a brief review of the theoretical foundations of the concept followed by considering the evidence for correcting experiencing as a common factor using our inclusion and exclusion criteria. We then provide a definition for a common factors (CF) therapy form of corrective experiencing followed by discussing interventions that facilitate corrective experiencing using several key elements. These elements include addressing emotions (by facing, expressing, or regulating them), an emphasis on the experiencing or active process, and a focus on the experiencing having contrast with history or expectations (see Figure 4.1). In both this chapter and the next, we repeatedly refer to the need for both emotional and cognitive components to these interventions, but we emphasize emotion in this chapter. We leave the latter, the cognitive reflection on the corrective experiencing, for our chapter on insight (see Chapter 5, this volume).

## OVERVIEW OF CORRECTIVE EXPERIENCING

We arrived at the term *corrective experiencing* to describe this overarching change principle related to working with emotions in therapy. We started with the Penn State definition (from the group gathered by Castonguay & Hill, 2012) of *corrective experiences* (note the plural noun ending): "CEs [corrective experiences] are ones in which a person comes to understand or experience affectively an event or relationship in a different and unexpected way" (Castonguay & Hill, 2012, p. 5). This definition, however, uses "experience affectively," and we wanted to highlight emotions even more strongly. The experiences in question tend to include both emotional experiences and a cognitive element, as we show later, with the two change principles highly related as corrective experiencing and insight.

Our definition of corrective experiencing, which we explore in detail later, includes the involvement of intense emotion, an active experiencing of the emotion by the client, and the contrast to the client's past experience or expectation. However, exploring this change principle in detail requires some foundational ideas regarding emotions, how humans experience them, and how they figure in the work of therapy. As we have seen in the two examples at the beginning of the chapter, emotions can be deeply and intensely felt, are salient in context or relationship with other individuals, and, when contrasted, can be vehicles for making meaning and change. We explore the topic of emotions and change in therapy, then address inclusion and exclusion criteria for the change principle, define the change principle, and finally outline intervention strategies associated with the change principle.

## Emotions and Change

We need not be terribly surprised that intense emotions are at play in therapy because, as we indicated in Chapter 1, demoralization—and the emotional distress that word encompasses—comprises the primary reason clients present for treatment and the primary target for CF therapy. Emotions are often activated through the therapy process, often by the therapy process itself. Perhaps emotions are released like an uncorked bottle, perhaps emotions lead us to revise what we had expected (see Constantino & Westra, 2012, for this illustration), but it seems clear that these corrective experiences involve emotions.

Recent developments in understanding emotions may be especially valuable in understanding how corrective experiencing interplays with emotions. According to a current theory of constructed emotion (Barrett, 2017), we have active roles in our emotional experiences. Barrett described emotions this way:

> [Emotions] are not triggered; you create them. They emerge as a combination of the physical properties of your body, a flexible brain that wires itself to whatever environment it develops in, and your culture and upbringing, which provide that environment. Emotions are real, but not in the objective sense

that molecules or neurons are real. They are real in the same sense that money is real—that is, hardly an illusion, but a product of human agreement. (Barrett, 2017, Location No. 111)

Our brains are constantly simulating not only what is happening in the world around us but also what happens inside the body. When the body experience gets interpreted by the brain, based on experience and emotion concepts, it uses the emotion word to describe it and give meaning to the sensations experienced (Barrett, 2017, p. 31).

Barrett (2017) argued persuasively that we construct our emotional experiences with our brains, not reacting to the world but actually constructing the world and assigning meaning that is connected to our brain's experience of the past, context, and culture. Surely, emotional changes, if they are to occur in the context of therapy, will require emotional activation. If the therapeutic endeavor hopes to reconfigure meaning in less painful and less disruptive ways, emotions will need to be reconstructed. Activation and new meaning assignment are essential for this to occur. As Kegan (1982) wrote persuasively about emotion as grounded in our experience as physiologically evolved,

Affect is essentially phenomenological, the felt experience of a motion (hence, "e-motion"). In identifying evolutionary activity as the fundamental ground of personality I am suggesting that the source of our emotions is the phenomenological experience of evolving—of defending, surrendering, and reconstructing a center. (pp. 81–82)

Reconfiguring meaning in therapy may involve just such emotions and motion about reconstructing a center.

## Emotions and Cognition

Alexander and French (1946) understood how the process of psychoanalysis involved the reconstruction of meaning through emotions. They wrote that the purpose of psychoanalysis (prior to the formal development of other schools of therapy) was "inducing emotional discharge in order to facilitate insight, and exposing the ego to those unresolved emotional constellations which it has to learn to master" (p. vii). Note the two parts, which we take to heart in our own conception of corrective experiencing and insight: inducing emotion and facilitating insight. For them, the target of the new experiencing was trauma from the past, and the experiencing could happen either in the therapy office or "parallel with the treatment in the daily life of the patient" (p. 66). The transference, or the emotional relationship between analyst and patient, was for them a mechanism for identifying outdated patterns, whereupon the therapist "has an opportunity to help the patient both to see intellectually and to *feel* the irrationality of his emotional reactions" (p. 67).

More contemporary psychodynamic work on corrective experiencing also used this emotion versus cognition split. In Levenson's (1995) time-limited dynamic psychotherapy, the goal was stated to be twofold: "1) providing a *new experience* for the patient and 2) providing a *new understanding* for the patient" (p. 40). Levenson clarified,

> *New* is meant in the sense of being different from and more functional (i.e., healthier) than the maladaptive pattern the patient has become accustomed to. And *experience* emphasizes the affective-action component of change—behaving differently and emotionally appreciating behaving differently. (pp. 40–41)

The actions in dynamic therapy have to do with the client having a different sense of themselves and of the therapist, the focus on interpersonal relating in the evocation of dynamic elements, and the therapist attempting to "subvert the patient's maladaptive interactional style" (p. 43). Levenson also referenced a statement usually credited to Frieda Fromm-Reichmann: "What the patient needs is an experience, not an explanation" (p. 42).

From these perspectives, one can understand the importance of emotion in a novel experience that provides a significant contrast for the client. The bifurcation between experiencing and understanding is also useful for our purposes. The current chapter focuses on the experiencing, which can be seen as primarily involving emotional moments, and insight, which can be seen as primarily cognitive and is taken up in the next chapter. The distinction may be mainly academic, however, as the degree of overlap in the concepts may make it difficult to distinguish corrective experiencing from insight in many cases.

In fact, the two factors are typically expected to accompany one another. According to group therapy experts Yalom and Leszcz (2005) as they highlighted the importance of the corrective experience, ". . . *the evocation and expression of raw affect is not sufficient*: it has to be transformed into a corrective emotional experience" (p. 28). They described that the experience (in group therapy, the experience is emotional and focused on the here and now) also needs a reflecting back on the experience, a "self-reflective loop" (p. 30). They also referred to this as reality testing, a sort of cognitive or intellectual component of the process. They noted that Freud started with describing catharsis—releasing repressed emotion through expression—as treatment as early as 1895. As Yalom and Leszcz (2005) pointed out, however, "It was not long before Freud recognized the error: emotional expression, though necessary, is not a sufficient condition for change" (p. 31).

Corrective experiencing seems from these descriptions to be a sort of experiential learning. Explicit, cognitive understanding or knowledge can imply knowing a thing, but this differs from doing a thing, which would be implicit or applied knowledge. One may also contrast the top-down versus bottom-up approaches (also called "high road" and "low road" emotional processing by L. S. Greenberg, 2012, p. 698). A top-down approach involves generating a new understanding, whereas a bottom-up approach is developing a new experience.

Emotions from the bottom-up may benefit from an exploration from an evolutionary perspective. Grounding emotions within evolution focuses on how they are adaptive, functioning to enhance survival, and are therefore not something to be avoided or tightly controlled (see L. S. Greenberg, 2012). From this evolutionary perspective it may be less helpful to distinguish emotions as negative and positive or even to distinguish between adaptive and maladaptive, because this could undermine the definition of emotions as basically adaptive. Rather, distressing emotional states (demoralized states) tend to be adaptive emotions that are amplified or dysregulated due to being either overactivated or excessively avoided. Compare this amplified adaptive response with allergies, in which the body's immune response (an adaptive function) goes into overdrive.

Our purpose here is not to reformulate or propose a general theory of emotions but to make a comparison that can be clinically useful. Consider our emotions as adaptive, and challenges with emotions reflect overfunctioning of a naturally adaptive response. For example, anxiety appears to be an overfunctioning adaptation for threats in the environment—in other words, the fight-or-flight response in overdrive. Depression may represent an amplified response to loss or exhaustion, requiring slowing down for rest and the reconfiguration of relationships and meaning. Shame may be a magnified adaptive response to group-based rejection, in the interest of reconnecting with the group in a way that rectifies and reinforces group norms. By having novel experiences with emotions that are corrective, the client can move toward feeling less hopeless or helpless and less demoralized, all the while moving toward remoralization.

Emotions figure prominently in change processes in therapy and form the core of our understanding of corrective experiencing. Physical and often raw emotions refer to our "somatically felt subjective experience" (Fosha, 2009, p. 287). As L. S. Greenberg (2012) pointed out, emotions are vehicles for connection, for meaning making, and are central to therapeutic change (pp. 704–705).

In the next section, we review our inclusion criteria for this change principle of CF therapy and present a definition that is transtheoretical in nature.

## INCLUSION CRITERIA FOR CORRECTIVE EXPERIENCING

To be considered a bona fide therapy, CF therapy needs specified components, and each change principle must meet our established criteria. Here we take each criterion in turn to show how corrective experiencing aligns with our requirements.

### Research Evidence in Support of Corrective Experiencing

Although corrective experiencing is not as heavily studied as is the therapeutic alliance, considerable research has been conducted on emotional experiences, corrective emotional experiences, and exposure therapy. Typically these are not considered together under an umbrella term of corrective experiencing when they are the subjects of empirical research. However, we consider them together here. We do this from the perspective of CF therapy, that the CF metatheory points to a common principle that can be translated to a specific change principle (corrective experiencing) and specific interventions associated with that change principle. By doing this, we are not suggesting that all of these ideas are merely exposure therapy or merely corrective emotional experiences. Rather, we are proposing that these ideas that have historically been confined to separate theoretical orientations have a common thread, that the common thread can be conceptually organized as a change principle, and that the change principle can be applied by a therapist with a client using specific interventions.

Unsurprisingly, emotion-focused therapy (EFT) researchers have done considerable work to address the evidence for emotional work in therapy. We recommend L. S. Greenberg's (2012) review of evidence for emotional work in therapy based on empirical studies and conceptual rationale. In one notable study of emotional work in therapy, Carryer and Greenberg (2010) coded emotion episodes in therapy based on whether they demonstrated moderate to highly aroused emotional expression. They found that these episodes of emotional expression predicted therapy outcomes for the clients, with a stronger predictive value even than the working alliance, but showing a nonlinear relationship. In other words, they found an optimal level of emotional expression, that a 25% frequency of highly aroused emotional expression was most therapeutic. This suggests that whereas moderate emotional arousal can be very helpful, too much arousal may be undesirable.

Corrective experiencing has been shown to be associated with outcome, but the findings are more nuanced than a simple correlation would suggest. L. S. Greenberg (2012) emphasized the importance of emotional processing based on several studies that found emotional processing predicted outcome especially during the middle or working phase of therapy. In his review he also found that the cognitive-processing element of corrective experiencing was essential to having the experience be therapeutic. Grosse Holtforth and Flückiger (2012) found evidence that pointed away from singular "big bang" or "aha" moments and more toward a change process as a series of assimilations and that mastery was needed to benefit from these. They described the change process as "fading in adaptive behaviors and fading out problematic behaviors" (p. 330). Some researchers found that clients may not recall or have experienced salient emotional moments in their therapy, possibly suggesting that corrective experiencing is a sufficient but not a necessary condition for change. Anderson et al. (2012) found that a majority of (but not all) clients could identify discrete corrective experiences in their therapy.

Peluso and Freund (2018; see also Peluso & Freund, 2019) conducted a meta-analysis of emotional expression in therapy and its relation to outcome. They estimated a medium to large effect ($d = 0.85$) between the client's expression and outcome (notably, they found a significant medium effect size, $d = 0.56$ for therapist's expression and outcome). However, conditions may need to be right for corrective experiencing to occur. Caspar and Berger (2012) pointed to the need of being at a medium arousal state, consistent with L. S. Greenberg's (2012) review. In addition, Caspar and Berger found that a good therapeutic relationship can help to either increase or reduce arousal, suggesting that the therapeutic relationship is instrumental in any change wrought through corrective experiencing.

Exposure, perhaps the best researched principle among the interventions we consider under the umbrella term of corrective experiencing, has a long history as a behavioral intervention. Emmelkamp (2013) extensively reviewed outcome literature on behavioral treatments by diagnosis and highlighted exposure as a key element across diagnoses that contributes uniquely to outcome. Though more behavioral than cognitive, he noted that cognitive and acceptance-based approaches use exposure as an important component of treatment. He described strong evidence for exposure as a treatment of choice for anxiety disorders. For depression, however, he found that behavioral treatment (i.e., without the "cognitive" in cognitive behavior treatment) still resulted in changes to cognitive experiences of clients. He cited this as a nonspecific effect but later hailed calls to focus on principles of change, focusing on processes rather than focusing excessively on distinct diagnostic categories (p. 376).

A classic tome for cognitive behavior therapy (CBT) practitioners, Barlow's (2014) *Clinical Handbook of Psychological Disorders* included exposure elements in most of the chapters (which are organized, as is Emmelkamp's, 2013, review, by diagnosis). For example, in that handbook Craske and Barlow (2014) highlighted how exposure appears to be "the most powerful component" in CBT for panic disorder and agoraphobia (p. 26). In a separate vein with depression treatment, the same theme can be found. For a transdiagnostic model of therapy for depression, exposure is a key element (Payne et al., 2014, p. 250).

Evidence for exposure as an effective practice is perhaps best known in the extensive career of Edna Foa. Foa used emotional processing theory to propose an explanation for how exposure works effectively for anxiety patients (see Foa et al., 2006). Modifying a fear structure is the focus according to this theory, but the requirements include two main elements: "activation of the fear structure and incorporation of new information that is incompatible with the pathological elements of the fear structure" (Foa et al., 2006, p. 7). This same emotional processing theory, according to Foa and other research (A. M. Hayes et al., 2005), may help account for exposure being an effective element in treatment for depression.

The volume of studies on exposure is extensive (see Emmelkamp's 2013 review); however, one of Foa's studies seemed especially notable for our purposes. Studying exposure for posttraumatic stress disorder (PTSD), Jaycox et al. (1998) noted different patterns of distress, emotional engagement, and habituation. They found the most effective pattern was one with high initial engagement (emotional activation beginning early in treatment) and gradual habituation between sessions. This seemed highly consistent both with Foa's emotional processing theory and with our dual elements of corrective experiencing, one focusing on emotional activation and the second more on cognitive change postactivation to promote lasting change.

Other elements we include under the umbrella term corrective experiencing include mindfulness, diaphragmatic breathing, and behavioral activation. Each of these presents a contrasting emotional experience for the client that is novel and serves to regulate emotions. For evidence of the effectiveness of mindfulness-based therapies, turn to a comprehensive meta-analysis finding mindfulness moderately effective (effect size of .53 in wait-list controlled studies, .55 in pre–post studies; Khoury et al., 2013). Relaxation training, with diaphragmatic breathing as the key component, has been shown in meta-analysis to be effective with or without CBT added, which seems unsurprising given our Chapter 1 (this volume) review of the contextual model (Thorp et al., 2009). Similarly, a meta-analysis of behavioral activation alone versus cognitive therapy showed both treatments as effective, though not differentially effective (Cuijpers et al., 2007). Evidence shared by Foa et al. (2006) suggested that exposure treatment for PTSD also helped decrease anger, guilt, and shame (see Cahill et al., 2003).

Though the terms we have presented here are not always combined under the umbrella term of corrective experiencing, we have shared a taste of the extensive literature in support of corrective experiencing as a change principle that is associated with positive outcome in therapy. We turn now to highlight how different schools of therapy utilize this principle of corrective experiencing, though perhaps using different language to describe the phenomenon.

## Conceptually Present in Most Therapies

Jerome Frank (1961) noticed many decades ago that emotional experiences were common across therapeutic orientations, even though they differed as to how these emotions were evoked and addressed. He wrote,

> Different types of psychotherapy tend to arouse patients emotionally in different ways. Among these are the requirement that the patient place himself in situations, or carry out acts, that he fears; the facilitation of emotional reliving of traumatic early life experiences; the therapist's failure to respond to the patient's maneuvers as the latter expects; and the evocation of "transference" feelings to the therapist. At this point it seems appropriate to call attention to an often neglected aspect of most psychotherapeutic methods, which may stir patients emotionally in a helpful but nonspecific fashion. This exciting feature is their novelty. Novelty is pleasantly exciting in itself, as evidenced by our constant search for new experiences, and it also tends to inspire hope. It is a medical truism that all forms of treatment work best just after they are introduced. The major reasons for this seem to be the physician's emotional investment in the success of a procedure he has initiated and the ability of something new and untried, especially when recommended by an authority, to arouse the patient's hopes. (p. 144)

Key to Frank's understanding here is the client's experiencing of emotions in novel and possibly untried ways, highlighting what we have noted throughout this chapter as contrast in the experiences. Corrective experiencing may not have been an explicit element in the contextual model, but it can certainly be seen as a common factor. Goldfried (1980, 2012, 2019) has consistently included this concept in his descriptions of common factors and change principles. He cited an interview with therapists hailing from discrepant schools of thought (see Brady et al., 1980) to show how across the board they referred to the principle of "new experiences" in therapy "critical," "crucial," or "essential" to the work of therapy (as cited in Goldfried, 2019).

More recently, Castonguay and Hill (2012) edited the volume *Transformation in Psychotherapy*, dedicated to the topic of corrective emotional experiences, with chapter authors representing perspectives across orientations. Psychodynamic, relational, cognitive behavior, acceptance and commitment, humanistic–experiential, and person-centered approaches were represented, and together they worked toward a consensus in understanding corrective experiences. As they reviewed their collaborative work, they highlighted corrective experiences as including the "disconfirmation of a client's conscious or unconscious expectations . . . as well as an emotional, interpersonal, cognitive, and/or behavioral shift" (Hill et al., 2012, pp. 355–356). Earlier work by me (BMO) in the Castonguay and Hill volume highlighted the concept of contrast with corrective experiences (Anderson et al., 2012).

Corrective experiencing may appear differently in discrepant approaches, especially with regard to the target. The target typically represents expectations (of the client always, but sometimes also the therapist's expectations) that are disconfirmed through a contrasting experience and through the evocation of emotions. Psychodynamic and relational perspectives highlight the relationship itself as the vehicle for corrective experiencing, that the client addresses a painful relational past with a sympathetic and benevolent therapist. Behavioral work focuses on exposure, that the corrective element is found through confronting feared stimuli, the resultant emotional activation, and habituating to the stimuli. S. C. Hayes et al. (2012) described a cognitive behavior view of corrective experiencing as involving "a challenge to expectations that are based on prior experiences, an increase in dissonance and affective arousal, and a new perspective and change in affective responses that often manifests in behavioral changes in the person's life" (p. 80). Practical skills can be taught in this and a variety of perspectives to give new experiences via regulating emotions in healthy ways. Acceptance and commitment therapy (ACT) focuses on experiential avoidance and confronting this experience by increased presence through mindfulness. Dialectical behavior therapy (DBT) focuses on learning emotion regulation and building skills to have healthier relationships via interpersonal boundaries. Humanistic therapies (e.g., EFT) focus squarely on the emotional experiencing of the client, highlighting unacknowledged emotions and helping them to express these emotions.

Each of these major approaches to therapy encourages new, contrasting experiences that are emotionally laden. We recommend reviewing Castonguay and Hill's (2012) volume to explore how each approach may describe corrective experiencing. For CF therapy, the overarching change principle is corrective experiencing, regardless of how the various schools of thought may use specific, theory-laden language to describe their interventions. CF therapists would focus on the change principle as their primary consideration.

## EXCLUSION CRITERIA FOR CORRECTIVE EXPERIENCING

We have already shown that the broad schools of psychotherapy ascribe to the change principle we are calling corrective experiencing. The principle is not the sole province of any single theoretical orientation (i.e., no single school of thought has exclusive claim to the principle). We have also given general descriptions of how corrective experiencing is positively associated with client outcome, often the key change principle. Empirical evidence is not lacking, especially considering exposure interventions under the umbrella of this change principle.

With regard to potential redundancy with other change principles, we propose that corrective experiencing offers a parsimonious description for a common thread across therapies. Though corrective experiencing may occur within the context of the dyad (the therapeutic relationship), it is important to note that the experiencing occurs for the client. Corrective experiencing and therapeutic relationship are therefore not synonyms. It is also not synonymous with motivation, though a corrective experience can often contribute to client motivation for change. We have highlighted how there is considerable overlap with our change principle of insight. To avoid redundancy with this concept, we distinguish between emotional and cognitive change experiences. Whenever the primary focus is a new emotional experience, we apply the term corrective experiencing. Whenever the primary focus is new cognitive awareness or understanding, we apply the term insight.

## DEFINITION OF CORRECTIVE EXPERIENCING

We aim to use terminology that crosses theoretical boundaries, that conceptualizes the change principle to allow for variability across boundaries and flexibility in application, and that offers parsimony without redundancy. As previously shared, for this change principle we began with the Penn State definition of corrective experiences (again, note the usage of the plural noun): "CEs [corrective experiences] are ones in which a person comes to understand or experience affectively an event or relationship in a different and unexpected way" (Castonguay & Hill, 2012, p. 5).

We found this definition to be workable across theoretical orientations and therefore highly consistent with our purposes. However, as we have reviewed relevant material in our attempt to understand the phenomenon, we found aspects that could be more strongly emphasized while retaining the transtheoretical language. We review several such aspects that we wish to incorporate in a CF therapy definition.

One aspect of the definition that could be adjusted reflected the term itself. *Corrective experiences* implies discrete moments. However, we want to emphasize the phenomenon as more active, ongoing, continuous, in process, or taking place across time. Siegel (2009) described *emotion* as more like a verb than a noun. For this reason we prefer more kinetic grammar to be employed with the use of the gerund form, corrective experien*cing*, rather than the more static plural noun, experience*s*. The gerund implies an active process rather than a reflective process, which would be more appropriate for the insight factor or change principle in the next chapter. By highlighting emotional experiencing, we highlight how clients often go through an active process. The difference lies in experience versus thoughts about an experience. The term can also highlight how experiencing occurs both in and out of the therapy office, and therefore the term does not refer merely to the single moments during a face-to-face encounter with a therapist. Pascual-Leone and Yeryomenko (2017), in a meta-analysis of experiencing, found that client experiencing is a small to medium predictor of outcomes and likely a common factor. What matters most is the client's engaging in their experience, regardless of whether or not the therapist is present, even though this experiencing is often occurring at the direction of or with the assistance of the therapist.

We also wished to emphasize emotions with our definition. By doing so, we find it highly consistent across therapeutic orientations. We also emphasize how corrective experiencing is a bottom-up factor rather than top-down factor (i.e., more suitable for our insight chapter). Emotions ground us in physiology, in the adaptive functions given us through evolution, as representing a fundamental aspect of life. Clients experience emotions in their bodies as a felt sense of reality of which they may or may not be fully aware. Emotions closely align with our definition of pathology for CF therapy: demoralization. Emotional learning is "warm" learning, whereas cognitive insight is "cool" learning.

We wished to emphasize an aspect that is already found in the Penn State definition but to tinker with it slightly. The words "different and unexpected" highlight how the experiences referred to are corrective. These are often novel experiences. Primarily, however, these emotional experiences contrast with what the client expects. The contrast can be illustrated by showing how on the one hand, a person expects and predicts that if they engage in a given behavior, a certain outcome will occur. Then on the other hand, when a person actually experiences the behavior or intervention, the actual emotional outcome thwarts the expectation. We wished to highlight both novelty and contrast in our definition. Note that the expectation language closely relates to cognition associated with emotions, and the more cognitive aspects are taken up in our chapter on insight (see Chapter 5).

Finally, we aimed to incorporate CF therapy language in our definition. Because the primary target of CF therapy involves demoralization, corrective experiencing can be useful only to the degree that it promotes change toward remoralization. The word "corrective" is useful in that it highlights both contrast and remedial change. We also incorporated remoralization in our definition. As clients engage in emotional experiences that are novel and contrasting, they are likely to feel less hopeless and helpless, moving toward remoralization.

For the purposes of CF therapy, we use the following definition.

### COMMON FACTORS DEFINITION OF CORRECTIVE EXPERIENCING

*Corrective experiencing* refers to when a client engages with their felt emotions in a novel approach that contrasts with their expectations and contributes to remoralization.

## INTERVENTION CONCEPTS FOR CORRECTIVE EXPERIENCING

Translating the CF metatheory to specific interventions requires that corrective experiencing not merely be a change principle but also be translated into specific, actionable interventions for use by CF therapists. As with the other change principles (therapeutic relationship, motivation, insight, and self-efficacy), this intervention approach emphasizes attention to the change principle, as this is the lens of CF therapy. The CF therapist seeks to employ specific interventions to evoke this change principle with their client. In this section, we give an overview of corrective experiencing intervention, followed by outlines of specific interventions to evoke this change principle with a client. The broad categories of corrective experiencing interventions include confronting, expressing, and regulating. We also offer deliberate practice exercises for the aspiring CF therapist to hone their skills with the interventions.

Therapists can use corrective experiencing, as with any of the guiding change principles of CF therapy, as a heuristic (see Lazarus & Wachtel, 2018). Think of heuristics as practical mental shortcuts to more complex ideas, like a general guideline. When working with clients, the change principles can readily come to mind to guide intervention decisions. As clients progress in therapy (and therapists use routine outcome monitoring to continuously assess progress), therapists can use the rubric of CF therapy change principles to determine how to apply interventions.

We offer several questions to guide therapists in the use of the heuristic of corrective experiencing:

- How is my client currently expressing their emotions? How am I as their therapist supporting and helping them express their emotions? How might they be holding back or struggling against their emotional experiences?

- How can I support my client in confronting experiences that they may be avoiding or resisting?

- What kind of emotional experience could be novel yet corrective for my client? How can I support the expression of their emotions? How can I support them in learning to regulate emotions or soothe themselves?

- I am hoping to support my client as they try to understand their experience in a way that can be more helpful to them. Can I help direct them toward emotional experiences that can help them move in the direction they want to go?

Questions like these may prompt therapists to choose interventions that promote corrective experiencing. A therapeutic relationship, consistent with ideas described in Chapter 2, can promote corrective experiencing. Even in an initial session, as a therapist listens reflectively to a client describing their distress, the expression of emotion can be corrective. Often clients express relief and optimism at the end of an initial or a single session, having expressed their concerns to a listening therapist and discussed how to proceed. Therapists can watch for similar opportunities as therapy progresses, attending to moments when clients would benefit from interventions that are consistent with corrective experiencing.

To further establish the big picture of corrective experiencing, we highlight the issue of contrast. This chapter's interventions shift our perspective on the problem through contrast, reframing our relationship to the challenge. This reframing shifts us from what Watzlawick et al. (1974) called first-order change to second-order change. They described first-order change in terms of change within a system that does not change the system itself

(p. 10). Think of this as our initial attempts to change a problem, often using first-order solutions that may neutralize or exacerbate the targeted problem. A classic example of this problem-exacerbating first-order solution, popularized by ACT, is the finger trap. When you put your fingers in a finger trap, the intuitive response (first-order solution) is to pull outward, trapping your fingers inside.

Contrast experiences reframe the problem—and consequently the solution—in terms of second-order change, or changes to the system itself, or "change of change" (Watzlawick et al., 1974, p. 11). Engagement with the problem then occurs on different terms than previously encountered, and the contrast and novelty can be very powerful, especially when paired with strong emotional experiences. With the finger trap, the second-order solution is to relax the fingers and move them toward the center.

The outline of first- versus second-order change can provide us with a general model for corrective experiencing. Using Watzlawick et al. (1974) as a model, Fraser and Solovey (2007) showed how identifying a first-order solution that is in use by a client can inform how a therapist addresses with the client the potential for a new experience on the second order that can induce second-order change. For example, a common first-order solution to the experience of anxiety is to avoid situations that make a person anxious. Snakes make me (RJB) anxious; I avoid snakes, and consequently I avoid anxiety. The first-order problem is solved. However, it is abundantly clear that avoidance behavior amplifies anxiety over the long term. The behavioral insight that overcoming anxiety involves confronting feared stimuli (e.g., snakes) rather than avoiding them is a clear example of a second-order solution replacing a maladaptive first-order solution. The relationship to the problem is reframed. My therapist might tell me as I work on my fear of snakes that the more important problem to address is not snakes but my avoidance of snakes.

Corrective experiencing involves contrasts in this manner, as outlined by Fraser and Solovey (2007). They offer several different types of contrast (using the term *client* in lieu of their term *problem-solver* will aid understanding):

- If the first-order solution is *to go away from the problem*, then the second-order solution will have something to do with *going toward it*.

- If the first-order solution is *to overpursue the problem*, then the second-order solution will have something to do with *stopping and reversing the pursuit*.

- If the first-order solution is *to not attend to the problem*, then the second-order solution will involve *acknowledging the problem* and *taking necessary problem-solving action*.

- If the first-order solution involves *making the problem overly complex*, then the second-order solution will involve *simplifying the problem and narrowing problem-solving efforts* down to the problem at hand and clarifying the problem's parameters.

- If the first-order solution is *to overintervene* with normal ups and downs of daily living, then second-order solutions will involve *tolerating and accepting* the amount of unpleasantness that is a natural part of the human condition.

- If the first-order solution *reads too little into the difficulty*, or *simplifies the problem so much as to trivialize it*, then the second-order solution will *honor the complexity of the problem*. To honor complexity entails both respecting and assisting the problem solver with building an understanding that clarifies the problem and its parameters in a way that is understood by the problem solver. (pp. 53–54; italics in original)

The novel, contrasting aspect of corrective experiencing can be seen in each of these examples. Target problems are reframed, and clients have different, contrasting experiences in relation to their initial target problems. One can see in their examples how interventions such as exposure, emotional evocation, distress tolerance, and behavioral activation show contrast and second-order change.

Throughout each intervention that follows in this chapter, the therapist can use the heuristic of corrective experiencing, focusing on the questions we have proposed or seeking for ways to bring about contrasting second-order change. This heuristic or lens is more important than fidelity to a particular school of thought or theoretical orientation. Corrective experiencing interventions can be used as described in this framework, or they can be borrowed from established therapeutic interventions. In several tables later in this chapter, we offer examples of corrective experiencing interventions and note resources for more complete instructions on their use. Note the major categories of interventions include confronting, expressing, and regulating, all referring to activities of the client during these interventions that fall under the umbrella of corrective experiencing.

## Confronting

### PRINCIPLE 4.1

Therapists help clients to move toward corrective experiencing by noticing current patterns, including content that may have been avoided, and offering novel or contrasting experiences.

As Fraser and Solovey (2007) pointed out, a common first-order solution to distress involves avoiding it, which unintentionally increases distress. Confronting involves moving toward rather than avoiding distress, in the interest of putting a second-order solution in place that will greatly improve a client's distress. Behavioral theorists, researchers, and therapists have laid considerable groundwork with this core idea as they have described exposure therapy. However, confronting undesirable emotions or distress has a similarly long history in psychodynamic and humanistic approaches to therapy as well in more general terms than behaviorists may espouse. In addition, third-wave cognitive behavior ideas (ACT, in particular) have taken the key issue, avoidance, and translated beyond the original behavioral concept of avoidance to encompass the much broader concept of experiential avoidance. Table 4.1 summarizes multiple confronting interventions from a variety of theoretical approaches.

As our corrective experiencing definition indicates, confronting involves a contrast for the client. The client experiences a contrast between avoidance and facing something that is feared. Behaviorists describe this as undermining the reinforcement pattern that avoidance behavior induces. In other words, avoidance behavior is learned and reinforced, and the distress is maintained (see Krypotos et al., 2015).

This relationship can be especially clear with anxious avoidance, including phobias, OCD, or PTSD. However, avoidance of distressing emotions can also be present in distress that is primarily depressive, similar to the experiential avoidance concept. Behavioral activation can present an opportunity for a depressed client to confront novel experiences that contrast with depressive avoidance. Mindfulness (see the Regulating section of this chapter) presents an opportunity to confront emotional experiences by increasing awareness, acknowledgement, and acceptance of the present moment. In A. M. Hayes's integrative approach to depression (focusing especially on behavioral and cognitive elements of avoidance and rumination), the overarching strategy is "exposure to avoided material, guid[ing] clients in processing difficult emotions and experiences. It also focuses on developing hope; healthy views of the self; and healthy lifestyle behaviors related to exercise, diet, sleep, and mindfulness meditation" (A. M. Hayes et al., 2005, p. 114). Note the contrast element. Psychodynamic or humanistic therapists may focus on the avoidance of repressed or unexpressed emotion (see the Expressing section), emphasizing activation and expression to move toward resolution.

Clients may feel motivated to persist in the avoidance pattern and reluctant to confront distressing emotions or other stimuli. With exposure work, barriers can still be emotional: extreme anger, emotional numbing, and overwhelming anxiety (Jaycox & Foa, 1996). These emotions can be addressed

**TABLE 4.1. Example Confronting Interventions**

| Intervention | Broad theoretical categories | Specific theoretical approaches | Additional resources |
|---|---|---|---|
| Exposure | Behavioral<br>Cognitive behavior<br>Mind-body | Exposure and response prevention | Foa et al. (2012), *Exposure and Response (Ritual) Prevention for Obsessive-Compulsive Disorder: Therapist Guide* |
| | | Systematic desensitization | Abramowitz et al. (2019), *Exposure Therapy for Anxiety: Principles and Practice* (2nd ed.) |
| | | Interoceptive exposure | Craske & Barlow (2014), "Panic Disorder and Agoraphobia" |
| | | Prolonged exposure<br>Cognitive processing therapy | Foa et al. (2019), *Prolonged Exposure Therapy for PTSD: Emotional Processing of Traumatic Experiences* (2nd ed.)<br>Monson et al. (2014), "Posttraumatic Stress Disorder" |
| | | Eye movement desensitization and reprocessing | Shapiro (2018), *Eye Movement Desensitization and Reprocessing (EMDR) Therapy* (3rd ed.) |
| Corrective emotional experience<br>Immediacy | Psychodynamic, relational | Time-limited dynamic psychotherapy | Levenson (1995), *Time-Limited Dynamic Psychotherapy: A Guide to Clinical Practice* |
| Experiential focusing<br>Expansion | Humanistic, third wave | Emotion-focused therapy<br>Acceptance and commitment therapy (ACT) | Elliott et al. (2004), *Learning Emotion-Focused Therapy: The Process-Experiential Approach to Change*<br>Gendlin (1981), *Focusing*<br>Harris (2019), *ACT Made Simple: An Easy-to-Read Primer on Acceptance and Commitment Therapy* |
| Behavioral activation | Behavioral<br>Cognitive behavior | Behavioral activation | Martell et al. (2022), *Behavioral Activation for Depression: A Clinician's Guide* (2nd ed.) |

through modifying exposure strategies or adapting other therapeutic interventions. Motivation work could be essential in helping to roll with the resistance and explore these barriers so a client can move in the direction of change.

Part of the purpose of confronting is to activate emotions. Exposure experts point out that activation is necessary but not sufficient, and "emotional processing requires the presence of information that disconfirms the erroneous elements in the structure" (Foa et al., 2006, p. 7). Confronting may occur in the therapy office, but it may be especially powerful outside of the therapy office. Exposure experts point to the between-session progress through exposure practice being especially effective in leading to habituation. Behavioral activation necessarily occurs outside of the therapy office.

Confronting may relate directly to content that arises through the therapeutic relationship, including how the client relates to the therapist. Psychodynamic therapists would view this as the transference. Interpersonal therapists may address this by highlighting the "real relationship," and CF therapists may use the microcounseling skill of immediacy to gently confront the client with this content, which may bring up emotions and potential insights for the client.

### Confronting Framework

CF therapists may use what follows as a general, transtheoretical framework to guide their thinking in order to enact confronting interventions with their clients. CF therapists may see fit, however, to use even more specific interventions from any of a host of other schools of thought (listed in Table 4.1). In this way, the principle provides the framework, which can be flexibly applied by the CF therapist.

1. CF therapists engage in *active listening* (as discussed in Chapter 2, on the therapeutic relationship) while listening for content that could be relevant for corrective experiencing. One may notice avoidance behavior and ask oneself what sort of emotional experience the client could have to contrast with their current experience. If anxious, could they have a new exposure experience to confront what is feared? If depressed, could they interact with others in new ways? If emotionally overregulated, could they confront their inner world? What kind of relational experience could they be reluctant to engage?

2. CF therapists highlight their observation with their client. For example, they could use the microskill of immediacy to describe the present moment. This could include "inquiring about or disclosing immediate feelings about the client, self in relation to the client, or the therapeutic

relationship" (Hill, 2020, p. 81; therapists may choose to practice the skill of immediacy using deliberate practice, see Table 4.2). The therapist could highlight avoidance behavior, giving a rationale for how avoidance reinforces and maintains distress.

3. CF therapists ask for permission to address this content more directly, while assessing the client's willingness to engage with the content in a new way. Confronting refers to the client's confronting and therefore refers to what the client does, not the therapist. Insisting the client confront distressing content without rationale or without permission could be injurious rather than therapeutic and at a minimum will likely lead to an increase in defensiveness. See the deliberate practice instructions in Table 4.3 on inviting to exposure.

4. CF therapists meet the client at their current motivation, rolling with the resistance to help the client work through perceived barriers. Numbing, extreme anger, or increased anxiety may be present (Jaycox & Foa, 1996) and need to be addressed to help the client prepare for exposure therapy or other difficult confronting work. See the chapter on motivation (Chapter 3) for more specific interventions.

5. In collaboration with their client, CF therapists plan and assist with carrying out the plan for the client to confront content. They may collaboratively generate a fear hierarchy for exposure via systematic desensitization. They may collaboratively create a list of planned activities for behavioral activation. They may use focusing interventions to help the client confront unacknowledged emotion. They may use expansion ideas to help the client confront and accept the emotion with or without active expression. They may coach the client through a mindfulness practice to address experiential avoidance.

6. CF therapists track the client's level of emotional activation throughout the confronting. They may use a Subjective Units of Distress Scale (Wolpe, 1969) and encourage the client to name emotions and describe the intensity. The therapist needs to ensure that the intensity is therapeutic and not excessive, interrupting if needed to promote soothing and regulation.

7. CF therapists encourage soothing after confronting. Intense emotional experiences are usually exhausting. Therapists can help their clients prepare for this by soothing in the session or encouraging self-care immediately following the session.

**TABLE 4.2. Deliberate Practice Suggestions for Immediacy**

| Method | Descriptions |
| --- | --- |
| Video-assisted observation of your work | • Watch your session, paying attention to the following:<br>  – Notice your inner experience while watching, describing out loud the emotions you notice while listening to your client and yourself. Pause at moments that were challenging in the session and identify your own emotion.<br>  – Notice your client's nonverbal behavior, including body language and tone of voice.<br>  – Notice your client's statements about the challenges they are wanting to address. Notice what they may be overtly or covertly asking for from you as the therapist.<br>  – Notice how the client relates to you. See if you can describe the moment-to-moment relating: for example, "[Client name] is becoming frustrated with how the conversation seems to be going in circles" or "[Client name] is deferring to me, soliciting my advice as an expert rather than trusting their own experience."<br>• If video content feels overwhelming, consider covering the screen and listening only. Alternatively, consider turning down the audio and watching only the visual stimuli.<br>• Identify key moments to share with a consultant, trying to identify and move through any defensiveness you may feel about sharing this. |
| Getting consultant feedback[a] | • Determine whether your relationship with your consultant is sufficiently supportive and safe for soliciting feedback openly. Consider working through defensive reactions with your consultant.<br>• Watch the session with your consultant, showing moments that seemed especially challenging.<br>• Request assistance with immediacy in particular. Consider asking your consultant how they may practice immediacy in the challenging moments.<br>• Role play difficult moments repeatedly, practicing using client-focused language to describe what is happening. Find words to use to rehearse saying as if to your client. |
| Setting small incremental goals | • Perhaps with your consultant's help, identify your current comfort level and competence with immediacy. Then, identify a behavior to practice on your own that stretches you just beyond this comfort level. Try to ensure that your practice is neither too overwhelming nor too easy. Be as specific as possible when describing what you are going to practice. |
| Solo deliberate practice | • Dedicate sufficient time to practice on your own.<br>• Use the session video to practice saying immediacy statements out loud.<br>• Notice how comfortable/uncomfortable the practice is and adjust the practice as needed. |

*(continues)*

**TABLE 4.2. Deliberate Practice Suggestions for Immediacy (*Continued*)**

| Method | Descriptions |
|---|---|
| Feedback-informed treatment | • Use outcome measures at each session to determine how the client is progressing in treatment. Immediacy may be used to discuss progress feedback with a client: for example, "Looking at your survey results, it appears that you've been experiencing more distress this week—can we talk about that?" |
| | • Use process measures to discuss what is happening in therapy using immediacy to talk about the process: for example, "Looking at your survey results, I'm wondering about whether we're working on the things that you want to address" or "Looking at these results, I'm wondering about how you're feeling about whether this process can help you." |
| | • Practice saying these interventions out loud, using immediacy to bring the feedback to the therapy interaction. |

*Note.* See also Hill's (2020) *Helping Skills* volume with chapters that discuss immediacy (Chapter 13), using challenges (Chapter 11), and other skills in an insight phase of therapy.
[a]We use the word "consultant" in this and other deliberate practice tables for brevity. We mean this to refer to mentors, supervisors, trainers, colleagues, or other experts as appropriate to the skill being practiced.

**TABLE 4.3. Deliberate Practice Suggestions for Inviting to Exposure**

| Method | Descriptions |
|---|---|
| Video-assisted observation of your work | • Watch your session looking for the following moments: |
| |    – Identify when the client is describing the challenge and looking for solutions. These may be openings for invitations to a new experience. |
| |    – Identify when the client is describing avoidance behavior, especially when frustrated by their avoidance behavior. |
| |    – Notice when the client is focused on a treatment goal (e.g., addressing anxiety) versus on tangents and could be invited back to their desired focus of treatment. |
| | • Listen to your invitations to exposure. Pay attention to whether it is an open invitation or more commanding. Pay attention to whether the invitation is specific. Pay attention to how your client responds to your invitation. |
| | • Listen to how you offer rationale for exposure to your client, including how you describe avoidance and how you describe exposure practice. Notice at which moments the client may show signs of ambivalent motivation to engage in exposure practice. |
| | • If video content feels overwhelming, consider covering the screen and listening only. Alternatively, consider turning down the audio and watching only the visual stimuli. |
| | • Identify key moments to share with a consultant, trying to identify and move through any defensiveness you may feel about sharing this. |

**TABLE 4.3. Deliberate Practice Suggestions for Inviting to Exposure (*Continued*)**

| Method | Descriptions |
|---|---|
| Getting consultant feedback | • Determine whether your relationship with your consultant is sufficiently supportive and safe for soliciting feedback openly. Consider working through defensive reactions with your consultant. |
| | • Watch the session with your consultant, showing moments that seemed especially challenging. |
| | • Request assistance with exposure invitations in particular. Consider asking your consultant how they invite their clients or describe the rationale for exposure. |
| | • Role play invitations to exposure, practicing using client-focused language to meet the client at their level of motivation. Find words to use to rehearse saying as if to your client. |
| Setting small incremental goals | • Perhaps with your consultant's help, identify your current comfort level and competence with invitations. Then, identify a behavior to practice on your own that stretches you just beyond this comfort level. Try to ensure that your practice is neither too overwhelming nor too easy. Be as specific as possible when describing what you are going to practice. |
| Solo deliberate practice | • Dedicate sufficient time to practice on your own. |
| | • Use the session video to practice looking for moments to invite and stating the invitations out loud. Practice adjusting the language based on the client's motivation. |
| | • Notice how comfortable/uncomfortable the practice is and adjust the practice as needed. |
| Feedback-informed treatment | • Use outcome measures at each session to determine how the client is progressing in treatment. Exposure practices may be overwhelming, and discussing their progress with this can be very validating: for example, "Looking at your survey results, it appears that you've been experiencing more distress this week. I'm wondering how exposure practice went for you?" |
| | • Use process measures to discuss what is happening in therapy: for example, "Looking at your survey results, I'm wondering about whether our talk last week about exposure lines up with what you want in treatment" or "Looking at these results, I'm wondering about how you're feeling about practicing exposure." |
| | • Practice saying these interventions out loud, adjusting your language with the invitation as needed. |

*Note.* See also Sentio University for instructions for a deliberate practice exercise titled "Providing a Treatment Rationale" (https://sentio.org/instructions-for-dp-exercises).

8. CF therapists encourage cognitive processing after the experience. Catharsis tends to be less useful on its own, without a cognitive process following to internalize the experience. Please see the insight chapter for greater emphasis on interventions highlighting cognitive shifts. Therapists may highlight the contrast elements of the experience and encourage further efforts to engage in similar confronting outside of the therapy office.

## Sample Script

Corrective experiencing interventions can, of course, vary greatly based on what is needed by the client and the therapist offering the treatment. The following script is intended to illustrate just one way that corrective experiencing can proceed, with some of the important elements noted throughout:

CLIENT: I've been trying and trying to finish this project, but I just sit and stare at the screen. Not only do I struggle to finish things, I can't even get myself to do things I used to love. Depression has taken that away from me.

THERAPIST: So much loss, so much struggle. [*reflective listening*]

CLIENT: Yes, and I'm sick of it. It's like I'm stuck here and will stay stuck until I figure this out.

THERAPIST: Stuck is no fun, and I notice that we're talking about it as if it's the permanent state of things. I wonder if we could explore ways to get unstuck, maybe make it less permanent? [*invitation*]

CLIENT: Ummm, yeah, that'd be nice. Seems unlikely though.

THERAPIST: Unlikely. You're seeing this as unlikely to lead to "unstuck"?

CLIENT: Yeah, I can't get myself to do things, so how the hell am I supposed to get unstuck?

THERAPIST: Sounds very frustrating [*rolling with resistance*]. Like, "I try and I try and it's not working"?

CLIENT: Exactly. Why keep trying?

THERAPIST: Excellent question. What reason could we possibly come up with to keep trying?

CLIENT: Well, I guess I do want it to be different.

[The therapist and the client explore what improvements the client wants in their life.]

THERAPIST: Would it be okay with you if we explored a way to have new experiences, a way that's especially geared for when we're stuck like this? [*invitation repeated*]

CLIENT: I'm game.

[The therapist explains the rationale for behavioral activation. Both the therapist and the client write out a list of pleasurable activities, discussing when the client can engage in it each day. The therapist requests for the client to track their emotions throughout.]

THERAPIST: So we have a plan. I'm hoping you can be gentle with you as you're practicing this. Regardless of what happens, let's talk about this next time. The idea here is to have a different experience [*highlighting contrast element ahead of time, to be highlighted again at next session*].

Notice in both the framework and the sample script how the therapist is guided by the lens of the change principle, corrective experiencing, and gently and collaboratively works with the client to help them move toward confronting experiences. CF therapists may see fit to use more specific exposure approaches (see Table 4.1), and this is entirely consistent with the spirit of CF therapy. CF therapists use the change principle as a heuristic to inform the clinical decision to help the client move in the direction of confronting. To learn more about immediacy, including using deliberate practice to improve one's use of the intervention, please see Table 4.2. For exposure to work well, the process of inviting can be a point of intervention that benefits from practice. Accordingly, we have also prepared Table 4.3 to guide deliberate practice efforts with inviting. Next, we address expressing as another form of experiencing that can be therapeutic for clients.

## Expressing

### PRINCIPLE 4.2

Therapists facilitate the client's expression of emotion, especially when emotions have been inhibited and when emotions can be helpful in correctively transforming the client's experience.

Confronting interventions may highlight the contrast element of our definition of corrective experiencing. Expressing emotions focuses on the part of our definition that refers to how clients engage with their felt emotions. Table 4.4 summarizes a variety of interventions that can be used to help clients express emotions.

Clients meeting with a therapist for the first time, experiencing significant demoralization, often express their distress openly also for the first time. If not for the first time, the opportunity to openly share invites clients to actively express emotions. As described in our therapeutic relationship chapter (see

**TABLE 4.4. Example Expressing Interventions**

| Intervention | Broad theoretical categories | Specific theoretical approaches | Additional resources |
|---|---|---|---|
| Reflective listening | Humanistic | Client-centered therapy<br><br>Motivational interviewing | Rogers (1957/1992), "The Necessary and Sufficient Conditions of Therapeutic Personality Change"<br><br>Hill (2020), *Helping Skills: Facilitating Exploration, Insight, and Action* (5th ed.)<br><br>W. R. Miller & Rollnick (2013), *Motivational Interviewing: Helping People Change* (3rd ed.) |
| Two-chair or empty chair<br><br>Dyadic affect regulation | Humanistic<br><br>Psychodynamic | Emotion-focused therapy<br><br>Accelerated experiential dynamic psychotherapy | Elliott et al. (2004), *Learning Emotion-Focused Therapy: The Process-Experiential Approach to Change*<br><br>Fosha (2000), *The Transforming Power of Affect: A Model for Accelerated Change* |
| Compassionate self | Cognitive behavior | Compassion-focused therapy | Gilbert (2010), *Compassion Focused Therapy* |
| Grief therapy | | Grief therapy | Worden (2018), *Grief Counseling and Grief Therapy: A Handbook for the Mental Health Practitioner* (5th ed.) |
| Assertiveness training | Cognitive behavior<br><br>Third wave | | Linehan (2014), *DBT Skills Training Manual* (2nd ed.) |

Chapter 2), therapists can facilitate the active expression and deepening of emotion through active listening that emphasizes emotional reflections. The focus in this chapter is on the expression itself. Clients may experience an elevation of distress, but the expression of that distress is really the goal with the interventions we describe here. Therapists actively and intentionally encourage emotional expression with reflection and evoking interventions.

Expressing may help to enact a second-order solution or change—note that we are using the descriptive system given by Fraser and Solovey (2007)— to address emotions that may be working as first-order solutions. Three of their bullet points may be relevant here:

- If the first-order solution is *to not attend to the problem*, then the second-order solution will involve *acknowledging the problem* and *taking necessary problem-solving action.* . . .

- If the first-order solution is *to overintervene* with normal ups and downs of daily living, then second-order solutions will involve *tolerating and accepting* the amount of unpleasantness that is a natural part of the human condition.

- If the first-order solution *reads too little into the difficulty,* or *simplifies the problem so much as to trivialize it,* then the second-order solution will *honor the complexity of the problem.* (pp. 53–54; italics in original)

Emotional expression helps to acknowledge a problem so that action can be taken. It can help with tolerating and accepting unpleasantness in life, by openly acknowledging it in the safe environs of a therapeutic encounter. Exploring emotions tends to acknowledge and honor the complexity of problems, as emotions rarely occur in the singular but usually in the plural.

The relationship itself, especially in the initial session, can set the tone for creating space for emotional expression. Empathy forms the core attitude in developing and maintaining a therapeutic relationship but also helps to explore the client's experiences, worldview, and concerns. Therapists can then help clients to become "aware of things clients know only implicitly— that is, what they know at some level but do not fully know that they know" (Elliott et al., 2004, p. 113). Therapists help clients express these emotions, deepening the exploration through interventions such as reflecting feeling, processing their emotions, then transforming their emotions through expressive interventions such as empty chair or compassionate self. As Carl Rogers (1975) described empathy using Eugene Gendlin's perspective,

> He [Gendlin] sees empathy as pointing sensitively to the "felt meaning" which the client is experiencing in this particular moment, in order to help him focus on that meaning and to carry it further to its full and uninhibited experiencing. (p. 3)

Helping clients become aware of their emotions and then identifying them can be helpful in its own right. Cameron et al. (2014) reviewed therapeutic effects on alexithymia, or the diminished capacity to identify and express emotions, and found therapy (across therapeutic orientations) helped reduce alexithymia. As seen in our Regulating section, mindfulness can also help with alexithymia (Norman et al., 2019). However, expression may also include more than this. As L. S. Greenberg (2012) emphasized, "Expression goes beyond awareness. 'Putting one's body where one's mouth is' helps overcome avoidance of experience, undoes muscular constriction, and generates neuro-chemical and physiological changes, and all of these change self-organization and interactions" (p. 704). L. S. Greenberg (2012) also noted that emotion can be used to transform emotion. EFT and accelerated experiential dynamic psychotherapy (AEDP) are examples of therapies that focus on emotions as vehicles for transformation (see Fosha, 2000, 2009; Fosha et al., 2009). However, encouraging emotional expression for therapeutic purposes can be an element in therapy generally.

It is unsurprising that clients experience emotions in therapy, especially, as we have noted, because demoralization represents the primary focus and motivating factor for therapy. Talking about difficulties tends to arouse emotions. However, experiencing can occur without expressing the emotion (i.e., without the act of emoting; L. S. Greenberg, 2012). In an interesting study by Pos et al. (2017), they studied sessions of therapy and found that the act of expressing emotion mediated outcome more than did merely experiencing emotion. Even emotions often thought of as negative, such as anger, can be expressed when clients learn how they can be adaptive. L. S. Greenberg (2012) pointed out how anger may be expressed to therapeutic effect, including in depression and sexual abuse treatments, such as helping someone to develop self-efficacy and reattribute blame.

For expressing interventions, we focus on reflective listening (essential in the initial phase of therapy, though also important throughout), emotional processing (with grief counseling as an example), and evocative interventions that may be useful in working phases of therapy (with two-chair work as an example).

## Reflective Listening

The act of the client disclosing to a therapist followed by the therapist helping the client to address the felt meaning can be a corrective experience in its own right. (Refer to our discussion of reflective listening in Chapter 2 of this book.) Reflective listening promotes a sort of emotional unraveling and disentangling for the client, which is then experienced as corrective by the client.

Reflective listening can highlight key concerns for the client. Expressions of emotion can help the therapist to "follow the pain" to better understand what are the most important concerns their client is experiencing. It can lead to the therapist finding that the client is reluctant or avoidant to address certain concerns, which can then be gently confronted by the client with the therapist's assistance.

### Emotional Processing

Demoralized clients may have difficulty attending to difficult emotions for a variety of reasons. Therapy may work to overcome avoidance (see the Confronting section of this chapter) as well as to work through emotions by expressing and processing them. The intention of the therapist in these moments is to help clients activate the emotions that are implicit (sometimes on the surface of awareness or sometimes repressed) to acknowledge them and move through them. Much like a beach ball in water, when a person tries to keep emotions below the surface, the pressure increases to the degree that it would help more to express and address the emotion rather than avoid it. "Helping people overcome their avoidance of emotions, focusing collaboratively on emotions, and exploring them in therapy thus appears to be important in therapeutic change, whichever therapeutic orientation is employed" (L. S. Greenberg, 2016, p. 671). Perhaps grief work shows a clear example for facilitating the expressing of emotions by the client.

In grief counseling or grief therapy, a person is often seeking help after a significant loss and feeling overwhelmed or numb. Consistent with the dual process theory of grieving, the person is needing to focus on recovery-oriented stressors (i.e., stressors of daily life continue without consideration of the loss; for example, the survivor needs to maintain employment or responsibilities), often with few opportunities to focus on loss-oriented stressors (i.e., emotional overwhelm when grief is triggered by reminders of the loss; Stroebe & Schut, 1999). Grief therapy presents an opportunity to actively process the loss-oriented emotions. Worden (2018) emphasized a key principle of this work: "Help the survivor to identify and experience feelings," including anger, guilt, anxiety, helplessness, loneliness, and sadness (p. 94).

Therapists consider when clients are either avoiding emotions or feeling a strong urgency to share emotions. Holding space for emotions represents a key therapist task. As L. S. Greenberg (2012) wrote, "Emotional processing is best facilitated by the progressive increase and then fading away of expressed emotional arousal over the course of a session" (p. 700). Therapists can help to deepen emotion (i.e., through reflective listening, evocative interventions, focusing interventions, or other interventions) and take care to help the client regulate their emotions as the session progresses closer to the end. This may take the form of regulating or soothing focused interventions.

**Evocative Interventions**

Several therapies focus directly on evoking emotion in order to transform a client's emotional experience. EFT (Elliott et al., 2004) may use interventions such as Gendlin's (1981) focusing, an empty chair, or a two-chair intervention to help a client open up expressively to an emotional experience and to work with the emotions directly. In this way, a person can confront an imagined significant person with whom they have emotional unfinished business and work toward a new emotional understanding. In a similar exercise in compassion-focused therapy (Gilbert, 2010; Gilbert & Choden, 2014), a client learns to inhabit one's compassionate self and then confront one's critical self imagined in another chair, which is much more effective for self-criticism than expecting oneself to merely stop criticizing oneself. In ACT (Harris, 2013), working on mindful presence and acceptance can include an expansion exercise, including noticing the experience of the emotion in the body (very similar to Gendlin's, 1981, focusing) and making space for the emotion. In one contemporary dynamic therapy, AEDP therapists observe when clients are expressing emotion or just holding back emotion and help to facilitate expression to help transform through "dyadic regulation" (Fosha, 2000).

Evoking emotions is not so much about eliminating so-called negative emotions but more about working to transform emotions so that clients can remoralize. As L. S. Greenberg (2012) eloquently wrote:

> Although exposure to emotion at times may be helpful to overcome avoidance of emotion, in many situations in therapy, change also occurs because one emotion is transformed by another emotion, rather than the maladaptive emotion simply attenuating. In these instances, emotional change occurs by the activation of an incompatible, more adaptive, experience that undoes the old response. Note that this is not replacing the old emotion, but rather undoing it. Also, this transformation involves more than simply allowing or facing the feeling, leading to its diminishment. Rather, emotional change occurs by the activation of a new incompatible, more adaptive experience. (pp. 700–701)

L. S. Greenberg (2016) also emphasized that expressed emotion, not merely the acknowledgement of emotion, is important. However, L. S. Greenberg (2016) also highlighted that the focus is not catharsis per se, as it is not helpful "all the time for all people" (p. 675). CF therapists may choose to use emotionally directive and transformative interventions as are found in EFT, AEDP, or compassion-focused therapies. In these clinical situations therapists may see themselves as "emotion coaches" (L. S. Greenberg, 2016, p. 681).

Expressing emotions may be a focus in interpersonal skills. From this perspective, such as in DBT, the clinical goal is less about transforming emotion with emotion and more about learning to speak up to others about one's emotional states. Aggressive emotional expression (e.g., insults or other verbal attacks) may need to be regulated, but on the other hand being passive about one's emotional states can be ineffective in interpersonal relationships (Linehan, 2014). Therapists as emotion coaches can help clients identify their emotions and learn to express them assertively. Evoking the emotion may be necessary during a role play when this is practiced.

Overall, evocative interventions help clients to work on expressing as part of an overall clinical strategy for corrective experiencing. Therapists may be directive by coaching clients through these experiences that they may carry forward in treatment and into their daily lives outside of the therapy office. See the following sample script for expressing interventions to explore how many interventions from this chapter can be used for CF therapists to help clients express their way to transforming their experiences.

### Sample Script for Expressing

CLIENT: I go about my day and it's like I'm just going through the motions. I feel like my life is hollow!

THERAPIST: It feels hollow, like you feel empty inside [*reflective listening, inviting the client to deeper emotional experiencing with "you feel ____ inside"*].

CLIENT: Yeah, exactly. I don't want to feel like that. Just the last two months, since she left, it's been so empty.

THERAPIST: Empty inside, specifically since she's been gone? [*Client nods in agreement.*] What if we focus for just a moment on the feeling, the crux of this, how it feels in the body? Where are you feeling this? [*focusing intervention, evocative. If needed, the therapist could move toward a two-chair intervention targeting the numb feeling.*]

CLIENT: Like right here [*points to chest*]—just this dark cloud here.

THERAPIST: Okay, notice this dark cloud right here in the chest; this feeling has a sense of what's so difficult right now. If that dark cloud right there in the chest had words describing what's going on in your life, let that feeling tell us. . . .

CLIENT: [*pausing, tears in eyes*] Shit, I hate this. . . . Damn . . . like this feeling of alone. I fucking hate being alone and it's like this dark is telling me I'll be alone forever, so what's the point?

THERAPIST: Alone . . . [*reflecting and pausing*] and like a sense of sadness, of hopelessness.

CLIENT: Exactly. [*tears, crying*]

THERAPIST: This is so rough. And the hollow feeling kinda feels like there was this sadness underneath it all. Like this sadness is important. Let's make space right here and now for sad [*therapist encouraging emotional processing and/or expansion*]. . . .

[The client spends time expressing sadness over the loss of their relationship, with the therapist helping to express and explore by reflecting throughout.]

CLIENT: I used up half of your tissue box. I hadn't realized there was so much there.

THERAPIST: We've got plenty of tissues around here. I get the sense that these feelings were so important to share and move through. I wonder what this was like for you? What do you make of this and what's next for you? [*Move to cognitive loop and insight, encouraging soothing for regulation.*]

## Regulating

### PRINCIPLE 4.3

Therapists assist clients with learning to soothe and regulate emotions, especially when clients feel out of control and need a new experience of mastery and calm to remoralize.

Demoralization often involves intense emotion and, beyond the emotion, the sense that there is no control over the emotion. The word "overwhelmed" illustrates this exactly, suggesting that a person is overcome or overpowered by the feeling. The person is in a state of emotional dysregulation. Therapy often includes helping a client learn to manage distress by regulating difficult emotional states (see Table 4.5 for a list of regulating interventions).

Confronting the distress, as we have described in a previous section, promotes second-order change to overcome the first-order solution (avoidance) that may be exacerbating distress. However, prior to clients engaging in confronting, they often need skills in hand to feel confident in the face of what

**TABLE 4.5. Example Regulating Interventions**

| Intervention | Broad theoretical categories | Specific theoretical approaches | Additional resources |
|---|---|---|---|
| Diaphragmatic breathing | Mind–body | Yoga, health psychology, cognitive behavior therapy | See https://www.anxietycoach.com and Carbonell (2022), *A Breathing Exercise to Calm Panic Attacks*, for examples |
| Mindfulness | Mind–body, adapted from Buddhist meditation tradition | Mindfulness-based stress reduction<br><br>Dialectical behavior therapy<br><br>Acceptance and commitment therapy | Woods & Rockman (2021), *Mindfulness-Based Stress Reduction: Protocol, Practice, and Teaching Skills* |
| Grounding | Cognitive behavior<br><br>Third wave | Dialectical behavior therapy | Linehan (2014), *DBT Skills Training Manual* (2nd ed.)<br><br>Najavits (2001), *Seeking Safety: A Treatment Manual for PTSD and Substance Abuse* |
| Emotion regulation skills<br><br>Distress tolerance skills | Third wave | Dialectical behavior therapy | Moonshine & Schaefer (2019), *Dialectical Behavior Therapy: Vol. 1. The Clinician's Guidebook for Acquiring Competency in DBT* (2nd ed.) |
| Self-compassion | Cognitive behavior | Compassion-focused therapy<br><br>Self-compassion | Gilbert (2010), *Compassion Focused Therapy*<br><br>Neff & Germer (2018), *The Mindful Self-Compassion Workbook: A Proven Way to Accept Yourself, Build Inner Strength, and Thrive* |

they may be avoiding. For example, prior to any exposure interventions, clients need to be taught strategies to downregulate their intense anxious responses through diaphragmatic breathing. This often involves the kinds of contrast we have shown throughout corrective experiencing. A client feels anxious and out of control, and then when they practice deep breathing, they feel a sense of mastery and a sense of calm. Breathing may not eliminate panic or stop a panic attack in its tracks exactly, and the client will still need to practice tolerating and accepting distress (a second-order solution according to Fraser & Solovey, 2007); however, the novel experience of regulating one's distress can be highly remoralizing for the client, giving them a sense of self-efficacy.

Helping clients to regulate their distress often begins with helping them to understand the biological underpinnings of the human stress response. Therapists may find individualized ways to explain the fight-or-flight response characteristic of the sympathetic nervous response. Perhaps more important, therapists help their clients practice, helping them correctively experience the body's natural method of downregulation. Therapists do not merely talk about breathing; they can actually practice with the client, helping the client have the experience in the session. The client can then experience a sense of mastery and calm. Breathing retraining or teaching diaphragmatic breathing represents a foundational skill for exposure work and can be a helpful tool for many clients, regardless of diagnosis, to develop this sense of mastery and calm so they can engage in their lives or engage in the therapeutic work. In Table 4.5, we have noted one breathing resource for an accessible example, but also note that similar resources are widely available. CF therapists may see fit to practice specific ways to coach clients with diaphragmatic breathing.

Clients often benefit from having multiple strategies, such as both diaphragmatic breathing and grounding strategies (see Najavits, 2001). This can be especially helpful when clients find difficulty with any single strategy. Grounding the senses in the present moment can be especially helpful when a client feels overwhelmed when confronting their internal world. Clients benefit from experimenting with different methods, finding what works and building their sense of self-efficacy as they do so.

In DBT, emotion regulation is conceptually separated from distress tolerance as well as from mindfulness, though all seem consistent with our change principle of regulating as a facet of corrective experiencing. Distress tolerance emphasizes a willingness or acceptance, according to DBT principles. Mindfulness can not only indicate awareness but also cultivate an attitude of open observation that helps a person respond flexibly to distressing situations. Linehan (2014) emphasized that clients need to be guided to accept and feel their feelings when they are not too overwhelming but also to distinguish when the intensity of their emotions is so high that they become dysfunctional. Though L. S. Greenberg and Linehan come from different perspectives with regard to theoretical orientation, their comments echo one another. "Emotion needs to be activated to make sense of it, but it also needs to be protected against and regulated" (L. S. Greenberg, 2012, p. 701). Regulating can help a client then return to a state in which insight or cognitive learning can occur.

Mindfulness represents a regulating strategy, but if approached as such, clients can easily become frustrated. As discussed in our insight chapter (Chapter 5), mindfulness helps to cultivate an attitude of awareness and openness toward one's internal states. It can therefore cultivate a sense of willingness and acceptance, which can then be calming and soothing. However, initial (and sometimes ongoing) practice of mindfulness brings one into contact with emotions that may have been avoided and in this sense is more like a confronting experience (consequently activating more intense distress) than a regulating one. Clients can be coached to practice the attitude, which then helps them move toward rather than away from distressing experiences, which then indirectly leads to less distress. Clients may benefit from knowing that the mindful pathway is a less direct path to regulating than an intervention such as diaphragmatic breathing or grounding interventions.

When teaching mindfulness, remember that the change principle is for the client to engage in the experiencing. Talking about mindfulness will therefore be less useful compared with the client's experiencing mindfulness. Practicing mindfulness on their own after practicing with a therapist will be still more useful for a client.

Self-compassion strategies can be highly congruent with mindfulness and can enhance a client's ability to be accepting toward difficult emotions. Neff and Germer (2018) offered helpful strategies to use to build self-compassion over time. Gilbert's (2010) perspective emphasized the physiological grounding in the parasympathetic nervous response for self-compassion, activating our natural, evolutionary tendency for nurture. He also emphasized using self-compassion with anxiety, anger, and self-criticism. Gaining more experience and expertise with self-compassion strategies is highly recommended for CF therapists to help their clients have regulating experiences. As with breathing and mindfulness, it is essential that clients actually engage in the self-compassion experiences, because a mere explanation of what self-compassion is will likely be insufficient.

For practice helping clients with regulating, please see our deliberate practice methods for slowing down in Table 4.6. Please note how the practice

**TABLE 4.6. Deliberate Practice Suggestions for Slowing Down**

| Method | Descriptions |
|---|---|
| Video-assisted observation of your work | • Watch the video, paying particular attention to the following:<br>  – Nonverbal indications that the client is anxious, stressed, or shutting down<br>  – Nonverbal indications that you are anxious, stressed, or shutting down<br>  – Verbal indications of high distress<br>  – Moments when you could ask client to check in about their level of distress<br>• Practice responding to your own anxiety as the therapist during the session by stating therapeutic, anxiety-alleviating statements out loud while watching the video.<br>  – Practice rating your own anxiety in real time as you watch the video. Rate it and then describe what fears you may be experiencing: for example, "I'm afraid that I won't be able to help my client with ____."<br>  – Practice regulating your own anxiety while you listen to the client. Use diaphragmatic breathing, grounding, or other regulating skill that you find helpful for yourself.<br>• Practice inviting the client to become aware of their current distress: for example, by rating their anxiety in the present moment using a 10-point scale.<br>• Practice inviting the client to engage in a strategy that can help in the moment to regulate distress.<br>  – Vary the lengths of the invitation and explanation. Sometimes it may be helpful to give a thorough explanation of the sympathetic nervous response for the client to understand why it matters. Sometimes it may be helpful to jump right into a breathing practice because the client is so activated and having difficulty conversing.<br>• Identify moments of rupture or resistance, when a client feels that the strategy is not working for them. For example, clients may say something like, "I've tried breathing before and it's never helped." Practice responses to this that honor the client's resistance and help them move toward this or another regulating practice.<br>• Identify key moments to share with a consultant, trying to identify and move through any defensiveness you may feel about sharing this. |

TABLE 4.6. Deliberate Practice Suggestions for Slowing Down (*Continued*)

| Method | Descriptions |
|---|---|
| Getting consultant feedback | • Determine whether your relationship with your consultant is sufficiently supportive and safe for soliciting feedback openly. Consider working through defensive reactions with your consultant. |
| | • With your consultant, look for moments in the video to practice tasks described previously. |
| | • Ask for feedback on your responses to common resistance or rupture statements from your clients. Practice refining these responses. |
| | • Notice your own emotional reactions to particular client emotional content and request assistance in addressing them. If needed, work through them with a personal therapist. |
| Setting small incremental goals | • Perhaps with a consultant's help, notice when or how your own distress is activated and you find yourself past the boundary of your comfort level. Decide how to use solo practice to manage your distress outside of your therapeutic relationship with your client so you can competently respond to client distress. |
| | • Perhaps with a consultant's help, notice ways you can improve your invitations to slow down. |
| | • Learn multiple ways to approach regulating to help your clients. |
| Solo deliberate practice | • Dedicate sufficient time to practice on your own. |
| | • Use the session video or any other audio and/or video recordings of the client as stimuli for practice. |
| | • Practice coaching clients through breathing practices, slowing your talking rate and using a calming tone. |
| | • Notice how comfortable/uncomfortable the practice is and adjust the practice as needed. |
| Feedback-informed treatment | • Use outcome measures at each session to determine how the client is progressing in treatment. Notice how they are responding within session to slowing down and check in about how it goes outside of sessions. |
| | • Use process measures to discuss what is happening in therapy. Check in after a regulating practice to see how the client responded, checking to ensure that they feel comfortable practicing and that it can be effective for them. |

encourages therapists to address their own inner experience of anxiety or stress to successfully address their client's activated anxiety or stress. Helping clients have these experiences can help them soothe themselves and experience a sense of mastery, leading to self-efficacy and remoralization.

## SUMMARY

To reiterate, on the basis of our definition of corrective experiencing, CF therapists can help a client to engage with their felt emotions in a novel approach that contrasts with their expectations and contributes to remoralization. CF therapists may use any of a variety of interventions that focus on the client's corrective experiencing, with the common threads being the activation of emotion in a manner that is novel and corrective for the client. The change principle forms the lens for the therapist, who can select from confronting, expressing, or regulating interventions.

All of these categories of interventions refer to what the client, not the therapist, is doing, with the therapist's role being a coach or assistant to invite and help them through the experiencing. Ideally, clients continue their corrective experiencing outside the therapy session in their daily life. To the degree that these interventions are effective for the client, they will contribute to a client feeling a sense of self-efficacy in their life and feeling remoralized.

We have included tables of possible interventions that fit in these categories, but these are not exhaustive lists. We encourage therapists to discover and use any other interventions that are consistent with the change principles we have described. Reading additional materials and gaining more specific details for these interventions is also part of the CF therapy approach, as is improving one's practice using deliberate practice suggestions in the tables.

# 5

# INSIGHT, COMMON FACTOR 4

The origin of thoughts and ideas represents a full branch of philosophy: epistemology. Can reason guide us to a new thought or idea? Or do we arrive at new thoughts and ideas via our own sensory experiences? Epistemology fundamentally asks the question: How do we know what we know?

The classic story of reason as a guide to insight comes from rationalist philosopher Socrates's dialogue with Meno. Socrates demonstrates what he believes to be innate knowledge by inviting a discussion with a person enslaved by Meno and guiding the child through a geometry problem. Through careful, step-by-step questions—the likely basis of the term *Socratic questioning*—the child reasons his way to the correct solution. Socrates intimates that the child always knew the answer, and the questions merely called it forth.

Socrates's perspective may be especially illustrative for psychotherapy. Do humans carry the answers (or insights) to their questions and concerns within themselves? If so, therapy may be seen as an instrument for calling it forth. On the other hand, humans may be guided to the answers (or insights) with a teacher. Perhaps a therapist may actively seek to guide a client to find their insights through questioning and guiding to new experiences. A therapist

https://doi.org/10.1037/0000343-006
*Common Factors Therapy: A Principle-Based Treatment Framework*, by R. J. Bailey and B. M. Ogles

may also offer information to the client previously unknown to the client. Perhaps these methods offer the insights that produce a client's desired change and remoralization in therapy.

On the other hand, perhaps the empirical school of epistemology also offers a path to insight, via sensory experiences that pave the way for insight to occur. As discussed in Chapter 4 of this book, the corollary of corrective experiencing tends to be cognitive. The novel—often emotional—experience that comes through confronting, expressing, and regulating has its pairing with cognitive insight. Therapists and clients engaging in the work of therapy may find themselves arriving at new knowledge, gained through the process of experience.

In another entertaining but likely sensationalized story of insight from antiquity (see Biello, 2006), the polymath Archimedes was tasked with determining whether the monarch's crown was truly made of gold or whether the metalsmith cheated him. The apocryphal story finds Archimedes lowering himself into a bathtub, seeing the water displaced, recognizing how the crown's composition could be measured via displacement, and immediately exiting the bathtub without bothering for a towel, running home naked through the streets of ancient Syracuse shouting, "Eureka!" The insight occurred in a moment of understanding.

Insights may arrive in lightning flashes, in the moment when conditions are right for a person to draw the connection. In these moments, the previous perspective is turned on its head, and the person cannot unsee the connection. As E. J. Langer (2009) showed with a unique take on mindfulness, when a person's perspective becomes rote and routine, it is narrow and closed off to the possibilities of new perspectives on a problem. Shifting one's perspective, seeing a problem differently can open the mind to possibilities previously unknown.

Therapists may also notice blind spots, aspects of the client of which the client is unaware. The role of the therapist in effectively helping the client to understand and appreciate these blind spots can require the interpretation of assessments, careful and gradual uncovering over time, or deliberate confrontation in a moment. The experience of therapy optimally helps a client toward insight in ways that will contribute to a client's self-efficacy (see Chapter 6) such that the client can use the insight in their life.

Whether guided to insight or independently derived, whether gradually discovered or spontaneously realized, the new thinking a client finds through therapy represents significant change. This chapter is about the power of a thought or idea to change a person: to influence their feelings, to modify their behavior, to shift their patterns of self-evaluation, to alter their relationships, and to change their view of the world. This chapter is about insight,

**FIGURE 5.1. Common Factors (CF) Therapy Model With Insight Interventions**

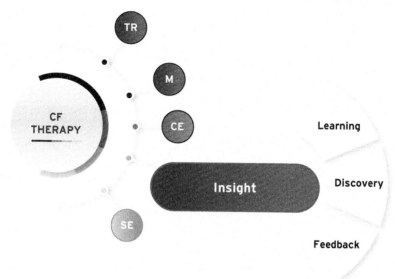

*Note.* TR = therapeutic relationship; M = motivation; CE = corrective experiencing; SE = self-efficacy.

understanding, awareness, or inspiration as a common pathway to improvement in psychotherapy. We first provide some conceptual background for insight as a common factor, including establishing the fact that insight meets our criteria as a common factor. We then develop a common factors (CF) definition of insight followed by describing interventions within three broad categories: learning, discovery, and feedback. As in previous chapters, we cannot cover all forms of intervention that lead to insight, but we provide examples from across the spectrum to illustrate how insight can be facilitated from a CF perspective (see Figure 5.1).

## OVERVIEW OF INSIGHT

Including insight as a common factor has been a thesis of researchers and theoreticians previously, having been included on lists of possible common factors. Wampold et al. (2007) proposed that "insight involves obtaining a functional understanding of one's problem, complaint, or disorder through the process of psychotherapy, and that insight is a beneficial common factor present in and critical to all psychotherapeutic orientations" (p. 119). They acknowledged that their definition and conceptualization of insight builds on the significant literature about common factors where insight, or some variation on the term, is routinely included in theorists' or researchers' conceptualizations of how the common factors manifest across therapeutic orientations. We say more later about insight both as a common factor and as a theoretical mechanism of change within various orientations.

A key element of change in life and therapy involves awareness, insight, knowledge, or learning. Insight as an element of change is central to some theoretical orientations (e.g., psychoanalysis) and an important component of other theoretical orientations that emphasize other aspects of change. Cognitive therapies emphasize cognitive change as a central element of therapy that clearly runs consistent with insight as we discuss here. For our CF approach to treatment, it is noteworthy that multiple researchers have identified insight, or a similar synonym, as a therapeutic component that is both transtheoretical and empirically supported. For example, Goldfried's (1980) third of five principles that are common across orientations is "increasing the patient's awareness and insight" (Eubanks & Goldfried, 2019, p. 89). Similarly, Lambert and Ogles (2004) produced a table of common factors using three main headings, one of which is Learning Factors, which includes elements such as insight, feedback, cognitive learning, and advice (p. 163). Prochaska and Norcross (2018) also identified "consciousness raising" as a transtheoretical process of change emanating from the "insight or awareness therapies" in their integrative model of psychotherapy (p. 8). They further divided consciousness raising into two categories—feedback and education—depending on whether the information or awareness is directed toward the client's actions or experiences (feedback) or focused on environmental events that are relevant to the client (education). Tschacher et al. (2014) conducted both a review of the literature and a survey of experts to develop a taxonomy of common factors. They included four factors in their taxonomy that have some direct or indirect relevance to insight as a common route to change: insight, assimilating problematic experiences, cognitive restructuring, and mentalization. Frank and Frank (1991) listed several functions of a therapeutic myth and ritual, one of which, "providing new learning experiences," fits into our conversation about insight and shows how learning experiences are associated with healing or remoralization (p. 45). Clearly, insight, either directly or in some synonymous form, appears repeatedly in the literature exploring factors common across therapeutic orientations.

Insight as an agent of change has long been evident in psychoanalytic therapies (S. B. Miller, 1992) and refers to the well-known idea of making the unconscious conscious (Messer & McWilliams, 2007). For example, Greenson (1967) stated that "it is characteristic of all techniques that are considered analytic, that they have the direct aim of increasing the patient's insight about himself" (p. 37). Indeed, therapies evolving from Freud's work have sometimes been labeled insight-oriented therapies. More recent therapy manuals in the psychodynamic tradition may refer to insight using different terms, but the essence is the same. For example, Luborsky (1984) referred to the first curative factor in supportive–expressive psychotherapy as "self-understanding" (p. 21). He continued:

> The main preliminary to the patient's improvement is an increase in *under-standing*. The focus of the understanding tends to be around the present symptoms and the associated relationship problems. The reexperiencing with the therapist in the "here and now" of the conflictual relationship problems gives the patient the most impetus toward meaningful *insight* and permits greater freedom to change. . . . The *insight* becomes progressively more meaningful to the patient as new editions of the relationship problems are repeatedly worked through with the therapist and others. (p. 22, emphasis added)

Similarly, Strupp and Binder (1984) indicated that "change is presumed to occur as a result of insight into the connection between current patterns of maladaptive behavior and their origin in childhood conflicts" (p. 22). Like Luborsky, they describe therapy as an interpersonal process that helps the "patient *see* what he or she is doing while doing it" followed by helping them to "*rewrite, modify,* and *correct* the assumptions" underlying their interpersonal interactions in therapy (p. 38, emphasis added). They also suggested that the

> process is greatly facilitated by the therapist's consistent and reliable behavior as a fellow adult who, through his or her actions disconfirms a number of the patient's anachronistic and false assumptions about reality; that is, about the behavior, motives, and so on of others. (p. 38)

As you can see, both manuals refer to helping the client understand, see, or gain insight about current relationship patterns or styles that originated in earlier (often childhood) experiences so that client assumptions and patterns of relating can be modified. Although not described specifically using these terms, an implicit assumption of this interpersonal process includes the connection of current interpersonal interactions to historical experiences or patterns of behavior.

Because of this rich history with the term *insight* in psychoanalytic theory, sometimes researchers and clinicians from other therapy orientations are reluctant to use the term as an element of change in their models. However, when thinking more broadly about the influence of ideas, cognitions, awareness, feedback, and education as forms of or synonyms to insight, it is only natural to consider insight as a factor common to other therapies, especially cognitive therapies that focus specifically on helping clients to think differently about events in their lives. This is clearer in the most definitive work regarding insight, the book *Insight in Psychotherapy* (Castonguay & Hill, 2007), which evolved from a working group of psychotherapy researchers from various therapeutic orientations that met in three meetings over 4 years culminating with the 20 chapters published in the final product. Included in this work are chapters about insight from several perspectives (e.g., cognitive behavior and common factors). Importantly, the final chapter of the book represented the group's best effort to establish a consensus definition for insight, processes for gaining insight, and research questions deserving of future study. Before turning to a CF definition of insight, however, we must first tackle the difficult distinction between insight and corrective emotional experiencing (described in Chapter 4).

## INCLUSION CRITERIA FOR INSIGHT

To be considered a bona fide therapy, CF therapy needs specified components, and each change principle must meet our established criteria. Here we show how insight aligns with our requirements.

### Research Evidence in Support of Insight

Although there is considerable theory about the essential role of insight as a mechanism of change both within and across orientations, there is much less research to support the idea. In a recent meta-analysis of 22 studies meeting specified methodological criteria, Jennissen et al. (2018) found a moderate effect size ($r = .31$) between insight and outcome. Insight was assessed from both clinician ratings and self-ratings, and outcome was assessed in a variety of different ways across studies (e.g., symptoms, interpersonal relationships). Although this first systematic review and meta-analysis provides an excellent starting point, the authors acknowledged that there is much to learn about the role of insight not just as a correlate of change but also as a mechanism of change.

A decade earlier, Connolly Gibbons et al. (2007) reviewed five types of empirical studies of insight:

- insight as a patient personality dimension (the tendency to be insightful),
- gains in insight during therapy and their relationship to outcome,

- insight in relationship to other therapy process variables,
- therapist interventions that promote the development of insight, and
- methodological studies of insight.

A comprehensive summary of their findings (and the many questions raised but unanswered in the literature they reviewed) is unnecessary for the purposes of this book. Their findings, however, do lend sufficient empirical support to the idea of insight being related to outcome. As a result, we are confident about including insight as a common factor that meets our inclusion criteria. For example, they concluded, in reference to the second type of study listed earlier, that "the results of some studies provide some empirical support for one of the main theories of psychotherapy: Improvements in symptoms and life functioning are possible if insight is gained, at least when longer term outcomes are examined" (Connolly Gibbons et al., 2007, p. 152). Although they raised several definitional and methodological concerns and made important recommendations regarding future research on insight, the findings they reported based on a relatively limited available literature support the idea of insight being a cross-orientation factor that is related to outcome.

## Insight Is Conceptually Present in Most Therapies

As described previously, insight has a strong historical connection to psychoanalytic therapy but is also central to cognitive therapies. Whereas the overlap between corrective experiencing and insight is significant—and from a humanistic perspective, possibly a complete one—it is clear that an emphasis on the new thinking or cognitions that come with corrective experiencing represents insight. Insight is present in most therapies at the conceptual level as well as the focus of specific interventions.

When connecting specific interventions to insight (and three other common factors that relate to cognitive pathways to change: assimilating problematic experiences, cognitive restructuring, and mentalization), Tschacher et al. (2014) found some overlap in certain interventions (e.g., reality testing, which was considered by the experts to influence all four of the factors), whereas other interventions were uniquely connected to a single common factor (e.g., transference interpretation, resistance interpretation, and focusing, which were related only to facilitating insight). This work provides a natural transition into the remaining portions of this chapter where we provide examples of interventions that match up with our CF therapy conception of insight.

## EXCLUSION CRITERIA FOR INSIGHT

We have already shown that the broad schools of psychotherapy ascribe to insight as a change principle. One potential issue involves that overlap between insight and emotional experiencing. In this respect, corrective emotional experiencing has many similarities to insight. We thus provide a modest description of the separation for these two factors here.

Descriptions of the therapy process leading to insight can sound very much like a corrective experience. Strupp and Binder (1984) described a therapeutic process of relationship enactment with the therapist that helps the client see what they are doing and provides the opportunity for them to rewrite, or correct, the relationship pattern. This enactment and correction could be described as insight that is followed by corrective experiencing. Similarly, Luborsky (1984) described the importance of connecting past and present relationships to make them emotionally relevant: "Past relationships gain in meaning when they are related to current ones. Keeping the relevance of the present in sight is one way for the therapist to ensure that the insight is emotionally meaningful and not just intellectual" (p. 22).

In a psychoanalytic paper, S. B. Miller (1992) repeatedly addressed the question of insight with and without emotion along with considering change with and without awareness/insight. It would be convenient if the oversimplification that corrective emotional experiencing was change originating in emotion and that insight was change originating in cognition was accurate. Unfortunately, or fortunately, depending on one's perspective of human complex nature and functioning, both processes are significantly overlapping. Certainly, from a humanistic perspective, an emotionally focused intervention may, and some may say must, involve some cognitive awareness, understanding, or insight to be fully meaningful and impactful. For example, L. S. Greenberg (2021) clearly articulated this in his book:

> The process of arriving at, allowing, and accepting emotions, however, is not enough to deal therapeutically with painful emotion. In addition to arriving at emotions, therapists also need to help clients leave certain painful emotions by activating new adaptive emotions that help change the old emotions. Clients need to consolidate their experiential change in new narratives consisting of new views of self and world. (pp. 20–21)

Similarly, insight does not lead to change through cognition independent of emotions (as if we were robots that process intellectual algorithms separated from complex feelings). Indeed, some have argued that "insights are effective only when they are accompanied by, or wedded to, affect" (Hammer, 1990, p. 19).

Although it might be nice for pathways of change to be purely cognitive or affective, the reality is that cognition, behavior, affect, physiology, and other domains of human functioning are highly interrelated and interactive despite our intellectual wish for more simple explanations. For now, we are not taking a deep dive into this complicated idea. Rather, we approach these two common factors from a very pragmatic point of view, with the idea that interventions evolving from each of them include the whole person (emotions and cognitions and other part-person intellectual distinctions, too), but we emphasize one or the other (i.e., emotion or cognition) as the primary or initial pathway to change. For this chapter, that pathway is a cognitive, intellectual pathway, but one must be mindful that emotions are present and must be considered and incorporated into treatment.

We have also endeavored to distinguish corrective experiencing from insight by focusing first on emotional experiences and second on cognitive changes through the work of therapy. By making this distinction, we reason that what might otherwise be a redundant factor—therefore excluded from CF therapy—instead offers a unique aspect of change that is commonly held and celebrated across orientations. Holding the two aspects of change—the emotional and the cognitive—together but separate is a challenging task. Including each of them as change principles, blending into one another, represents as parsimonious a representation as possible.

## DEFINITION OF INSIGHT

Our goal throughout this book has been to use terminology that crosses theoretical boundaries, conceptualizes the change principle to allow for variability across boundaries and flexibility in application, and offers parsimony. A dictionary definition of *insight* includes phrases such as "the power or act of seeing into a situation" or "the act or result of apprehending the inner nature of things or of seeing intuitively" (Merriam-Webster, n.d.). Castonguay and Hill (2007), pursuing a consensus definition among a group of psychotherapy researchers, stated:

> Insight usually is conscious (as opposed to unconscious or implicit) and involves both a sense of *newness* (i.e., the client understands something in a new way) and making *connections* (e.g., figuring out the relationship between past and present events, therapist and significant others, cognition and affect, or disparate statements). Hence, most of us agreed that we could define insight as a conscious meaning shift involving new connections (i.e., "this relates to that" or some sense of causality). (p. 442)

In an exceptionally thorough analysis of the meanings of insight, Elliott (2007) identified three main categories of insight language: perceiving/sensing, entering/penetrating, and coming into possession. He concluded that insight is organized around the notion of perceiving or sensing an idea through one of two "complementary visions" of what it means to perceive or sense: either through entering or through possessing (p. 172). In an earlier article Elliott et al. (2001) suggested that insight includes four major elements: metaphorical vision, connection, suddenness, and newness.

For the purposes of CF therapy, we combined these ideas to arrive at the following definition for insight as a common factor.

## COMMON FACTORS DEFINITION OF INSIGHT

*Insight* refers to when a client becomes consciously aware of (discovers), educated about (learns), or is confronted with (feedback) a new way of perceiving or thinking (often through connections to known ideas or experiences) about themselves, their relationships, or the origins of their distress in a way that catalyzes hope and contributes to remoralization.

## INTERVENTION CONCEPTS FOR INSIGHT

As in previous chapters, this portion of our discussion on insight is focused on identifying change principles and specific, actionable interventions that can be used by CF therapists. As we have mentioned before, therapists can use insight as a heuristic (see Lazarus & Wachtel, 2018, p. 391) for working with their clients to determine the appropriate interventions that are needed in the specific circumstance.

We offer several questions to guide therapists in the use of the heuristic of insight:

- What information would be helpful to my client? How might I best provide that information to my client?

- Could brief psychoeducational modules be used to help my client learn more about their circumstance that would lead to change?

- How can I help my client to engage in a process of introspection, awareness, discovery, and self-understanding?

- What feedback could I give my client that would help them to understand how their thinking, emotions, and behavior are influencing them, others around them, and their circumstances?

- In what ways are my client's perceptions inaccurate? How can I help them to perceive their experiences in a more realistic way?

Questions like these may prompt therapists to choose interventions that promote insight. A therapeutic relationship, consistent with ideas described in Chapter 2 of this book, can help to create a safe environment where learning, self-discovery, and even difficult feedback or reality testing can be received in a way that promotes change. Note the major categories of interventions include learning, discovery, and feedback, all referring to activities of the therapist and client during these interventions that lead to the acquisition of insight.

## Preparation for Insight

Before we jump into the various interventions that may lead to insight, it may be helpful to briefly discuss strategies that can be used to prepare for insight. Hill et al. (2007) suggested five stages of insight attainment: (a) setting the stage for insight, (b) preparation for insight, (c) markers of client's readiness for insight, (d) promotion of insight, and (e) consolidation of insight. The interventions that we describe later come largely in Stage 4, promotion of insight. Much of what we describe in Chapters 2 and 3 regarding the therapeutic relationship and motivation could be considered preparation for insight. Hill et al. (2007) described a number of potentially useful interventions that could help the client be more receptive to insight-oriented interventions, such as

- reducing client inhibitions;
- decreasing client avoidance or defenses;
- encouraging client introspection and exploration;
- helping clients "activate relevant schema" by helping them to identify thoughts, consider assumptions, or think about their beliefs;
- increasing client arousal to an optimal level; and
- increasing clients' state of dissonance in anticipation of insight. (p. 447)

Of course, a variety of other techniques might be used to set the stage for and prepare the client for insight. Much of this planning should consider the client's state and trait level receptivity. Awareness of client markers (Hill et al.'s, 2007, Stage 3) may help to determine when the client is ready for insight-oriented interventions. These markers might include client statements such as "I am confused why this happens to me," "I want to know how I can handle these situations better," and "Is it possible that my reaction is related to ____?" or other statements that reflect a desire to understand themselves, others, or situations better. As Hill et al. (2007) suggested,

"Puzzlement seems to motivate active self-exploration, which can lead to new emotional awareness and insight" (p. 447). With this background and preparation, we now turn to insight interventions grouped within our three categories: learning, discovery, and feedback.

## Learning

Our first insight domain represents the benefits of learning through the informal provision of information and more formal educational processes. At the most basic end of the continuum and often with less need for emotional engagement, the therapist can provide basic information that may be helpful for the client. In a more formal and sometimes structured way, educational modules or outlines may be used to give the client insight through education.

### Basic Information

> **PRINCIPLE 5.1**
>
> At a very elementary level, psychotherapy is an opportunity to learn, and sometimes the provision of basic information in and of itself can lead to change.

Sometimes change occurs when the therapist provides straightforward and basic information. The idea of providing basic information to the client brings to mind a case recounted by one of my (BMO's) graduate school clinical supervisors. The supervisor presumably told me this story to communicate the value of simplicity and parsimony in therapeutic interventions—at least, as I recall the incident and remembering my excessive complication in reporting about the case being discussed in supervision. Here is how the story went. A brand-new college student was once referred to the supervisor for treatment. The referral source indicated that the student had emotional distress in the form of depression and anxiety that was disrupting the student's adjustment to life away from home and parents and adaptation to college life. As the supervisor met with the student/client, he began to see that the client had no prior exposure to a college campus and that his parents could provide little support because they also had no experience with higher education. The supervisor soon realized that the client needed very basic information about how to negotiate a college campus. As a result, during the next session he went for a walk with the client around campus to show him what resources were available to students and where these various services on campus were located. In addition, they walked to each of the buildings where the client had classes to show him where each classroom was located and how to get there. Although school was already in session, the client's anxiety had prevented him from attempting to attend class up to that point. With this walking session around campus along with helping the client with a few administrative processes at the university, the therapy was immediately successful in improving the client's mood and helping him to become engaged as a student on campus. After only a few sessions, the client was feeling much better with regard to depression and anxiety and ended treatment having experienced significant changes in school functioning. As is illustrated in the example, and as any seasoned therapist knows, there are times when providing information can be quite helpful. And in some cases, such as the example, it can be sufficient to produce the needed and desired change.

One special form of information giving involves self-disclosure. In some circumstances and with some clients, a therapist's disclosure about their thoughts, feelings, or experiences may be helpful to the client. Self-disclosure can take many forms, and an extensive discourse on its merits is beyond the scope of this chapter. The key point is that, when appropriate, a therapist's self-disclosure may be helpful. For example, a self-disclosure may help the client to see their own problems as more common than unique—again, a sort of normalizing of issues similar to the universality principle in group therapy. Similarly, a self-disclosure may give the client hope that they can improve. A self-disclosure could provide a model for the clients to see and use in managing their own issues. Self-disclosures may also help to strengthen the connection between the client and therapist. At the same time, self-disclosures carry some ethical risks as boundary crossings. To mitigate those risks, Knapp et al. (2017) suggested that therapists

> (a) disclose infrequently; (b) intentionally self-disclose to normalize, model, or strengthen the therapeutic alliance; (c) ensure that self-disclosures focus on the needs of the patient; (d) observe how patients respond to self-disclosures; (e) decide to self-disclose on the basis of the impact on the patient, recognizing that some patients respond well to self-disclosure and others do not . . .; and, if the self-disclosure appear to be problematic, then (f) document self-disclosures and the clinical rationale behind them. (p. 108)

Providing information through self-disclosures or information giving is similar to, and overlaps with, two other topics of this book: role induction in the therapeutic alliance and expectation setting for enhancing motivation. Especially early in treatment, uncomplicated provision of information about the practical aspects of treatment, the typical symptoms and course of mental health disorders, and the expectations for treatment can be very useful for the client. For example, in the manual on interpersonal psychotherapy of depression (IPT), Klerman et al. (1984) suggested "giving the symptoms a name" so that clients can know that their symptoms are associated with a known disorder and that they are not "going crazy" (p. 83). Here is an excerpt from the example they provided about how the diagnosis could be conveyed to the client (with details modified to match the client-specific circumstances):

> The symptoms you describe are all part of being depressed. Your appetite and sleep are disturbed. You've lost interest in your usual activities. You're more irritated with your children and not getting along with your spouse. You can't imagine taking the job you were interested in before. You don't have energy and zest. This is all part of the clinical picture of depression. Your thoughts about death, your tiredness and feeling of futility, the question about where your life is going, your lack of energy, are part of the constellation of depression. The symptoms you describe are common ones for depressed persons. You are in the throes of depression. (p. 83)

Klerman et al. (1984) went on to suggest that the therapist similarly provide general information about depression and its treatment, including giving the patient the sick role, while also describing the recovery process. All of this is meant to help the client to understand that "depression is a disorder in which they are not fully in control but from which, with treatment, they will recover without serious residual damage" (p. 85).

We are not advocating for IPT here; rather, we are suggesting that in many instances basic information can be helpful to the client as a form of insight. The IPT example is just one of many that could be used to illustrate how the CF therapist can help their clients to improve simply by knowing more about their current symptoms and the course of therapy. Basic information in many other situations can be very helpful. For example, one of us (BMO) once provided a friend with basic information about the typical issues that stepparents encounter after he remarried following the death of a spouse. The friend later reported that just knowing what to expect and that other stepparents encounter similar situations with adolescent children was very helpful even without treatment (though the friend did later ask for a referral and sought treatment). The point is that sometimes providing basic information can be a catalyst for change.

Information may relate to multicultural concerns, diagnosis, life situation, relationship challenges, available resources, research findings, or even accurate sources of factual information. When working with a child once, one of us was able to relieve a child's anxiety by letting them know that when they stuck their hand with a pencil, while painful, they would not get lead poisoning because pencil "lead" is graphite. The information shared in a trusting relationship not only can be reassuring but can catalyze the work of therapy.

## Psychoeducation

### PRINCIPLE 5.2

Didactic instruction as a form of learning with or without applied exercises can facilitate insight leading to change in psychotherapy.

At a more formal level, some treatments can include psychoeducational components or modules in which specific principles, or concepts, are taught and then applied. We included this as a separate category from basic information within our learning subdomain of insight because it is more intentional, formal, and structured than is the informal delivery of information. An educational intervention is typically connected to a prepared lesson plan (or curriculum) that has clear learning objectives along with suggestions for practice and application. Still, these two learning subdomains are very similar and overlap to some degree.

Many forms of psychoeducation are available to help clients. Indeed, perhaps the most common form of educational help for clients is available through self-help books or bibliotherapy. For example, dozens of self-help books are available to help individuals with a variety of problems. Periodic reviews of bibliotherapy as either a self-help treatment or an adjunctive treatment for clients in therapy have been published over the years (see, e.g., Lenkowsky, 1987; Mains & Scogin, 2003; McCulliss, 2012; Sclabassi, 1973). It is not easy to characterize those findings because educational materials may be beneficial for some types of clients/problems and not others (Lenkowsky, 1987). Self-help has been found to be helpful in earlier studies for depression, mild alcohol abuse, and anxiety (Mains & Scogin, 2003). Many of these published books or other readings put together by therapists can be helpful for clients either separately from or integrated with ongoing therapy. The CF therapist can accumulate resources that can accompany their treatment.

An even more formal application of education is available in some treatment approaches or for some types of problems. For example, in Craske and Barlow's (2014) treatment for clients with panic disorder and agoraphobia, education is one of six components of treatment (education, self-monitoring, breathing retraining, applied relaxation, cognitive restructuring, and exposure).

Treatment in this cognitive behavior approach begins with education about "the nature of panic disorder, the causes of panic and anxiety, and the ways panic and anxiety are perpetuated by feedback loops among physical, cognitive, and behavioral response symptoms" (p. 24). The psychophysiology of panic and anxiety is also described in detail and accompanied by a very thorough handout. Similarly, fear (as an emotion) is distinguished from anxiety (a chronic state of tension). The purpose of the education is to "correct the common myths and misconceptions about panic symptoms . . . that contribute to panic and anxiety" (p. 24).

Other treatments include an educational component as part of their delivery, such as Lewinsohn's classic coping with depression course (Cuijpers, 1998; Donker et al., 2009; Lewinsohn et al., 1984). Similarly, other treatments such as assertiveness training, parenting skills training, and communication skills training are delivered in an educational format or include educational elements within the treatment model. The layout of these treatments often integrates some instruction by the therapist with role playing or some other form of practice and between-session homework where the skills are applied in daily life. The client then reports back on their experience with opportunity for further review, feedback, and practice before moving on to another skill.

The third-wave therapy, acceptance and commitment therapy (ACT; S. C. Hayes & Lillis, 2012), famously uses metaphors to communicate ideas in novel ways. On the basis of the theory that language can limit our understanding of our situations, the metaphors and concepts of ACT intentionally juxtapose the language we use with distress. These metaphors may be used in a framework of educating a client.

As with the previous Learning section on basic information, our use of examples within the learning/education domain that come from one orientation (cognitive behavior therapy [CBT] or ACT in this case) should not be interpreted as advocacy for a particular model or for an eclectic model of treatment (even though we have demonstrated throughout this book that a CF approach to treatment is very similar to other integrative forms of treatment). Rather, we are suggesting that the use of education or educational modules as a route to insight is a relatively common intervention pathway across orientations that can be used by the CF therapist when it fits with the client's circumstances (see Table 5.1 for some examples of learning-oriented interventions). The CF therapist recognizes that insight is a potent common factor of change. As a result, when the individual client circumstances warrant education as a corridor to potentially healing insight, they provide that

**TABLE 5.1. Example Learning Interventions**

| Intervention | Approaches | Resources |
|---|---|---|
| Psychoeducation | Cognitive behavior therapy | Barlow (2020), *Clinical Handbook of Psychological Disorders: A Step-by-Step Treatment Manual* (6th ed.) |
| Bibliotherapy[a] | Cognitive behavior therapy | Burns (2020), *Feeling Great: The Revolutionary New Treatment for Depression and Anxiety* |
| | | Barlow & Craske (2022), *Mastery of Your Anxiety and Panic: Workbook* (5th ed.) |
| | Interpersonal | Weissman (2005), *Mastering Depression Through Interpersonal Psychotherapy: Patient Workbook* |
| | Third wave | Linehan (2014), *DBT Skills Training Manual* (2nd ed.) |
| | | Harris (2008), *The Happiness Trap: How to Stop Struggling and Start Living: A Guide to ACT* |
| | | Gilbert (2019), *The Compassionate Mind (Compassion Focused Therapy)* |
| | | Forsyth & Eifert (2016), *The Mindfulness and Acceptance Workbook for Anxiety: A Guide to Breaking Free From Anxiety, Phobias, and Worry Using Acceptance and Commitment Therapy* |

[a]Far too many books are available to mention all that are important or frequently used. We provide some examples here to illustrate the breadth and utility of educational materials that can be used to supplement therapy.

education. Existing interventions that incorporate educational modules that are useful can be accessed and tailored to the task at hand. In this way, the CF treatment becomes very similar to other integrative therapies.

## Discovery

Our second domain for insight represents a client's process of becoming aware of themselves or their circumstances. Other words to describe this form of insight might include awareness, realization, self-understanding, or even epiphany. The pathway to this form of insight differs from learning/education in that awareness or discovery typically comes from within the client. In learning or education, the therapist, or another external source, such as a book in bibliotherapy, provides the insight. The therapist's role then

in self-discovery is to create the circumstances for or the treatment environment needed for the client to become more aware of themselves or other
external factors contributing to their demoralization. We divide discovery
into two further categories: awareness and self-understanding.

## Awareness

**PRINCIPLE 5.3**

An important potential route to insight involves the therapist creating the
circumstances or environment within which the client can gain insight by
becoming more aware of themselves or their circumstances.

Therapists can help a client to find hope and healing by creating an environment or situation within which they can become aware of the sources of
their dysfunction or potential pathways to healing. For example, one way a
CF therapist can help a client to gain awareness of their symptoms is through
self-monitoring. A client who wishes to decrease the frequency and intensity
of their headaches could be given a straightforward self-monitoring assignment that may lead to greater awareness of factors that contribute to the onset
and intensity of their pain (e.g., changes in sleep, foods consumed, weather
patterns, activity, exercise). The homework assignment to monitor and record
their symptoms along with other factors that precede, coincide with, or follow
these symptoms can lead to greater awareness (insight) about the causes
and consequences of the symptoms. Other behavioral interventions, such as
desensitization, may result in surprising and spontaneous insights (Cautela,
1965; Powell, 1996). Sometimes these connections can be powerful information that leads to improvement even in the absence of the therapist. Once
aware of contributors to their symptoms or situation, clients may return
to therapy to discuss these discoveries where they can be consolidated and
assimilated more fully. We say more about this later in the chapter.

Similarly, other types of homework can lead to client insight. For example,
after about eight or nine sessions working with a client, I (BMO) developed
a homework assignment to help a client gain awareness of her own experience relative to other women. In this case, the client entered treatment for a
recurring pattern of depression with some associated risky behaviors based,
in part, in thoughts of death and hopelessness about the future. The client
had been in treatment a few years earlier with a therapist in another geo-
graphic region related to childhood abuse and reported significant progress

in that treatment. As a result, she felt that the abuse should not be the central focus of this new bout of treatment. As the therapy progressed, it became apparent that a significant, daily precursor to her experience of depressed mood and subsequent actions (e.g., staying in bed, skipping work, ruminating about the awfulness of her life) had to do with how she felt when she first woke up in the morning. The client reported that she often woke up in the morning "feeling crappy." Her first instinct at that point was to launch into a cycle of feelings and thoughts that helped her to try and explain why she felt "crappy" in the morning and why she seemed to feel that way more often than do others. Her explanations often degenerated into final solutions such as "God allowed this to happen to me because I am defective" or "I'm fundamentally flawed and always will be." Her perception was then that she woke up feeling crappy more frequently than do others because there was something wrong with her.

To help her gain awareness of, appreciation for, and perspective about her mornings, the client and I developed together a survey/interview that the client was to administer to a diverse (age, family circumstance, race, economic status) group of 20 women with whom she was acquainted during the week between therapy sessions. The survey had perhaps a dozen items that included questions such as "How often in a typical week do you wake up feeling poorly?" or "What do you do if you feel unwell when you wake up?" The client excitedly returned to the next session with the results of her research. She began the discussion with the question "Did you know that most women often feel crappy when they wake up in the morning?" What followed then was a discussion of the client's insight into her own daily experience gained by becoming aware of other women's experiences. It was a powerful realization for the client to learn that she was more like other women than she was different. In essence, through the homework assignment involving others, the client had benefited from a change mechanism common in group therapy: universality, the idea that she was not alone but that others shared her concerns and challenges. On the basis of the insights gained through a relatively simple homework assignment, the client's self-perception and mood changed significantly. Instead of attributing her wakeup feelings to a fundamental flaw in herself, God's condemnation, or her difficult past, she recognized that she was more normal than she had supposed, and this insight made all the difference.

Awareness-building interventions may also be unstructured and exploratory. Therapists from across the gamut often encourage writing tasks to facilitate awareness, such as journaling, writing on a certain topic from the session, or writing out emotional content (Ruini & Mortara, 2022). Awareness may be facilitated by mindfulness practices (see also Chapter 4, this volume), in which the therapist may be encouraging corrective experiencing via a new emotional frame while also hoping that it leads to increased awareness and insight.

Perhaps the most common intervention that leads to awareness is reflective listening. In our conceptualization of discovery, the therapist creates conditions for insight in the therapy office. For example, within the context of a warm, safe, and healing relationship, therapist utterances, like reflective listening, allow the client to become aware of their values, preferences, or desires or to discover the way that events continue to influence them emotionally and intellectually. This can lead to greater awareness and understanding and subsequent change. When a client hears the therapist repeat back to them what they heard, it provides an opportunity for the client to have increased awareness and insight into their suffering. Clients may experience increased awareness, sensitivity, and empathy toward themselves and their circumstances.

We have already described the value of reflective listening as a method of engaging with the client and developing a healthy therapeutic relationship (see Chapter 2). Similarly, reflective listening is a common method of facilitating corrective emotional experiencing (see Chapter 4). Indeed, reflections as a therapist's verbal response mode are essential to therapy and serve a variety of functions. As an avenue to insight, the therapist creates an environment of trust and safety where a client is receptive to insights that might surface in the therapist's reflections. When a client hears the therapist's reflection—the therapist's conceptualization of what they just heard from the client—the client may gain new understanding about their own communication. This is a common route to greater self-awareness and discovery.

Reflections are the key ingredient in motivational interviewing (MI) that often leads to greater client awareness of their own motivations for change. Similarly, reflections are at the heart of humanistic approaches that help clients to better understand and align their behavior with their inner values, preferences, and desires. Reflections are also often considered in basic microcounseling texts and classes. For example, Cormier and Nurius (2003) suggested in their book on interviewing strategies that there are several potential purposes for a therapist reflection, including

- encouraging client expression of feelings,
- helping the client to be more aware of feelings,
- helping the client to acknowledge and manage feelings,
- helping the client to discriminate among feelings, and
- helping the client to feel understood.

In CF therapy, the reflection can serve any of these purposes, along with those already mentioned, such as engaging with the client, establishing the therapeutic relationship, and, for the purposes of this chapter, facilitating insight through greater self-awareness and discovery.

Of course, a variety of other techniques may be used to facilitate client awareness in addition to those described in this section. The CF therapist uses these and other interventions to help the client become aware of themselves and their circumstances as a route to change.

### Self-Understanding

**PRINCIPLE 5.4**

Another route to insight involves the therapist promoting opportunities for the client to hear and gain insight through self-exploration and therapist interpretations.

Another pathway to insight through discovery is self-understanding. We see this as different from awareness in that the insight comes more directly from therapist statements within therapy as opposed to coming from a variety of situations and circumstances, including those noted earlier, such as self-monitoring and homework assignments.

As described previously in the section on reflective listening (see Chapter 2), sometimes a client's exploration in therapy, as the therapist reflects back content, results in insight about themselves. Increased awareness about the explanations for demoralization, in both the past and present circumstances, can contribute to insight and remoralization. The emotional space of the therapeutic relationship can promote opportunities for the client to engage in self-exploration.

Self-understanding as a route to insight can be helpfully explained by turning to psychodynamic models of treatment. The primary mechanism of change in psychodynamic therapies is purported to be insight or self-understanding. This is described in a variety of ways, and, as noted earlier, it can sometimes overlap with our conceptions of corrective emotional experiencing. Perhaps the central potential dividing factor is the degree to which cognitive understanding, separate from emotional experiencing, can produce change.

An example of this can be seen in Strupp and Binder's (1984) description of the pattern of change in time-limited dynamic psychotherapy. They suggested that

the task of psychotherapy is (1) To create optimum (safe) conditions for the enactment of the patient's scenarios; (2) To allow them to be enacted (within limits); (3) To help the patient see what he or she is doing while doing it; (4) To restrict the enactment of complementary roles assigned by the patient, forcing the latter to rewrite, modify, and correct the assumptions underlying his or her scenarios. (p. 38)

The mechanism of change is described as seeing and understanding behavior while doing it and then modifying or correcting the underlying assumptions through interactions with the therapist. Although enactment infers a combination of cognitive, affective, behavioral, and especially interpersonal components, the initial, and perhaps dominant, idea is that awareness, self-understanding, or insight allows modification, which then alters the need for future enactment. This is "facilitated by the therapist's consistent and reliable behavior" (p. 38). Step 4 in this model fits better with corrective emotional experiencing (see Chapter 4, this volume), and Step 3 fits in this chapter about insight.

The CF perspective of this process is similar but without the theoretical framework of psychodynamic therapy. That is, the CF therapist creates a safe space through the development of a warm, trusting, therapeutic alliance, which then allows the client to be themselves in the relationship with the therapist. This provides the opportunity for the therapist to provide interpretations of the client's behavior, emotions, thoughts, or interactions (insight). In this CF framework, an interpretation is not the specific psychoanalytic notion of an interpretation but rather matches a more cross-orientation notion of interpretation like that included in Hill's (1986) counselor verbal response mode category system, which described an interpretation as

> a therapist statement that goes beyond what the client has overtly recognized and provides reasons, alternative meanings, or new frameworks for feelings, behaviors, or personality; it may establish connections between seemingly isolated statements or events; interpret defenses, feelings of resistance, or transference; or indicate themes, patterns, or casual relationships in behavior or personality, or relate present events to past events. (Hill et al., 1989, p. 285)

These interpretations or connections can be received as insight by the client that becomes transformative (see, e.g., the interesting analysis of a single case in Hill et al., 1989).

The CF therapist may productively use interpretations as a way to facilitate client insight. An interpretation typically moves beyond the reflection used to facilitate awareness by providing the therapist's view of patterns, connections, or alternative meanings for client consideration. Whereas a therapist reflection attempts to repeat back to the client the underlying meaning of their own expressions, an interpretation represents the therapist's considered judgment of factors that are contributing to the client's distress and is often received by the client as a new or previously unknown connection, pattern, or meaning. In other words, the client has gained insight! When a therapist provides an interpretation, they bring into the open an idea, pattern, or emotion that was previously vague, uncertain, or unknown by the client.

Therapist interpretations may look like the following:

- "I noticed that when you talk about your interactions with your boss, they sound very similar to ideas and emotions you express when talking about your relationship with your father."

- "You have been seeing me now for six sessions, and in that time, you have talked about everyone in your nuclear family except your mother."

- "It seems that each time you have a bad day, where you feel especially depressed, it comes right on the heels of an incident at school where you think of yourself as being intellectually incompetent."

- "When your son doesn't come to visit you, you question your worth as a mother."

Interpretations can take many forms, but in all cases, they are meant to help the client consider ideas, meanings, and connections of which they were previously unaware. They target insight with the idea that greater client awareness and understanding will provide them with the information needed to make emotional, intellectual, and behavioral change in future similar situations. In Table 5.2, we give suggestions for ways to use deliberate practice to improve one's competency with offering interpretations.

Other interventions may fit into our insight framework within the discovery and self-understanding domains. We do not go into any additional detail, but we do provide some examples in Table 5.3 and look forward to the continuing advancement of the CF model of treatment as others continue to apply interventions within existing or new categories.

## Feedback

### PRINCIPLE 5.5

Another route to insight involves the therapist providing feedback to the client. Like a mirror, feedback may facilitate insight regarding client emotions, behaviors, thoughts, or interaction patterns that allows the client to better see themselves and that leads to client change and remoralization.

**TABLE 5.2. Deliberate Practice Suggestions for Interpretation**

| Method | Descriptions |
|---|---|
| Video-assisted observation of your work | • Interpretations can often be closely associated with how you are conceptualizing a client's case. Briefly reviewing how you are explaining or conceptualizing a client's demoralization, including their history and any relevant factors, can help to prepare you to notice connections with what the client shares in session and possible interpretations. Watch a therapy session, paying attention to the following moments:<br>– Identify moments when a client talks about a key concern. Pause the video and consider any other related moments, especially moments when the client described the key concern.<br>– Consider how you are understanding the client's concerns. With the video paused or the volume turned down, practice describing your understanding to the client in your own words. Based on these practices, identify ways you could share an interpretation that would be most easily accepted and internalized by the client.<br>– Consider the question "What might my client not yet realize about what they are saying at this moment?" Consider their nonverbals, the therapeutic relationship, their motivation, and their emotional expression. Practice verbalizing your observations as if to your client.<br>– Write out a brief, bulleted list of your conceptualization of the client and their concerns. As you watch the video, pay attention to moments when you could make a connection between what the client is saying and how you are conceptualizing their case.<br>• Identify key moments to share with a consultant, trying to identify and move through any defensiveness you may feel about sharing this. |
| Getting consultant feedback[a] | • Determine whether your relationship with your consultant is sufficiently supportive and safe for soliciting feedback openly. Consider working through defensive reactions with your consultant.<br>• Watch the session with your consultant, briefly giving an overview of your conceptualization of the client's case. Ask for assistance, noticing moments when you could make interpretations.<br>• Request assistance with specific language used in interpretations. Experiment with different ways of phrasing and communicating an interpretation, asking for feedback from your consultant as to how you are coming across and how they believe the client might respond.<br>• Ask for specific interpretations your consultant would consider making to the client, referring to the specific moments you have identified from watching the video or recalling the session. |

**TABLE 5.2. Deliberate Practice Suggestions for Interpretation (*Continued*)**

| Method | Descriptions |
|---|---|
| Setting small incremental goals | • Perhaps with your consultant's help, identify your current comfort level and competence with interpretations. Then, identify a behavior to practice on your own that stretches you just beyond this comfort level. For example, you may practice using language that has varying levels of technical jargon or practice finding ways to offer interpretation without sounding condescending. |
| Solo deliberate practice | • Dedicate sufficient time to practice on your own.<br>• Use the session video to practice your target behavior with regard to reframing interventions.<br>• Notice how comfortable/uncomfortable the practice is and adjust the practice as needed. |
| Feedback-informed treatment | • Use outcome measures at each session to determine how the client is progressing in treatment. When progress feedback shows the client as not on track, checking in around how the client is interpreting their progress in treatment may be helpful. You may find it helpful to hear the client's explanation for their distress and offer your own interpretations as they describe how they see their concerns. |

[a]We use the word "consultant" in this and other deliberate practice tables for brevity. We mean this to refer to mentors, supervisors, trainers, colleagues, or other experts as appropriate to the skill being practiced.

**TABLE 5.3. Example Discovery Interventions**

| Intervention | Approaches | Resources |
|---|---|---|
| Self-monitoring | Behavioral | O'Donohue & Cummings (2008), *Evidence-Based Adjunctive Treatments* |
| Homework | Transtheoretical | Tompkins (2004), *Using Homework in Psychotherapy: Strategies, Guidelines, and Forms* |
| Writing | Transtheoretical | Ruini & Mortara (2022), *Writing Technique Across Psychotherapies–From Traditional Expressive Writing to New Positive Psychology Interventions: A Narrative Review* |
| Experiential focusing | Humanistic | https://focusing.org/felt-sense/what-focusing |
| Reflection | Transtheoretical | Hill (2020), *Helping Skills: Facilitating Exploration, Insight, and Action* (5th ed.)<br>W. R. Miller & Rollnick (2013), *Motivational Interviewing: Helping People Change* (3rd ed.) |
| Interpretation | Transtheoretical | Hill (2020), *Helping Skills: Facilitating Exploration, Insight, and Action* (5th ed.) |
| | Psychodynamic | Levy (1990), *Principles of Interpretation: Mastering Clear and Concise Interventions in Psychotherapy* |

To this point in the chapter, we described interventions that lead to insight that come in the form of learning (information or more formal and thorough education) or by a process of discovery through awareness or self-understanding. Insight can also come in a more direct format as interventions that provide feedback. Although feedback might sound emotionally challenging (like confrontation), we think of this more as an indication of the source of insight (from the therapist) than as a harsh or incriminating process. In the information domain of insight, the therapist provides the cognitive/intellectual data, but the data are typically about things external to the client, such as instruction about symptoms of depression, how therapy works, the difference between thoughts and emotions, or how to be assertive. In the awareness domain, the client discovers, recognizes, or realizes the insight—often about themselves—through assignments, self-monitoring, mindfulness, or exploration in a therapeutic environment that facilitates introspection. In the feedback domain, the therapist provides information about the client to the client. It is often feedback in an intellectual or cognitive form about the way the client thinks, behaves, or feels.

Feedback in psychotherapy takes a variety of forms and helps the client to be aware of aspects of the self of which they may be oblivious or unaware or may underemphasize. How do you know when you have spinach in your teeth? Without a helpful mirror, one might go minutes or hours without realizing that a dark green spot is changing your smile and distracting conversational partners. One quick word on the sly from a caring individual can quickly inform you of your unfortunate circumstance and provide you with the opportunity for correction, which you may or may not decide to do. Similarly, a variety of therapeutic interventions are available to help clients become aware of emotional, behavioral, cognitive, or interpersonal characteristics or patterns that may be as hidden to the person and as distracting to themselves or others in their circle of influence as is spinach in the teeth. We discuss here several examples of interventions that might be considered as falling in the feedback category, though there are obviously many others. The CF therapist can determine when feedback, in the context of a warm, caring relationship, is likely to lead to helpful, changing insight that benefits the client. At that point in time, the CF therapist can determine which type of intervention may be the most helpful delivery method. We do not consider all types of interventions where feedback can be provided, but we do provide several examples here. We organize our discussion by placing feedback interventions within one of two categories: feedback through data and feedback through the therapy process.

## Feedback Through Data

One of the ways therapists can give clients feedback is through the use of assessment tools or other instruments or devices that provide a different and useful perspective on client concerns, circumstances, or progress. Especially with newer technologies, data can be gathered in a variety of ways—too many to include in this brief section. As in prior chapters, our primary concern is with developing a heuristic for clinical conceptualization or guiding principles within which many interventions might fit. We describe a few forms of data-based feedback and expect that the CF therapist may add a variety of others to their tool kit depending on their typical clientele and clinical preferences.

*Biofeedback.* One obvious form of data-based feedback in therapy is biofeedback. The process of providing in-the-moment physiological data regarding client- and therapist-specified parameters can help the client be aware of such things as temperature, heart rate, galvanic skin response, and muscle tension, which are not easily quantifiable or personally noticeable in typical situations. With the visual or audio cues, the client can become aware of their levels of arousal or tension, which then provides them the opportunity to intervene and alter their typical reactions. As a result, biofeedback operates at least to some degree based on new awareness of previously unknown information and potentially the connections between the mechanism that is being monitored and other symptoms. In addition, biofeedback in a more abstract sense is a useful metaphor for the way in which feedback regarding psychological characteristics gives the client previously unknown information that allows them to establish new or different responses.

*Assessment as intervention.* Another method of providing data-based feedback to clients that can be common to all orientations is insight through assessment. This is especially relevant to psychologists who conduct psychological evaluations as part of the intake process (or when they conclude an assessment with intervention-oriented feedback), but it can also be relevant to other clinicians who use standardized measures to gather assessment data at the beginning of treatment. For example, Finn (1996) developed a manual describing a format for using the Minnesota Multiphasic Personality Inventory–2 (MMPI-2; Butcher et al., 1989) as a therapeutic intervention. The idea is that the client and therapist together establish collaborative goals/questions for the assessment in an initial interview, followed by the client completing the assessment. The client and therapist then meet for a feedback session in which the therapist provides feedback based on the

MMPI-2 combined with the data gathered in the initial interview. The client is given the opportunity to corroborate or modify interpretations as they consider together answers to the client's questions based on the assessment. As in other therapeutic interventions, the feedback session is facilitated by a collaborative relationship that helps to put the client at ease. With colleagues, Finn (Finn et al., 2012) later expanded on the MMPI-2 context to develop a broader guide for collaborative therapeutic assessment.

Finn (1996) was not the only one to consider assessment as a potential intervention. In fact, enough studies have been conducted on psychological assessment as a prospective therapy intervention that Poston and Hanson (2010) conducted a meta-analysis of the 17 available studies. They concluded that these studies "taken together . . . suggest that psychological assessment procedures—when combined with personalized, collaborative, and highly involving test feedback—have positive, clinically meaningful effects on treatment" (p. 203).

Similarly, interventions have been developed using MI where the clinician provides feedback regarding an assessment (often regarding the frequency and intensity of use of an addictive substance; see, for example, Stephens et al., 2002). One form of MI has been labeled motivational enhancement therapy, which is typically focused on resolving the client's ambivalence about entering treatment for their addiction. The client completes an initial assessment battery, followed by participating in a few sessions with a therapist. In the first treatment session, the therapist provides feedback regarding the findings of the initial assessment, stimulating discussion about personal substance use and providing the therapist the opportunity to strengthen any client self-generated introspective observations regarding the possibility of change. MI principles are used to strengthen motivation and build a plan for change, which often involves a recommendation to consider further treatment.

As can be seen from these examples, one potential CF intervention leading to insight involves the use of standardized assessment procedures to provide feedback to the client. The feedback has the value of both introducing an external source of information separate from the therapist, based on client responses, and opening the door to further conversation in treatment—so-called grist for the mill.

*Routine outcome monitoring.* Another form of assessment-oriented or data-based feedback that is a strong match with a CF approach because it has a natural fit with any therapeutic orientation is progress monitoring and clinical support tools through routine outcome measurement. Indeed, Norcross and Wampold (2011) included "collecting client feedback" as one of several elements of the therapeutic relationship that are "demonstrably effective" (p. 99). With the introduction of research-based outcome measures in practice, combined with technology that allows for routine administration, scoring, and reporting, the possibility of tracking a client's progress in therapy has become more common. Studies of feedback systems that provide data regarding a client's symptomatic improvement over time in therapy consistently found that the treatment is more efficient and improves outcomes—especially for clients who do not progress as quickly as statistical projections would anticipate (de Jong et al., 2021; Lambert et al., 2018).

Although routine outcome measurement is not technically a therapist intervention in treatment, once the therapist receives the feedback based on the client completion of the progress measure, they can then use that information in the therapy session. For example, the routine monitoring of client progress leads to "increased opportunities to reestablish collaboration, improve the relationship, modify technical strategies, and avoid premature termination" (Norcross & Wampold, 2011, p. 99).

Similarly, Page and Stritzke (2015) devoted a brief chapter to the topic of routine outcome monitoring in their book for trainees in clinical psychology. They described monitoring client progress as a therapeutic intervention and provided both the rationale for obtaining practice-based evidence and instruction about how to provide feedback to the client. Similarly, Lambert et al. (2019) recommended having an "explicit discussion with patients and problem solving with at-risk cases to provide additional benefits" (p. 623) beyond simply discussing their progress. They emphasized that progress monitoring and feedback had been especially helpful for clients who were not on track as expected.

For the CF therapist, a useful strategy would be to identify a method for gathering session-by-session data to track client change, often using a brief, global symptom-based measure that can apply to a broad range of clients. It is especially helpful if this can be collected electronically and compared using research-based algorithms with average client improvements to identify clients who are progressing as expected or not. However, even if the therapist does not use a system that includes a comparative feature, they can easily examine the session-by-session results to determine if the client is progressing. One of the reasons this is important is that there is strong evidence that therapists are poor judges of client deterioration (Hannan et al., 2005; Lunnen & Ogles, 1998; Lunnen et al., 2008; Page & Stritzke, 2015).

With session-by-session data, the therapist has some more objective evidence to help guide their decision making regarding the case and assessment data that they can use to start a conversation with the client to obtain important additional information to guide treatment. With some feedback systems, additional clinical support tools can be used in cases where the client is not on track, such as the Assessment for Signal Clients (see Lambert et al., 2007). Administration of this assessment can be especially helpful if an alliance rupture is in some way indicated as having a role in client deterioration or lack of progress because it gives the therapist an opportunity to have a conversation about the relationship and to potentially repair the breach. Of course, other potential reasons for the lack of progress (such as external-to-therapy factors, social isolation, or client factors) may play a role. Beginning the conversation opens the door to consider these issues and may bring additional insight into the therapy room. In Table 5.4, we offer suggestions for using deliberate practice to enhance one's ability to address feedback with a client.

In addition to our brief description of several data-based interventions that may be used to provide transformative feedback leading to insight, other interventions could be added to this CF domain. We anticipate future work may identify other categories of feedback or additional interventions that fit into any of the insight domains and look forward to seeing the evolution of the CF framework for therapy.

## Feedback Through the Therapy Process

Our second category of feedback is insight that is gained through therapist interventions related to behavioral, emotional, cognitive, or interpersonal interactions in the therapy process. In this form of feedback, the therapist identifies areas of potential feedback through the give-and-take of therapeutic conversations. For example, a therapist may notice that habitual client behaviors are connected to patterns for which in-session feedback may help the client to be aware of precipitating events. Similarly, the therapist may identify repeated unrealistic or idealistic thought patterns that if skillfully addressed through feedback may help the client to recognize and correct their views. Although emotion-filled events in therapy might also fit into this category, they have been more appropriately addressed in the Confronting section of the corrective experiencing chapter (see Chapter 4). There are many interventions directed at helping the client to gain insight through observations in the therapeutic process. We mention several examples here to provide the CF therapist with a few potential applications.

*Behavioral feedback.* One form of feedback evolving from therapeutic conversations and leading to insight has evolved from behavioral assessment and therapy where it is referred to as functional analysis of behavior. When conducting functional analysis, the therapist and client work together

**TABLE 5.4. Deliberate Practice Suggestions for Reviewing Feedback**

| Method | Descriptions |
|---|---|
| Video-assisted observation of your work | • Be sure to record video of moments when you review progress feedback with a client. Reviewing how you introduce the topic, the data you are sharing with your client, and the exploratory questions you ask can help you improve each of these skills. |
| | • Review the moment when you raise the topic with your client. Notice how your client responds, both verbally and nonverbally. Notice your own responses to the client. Pay particular attention to whether you feel responsible or defensive about your client's progress or lack of progress. |
| Getting consultant feedback | • Determine whether your relationship with your consultant is sufficiently supportive and safe for soliciting feedback openly. Consider working through defensive reactions with your consultant. |
| | • Discuss the most current progress feedback you have with your consultant. Notice any reluctance you may feel around sharing that the data suggest your client may be experiencing more distress rather than less distress as therapy progresses. |
| | • Discuss ways to address progress feedback with your client in ways that are more productive and not defensive. |
| | • Consult about possible actions to take based on the feedback. For example, consider how to adjust your conceptualization of the case. Consider ways to intensify treatment, such as adjunctive bibliotherapy, group therapy, and medication referral. Consider ways to gather more information, such as giving the client process-related measures for the therapeutic relationship and motivation for therapy. |
| Setting small incremental goals | • Perhaps with your consultant's help, identify your current comfort level and competence with addressing progress feedback with your client. Then, identify a behavior to practice on your own that stretches you just beyond this comfort level. For example, you may practice addressing situations when you believe the feedback you give will not be well received by the client. Or you may practice bringing up the feedback and asking open-ended questions of the client, avoiding the temptation to offer your conclusion first. |
| Solo deliberate practice | • Dedicate sufficient time to practice on your own. |
| | • Use the session video to practice your target behavior with regard to discussing feedback with your client. |
| | • Notice how comfortable/uncomfortable the practice is and adjust it as needed. |
| Feedback-informed treatment | • Use outcome measures at each session to determine how the client is progressing in treatment. Discussing this progress feedback with your client is essential to feedback-informed treatment. When progress feedback shows the client as not on track, a discussion is vital. You may also find it helpful to emphasize with your client the purpose of the outcome measure they are filling out on a regular basis, including how this is helpful information and how you use the data. |

to identify a target behavior that the client desires to change. They then examine incidents, sometimes through observation, where the behavior surfaces. They then locate antecedents and consequences of the behavior to learn the function of the behavior and the circumstances or events that work together to elicit and sustain the target behavior. Although we are using the word "behavior" here, the change target might be cognitions or emotions such as self-critical thoughts or depressive feelings, so long as the target can be monitored and recorded and the precursors and reinforcers can be identified. We are also using the behavioral language, but the CF therapist need not think of the analysis of behavior through the behavioral theory lens. Rather, their focus is on examining behavioral patterns with the client to help them gain insight into the factors that contribute to and maintain their behavior.

For example, a common target that clients consider together with their therapists is an addictive or habitual behavior. A client who wishes to quit smoking may work together with the therapist to develop a relapse prevention plan using an analysis of behavioral patterns. In the case of most addictions, and smoking in particular, the target behavior is easily identifiable as use of the addictive substance or, in this case, smoking a cigarette. The client and therapist then work together to examine past lapses where the client smoked to better understand the circumstances and events that led up to the smoking and the consequences that followed the smoking. Interventions are then developed to help the client better manage or cope with any prospective triggers and to alter consequences that can be reinforcing the smoking. We include this type of intervention in our insight chapter because analysis of behavior patterns may help the client to become aware of factors that contribute to or maintain the behavior of which they were not previously aware. A more detailed description of functional analysis is not provided here but can be pursued by the CF therapist who determines that such an examination of the client's desired changes may best benefit from this intervention strategy.

We realize that the purist behaviorally oriented clinician might argue that this exercise is related to classical and operant conditioning rather than any form of cognitive insight as the mechanism for change. From a CF point of view, however, we view the intervention as a form of feedback that provides insight about the mechanisms that contribute to maintaining the behavior and that provide an avenue for change.

Again, this point of view is subtly different from an integrative approach based on the idea that an analysis of change precursors and consequences is used in various orientations more than one might think (albeit described using different language) and is therefore common and not simply a combining of various orientations. Interested CF therapists can use the principle of thoroughly evaluating the situations and circumstances that lead to and sustain client behaviors, thoughts, emotions, and interpersonal patterns in an effort to gain insight for interventions that alter precursors or consequences and facilitate change.

*Cognitive feedback and reality testing.* Another common situation where insight can be helpful to the client involves their thinking patterns and perceptions of themselves, others, the world, and the future. One clear example of this was referred to in the chapter introduction: Socratic questions. Socratic questions can help the client to take a different perspective on themselves and their problems (Carona et al., 2021). These therapist intervention strategies are easily tied to CBT and new-wave CBT approaches but are also evident in other therapeutic orientations. Questions such as "Is there an alternative way to view your situation?" or "What would your best friend say about this situation if they were here in this room?" may help the client to see options to their situation allowing them to handle future similar situations differently. These questions help to make the client aware of or understand the way in which their view of a circumstance may influence their feelings and behavior. It helps them take a new and different perspective on events in their lives by evaluating their thoughts related to a specific event in their lives. J. S. Beck (2011) provided several questions that may help a client to gain insight through evaluating their thoughts, including the following:

1. What is the evidence that supports this idea? . . .
2. Is there an alternative explanation or viewpoint? . . .
4. What is the effect of my believing the automatic thought? . . .
5. What would I tell ____ (a specific friend or family member) if he or she were in the same situation?
6. What should I do? (p. 172)

These and many other questions that help clients to consider options and alternatives help them to gain new perspective and insight on the origins of and contributors to their issues. Many CBT-oriented books provide examples and training that can be studied and integrated into the CF practice. See our deliberate practice table (Table 5.5) regarding reframing interventions for more helpful suggestions.

The two-chair (or empty chair) technique originating in gestalt therapy can also be a form of perspective taking. Although the two-chair technique was also described in the chapter on corrective experiencing (see Chapter 4,

**TABLE 5.5. Deliberate Practice Suggestions for Reframing**

| Method | Descriptions |
|---|---|
| Video-assisted observation of your work | • Watch a therapy session, paying attention to the following moments:<br>  – Identify when your client uses language that demonstrates a fixed way of thinking about a concern. These are not necessarily the moments when a reframing intervention is best used, as the client may be in high distress and a reframing attempt may come across as invalidating. In this circumstance, make a mental note of the client's language. Then watch for language that you may address later in the session when the client may be amenable to considering alternative ways of considering their concern.<br>  – Identify when your client invites or may be welcoming to a new way of thinking about their concern.<br>  – Identify when you attempt a reframe, ask Socratic questions, highlight fixed mindsets, or use other interventions that are intended to help the client reframe their concern. How did your client respond? Are there any signs of defensiveness? Was the client ready for your reframe? How could your reframe (including the timing of the reframe) be improved in a way that the client could use it?<br>  – When you identify both language from your client to address and the optimum timing to encourage a reframe, practice offering a reframe out loud.<br>• Identify key moments to share with a consultant, trying to identify and move through any defensiveness you may feel about sharing this. |
| Getting consultant feedback | • Determine whether your relationship with your consultant is sufficiently supportive and safe for soliciting feedback openly. Consider working through defensive reactions with your consultant.<br>• Watch the session with your consultant, asking for assistance to notice both language the client uses that can be reframed and the optimum moment(s) for using reframing interventions.<br>• Request assistance with noticing defenses and resistance that may have eluded your notice in the reframe. Pay particular attention to moments when you experience the righting reflex and get help to see whether your responses roll with the resistance.<br>• Discuss possible strategies for reframing with your consultant (e.g., Socratic questioning, reflections with reframes embedded, identifying cognitive distortions) and find new ways to engage clients in this manner. |

**TABLE 5.5. Deliberate Practice Suggestions for Reframing (*Continued*)**

| Method | Descriptions |
|---|---|
| Setting small incremental goals | • Perhaps with your consultant's help, identify your current comfort level and competence with reframing. Then, identify a behavior to practice on your own that stretches you just beyond this comfort level. For example, you may practice using specific language for reframing, using specific interventions to reframe, or attuning to the client's responses after a reframing intervention. Try to ensure that your practice is neither too overwhelming nor too easy. Be as specific as possible when describing what you are going to practice. |
| Solo deliberate practice | • Dedicate sufficient time to practice on your own.<br>• Use the session video to practice your target behavior with regard to reframing interventions.<br>• Notice how comfortable/uncomfortable the practice is and adjust the practice as needed. |
| Feedback-informed treatment | • Use outcome measures at each session to determine how the client is progressing in treatment. When progress feedback shows the client as not on track, checking in around whether the client may be looking for new ways of thinking may be helpful. Exploring goals of therapy relative to thinking patterns and seeking new insights may also be helpful. |

this volume) as an avenue toward emotional change, it can also be fruitfully used as a way to help a client take another perspective on a relationship that leads to insight. For example, a client who had significant unresolved issues with her deceased mother participated in a two-chair experience during therapy where she engaged in a conversation with her mother. As she shifted chairs she began to think about and anticipate how her mother might respond. She immediately thought about what she might say in a similar circumstance to her own daughter in similar circumstances. The words that she then heard coming from "her mother" were not judgmental, harsh, or incriminating. Rather, she expressed understanding, support, and encouragement. As she accepted this alternative view of her mother's evaluation of her from the grave, she was also able to be less harsh with herself, and her anxious and depressive symptoms were alleviated to some degree. The insight gained from considering her mother's perspective in the two-chair exercise helped her change.

One might argue that the avenue of change in this exercise had more to do with corrective emotional experiencing than with insight. Clearly, emotions are present in this exercise, but for the purposes of this chapter, the insight gained through taking another's perspective also contributed to the change.

Conveniently, the CF therapist can use the two-chair technique without regard for the dominant avenue of change because both emotional and insight-oriented reasons are satisfactory if leading to change.

Other interventions that address client thinking patterns or reality testing could be included in this section in addition to Socratic questioning and the two-chair technique. The central idea is that the CF therapist may encounter situations in which the road to healing includes feedback regarding client thinking patterns or beliefs about the world. This feedback, or other forms of feedback in this broader section, take aim at producing client insight leading to correction, improvement, change, and remoralization (see Table 5.6).

## Consolidating Insight

Any of the interventions that we have described in this chapter—learning, discovery, and feedback—can lead to client insight and potential change. At the same time, one sudden epiphany or realization doesn't always translate

**TABLE 5.6. Example Feedback Interventions**

| Intervention | Approaches | Resources |
|---|---|---|
| Functional analysis | Behavioral | Sturmey (2007), *Functional Analysis in Clinical Treatment (Practical Resources for the Mental Health Professional)* |
| | | Marlatt & Donovan (2005), *Relapse Prevention: Maintenance Strategies in the Treatment of Addictive Behaviors* (2nd ed.) |
| Biofeedback | Transtheoretical | https://www.biofeedback.org/licensed |
| Chair work | Existential | https://transformationalchairwork.com/articles/transformational-chairwork |
| Cognitive feedback/ perspective taking | Cognitive behavior therapy | J. S. Beck (2021), *Cognitive Behavior Therapy: Basics and Beyond* (3rd ed.) |
| Routine outcome monitoring | Transtheoretical | Codd (Ed.) (2018), *Practice-Based Research: A Guide for Clinicians* |
| | | C. Evans & Carlyle (2021), *Outcome Measures and Evaluation in Counselling and Psychotherapy* |
| | | Ogles et al. (2002), *Essentials of Outcome Assessment* |
| Assessment | Transtheoretical | Finn et al. (2012), *Collaborative/ Therapeutic Assessment: A Casebook and Guide* |

into enduring change. As a result, therapeutic efforts may be required to consolidate, strengthen, and repeat the process in order to help the client assimilate the insight into their worldview and help them to adjust emotional and behavioral correlates. These efforts match with Hill et al.'s (2007) fifth and final stage of insight attainment. They suggested that strategies such as reinforcing client insight, helping the client explain the insight in a "clear and memorable form," and repeating the insight in a way that helps to generalize the awareness can help to translate the insight into an enduring influence on future behavior, thinking, and emotions. In addition, the chapter on self-efficacy (see Chapter 6, this volume) fits as a change-oriented principle that sequentially and conceptually builds on insight as a change mechanism.

## SUMMARY

In this chapter, we introduced various forms of interventions that may lead to change-oriented insight through learning, discovery, and feedback. Many other interventions might fit into this chapter, but an exhaustive list is beyond the scope of introduction to the CF model of treatment. Insight represents a change principle, and a CF therapist may use this change principle as a heuristic for choosing interventions consistent with the principle. Through setting the stage for and preparing the therapeutic environment using interventions from Chapters 2 and 3 and when recognizing markers of readiness for insight, the CF therapist can select among interventions leading to insight that are best suited to the client's clinical presentation. When insights are obtained, continuing work is often needed to consolidate or reinforce the intellectual awareness so that it can influence and inform emotions, behavior, and relationships. Many of the strategies that might help to build on initial insight can be found in Chapter 6 on the common factor self-efficacy.

# 6 SELF-EFFICACY, COMMON FACTOR 5

Frank and Frank (1991) pointed out in their contextual model that all therapies "enhance the patient's sense of mastery or self-efficacy" (p. 48) and "provide opportunities for practice" (p. 50). These ideas highlight how the point of therapy is to empower clients rather than create dependence in clients. By design, helping clients feel more capable of addressing their challenges can make the therapist obsolete. What began at the outset of therapy as two individuals working together for the benefit of the client needs to shift toward remoralization and the confidence of a single individual in managing the ups and downs of their life. As we point out as we define self-efficacy, therapists encourage their clients to apply therapy content and practice toward experiences that build a believable sense of empowerment, liberation, and mastery outside of therapy consistent with remoralization.

According to some, the narrative arc of therapy mirrors the hero's journey map of storytelling in fiction, theater, or film (see Williams, 2019). The hero's journey, originally described by Joseph Campbell (1949/2008), includes three phases of a change process for the hero: separation from the known world and initiation into a previously unknown world in which the hero addresses problems and undergoes personal changes and returns to the known world

https://doi.org/10.1037/0000343-007
*Common Factors Therapy: A Principle-Based Treatment Framework*, by R. J. Bailey and B. M. Ogles

as a transformed person. Celebrated stories with elements of the hero's journey include heroes such as Harry Potter, Luke Skywalker, and Frodo Baggins. The hero finds a mentor on the journey, such as Dumbledore, Obi-Wan Kenobi, or Gandalf. Williams (2019) highlighted how clients undergoing similar journeys learn "that in addressing their significant life problem, new polar-opposite skills will be required . . . [and] can only be learned through facing a series of increasingly more difficult trials" (p. 522). Perhaps therapists can be seen as these mentors assisting client–heroes on their journeys.

In the classic film *The Wizard of Oz*, Dorothy may be seen as a hero on a journey, leaving her family and the known world in Kansas for a fantasy adventure in Oz (Vidor et al., 1939). Her hero's return after surviving many adventures in Oz shows key elements of the way heroes return home changed and empowered. The good witch Glinda informs Dorothy that she has always had the power to return home via the magical ruby slippers. When the Scarecrow asks Glinda why she hadn't informed Dorothy of this fact earlier, Glinda responds, "Because she wouldn't have believed me. She had to learn it for herself" (Vidor et al., 1939). Dorothy describes what she has learned: "If I ever go looking for my heart's desire again, I won't look any further than my own backyard. Because if it isn't there, I never really lost it to begin with!" In a sense, she has learned that the answers do not exist "out there," with our happiness and solutions dependent on others and on external factors, but rather they exist "in here" within our own power. Her adventures left her confident and empowered, ready to face the realities in her home life.

Glinda as the hero's mentor in the hero's journey is like a therapist in another way. Whereas the Scarecrow, Tin Man, Cowardly Lion, and even the Wicked Witch each have analogues back at home in Kansas (the farm hands and the malevolent neighbor), Glinda does not. Dorothy in Oz uses fantasy to work out problems in her life; she gains experience and insight, but Glinda does not return to Kansas with her. Therapists do not typically enter the real lives of their clients. Therapy is designed not to replace relationships but to help clients with those real-world relationships. Therapy is designed to empower clients to become the heroes of their own lives, not to create dependence. The aspects of therapy that help most are the ones that the client can apply, master, and take home.

As Frank and Frank (1991) pointed out, mastery and self-efficacy and opportunities to practice are critical to the client deriving lasting benefit from therapy. Therapists overlook extratherapeutic events to their peril if they believe that what happens in the therapy office is most responsible for client change. Our (RBJ and BMO) former supervisors have been fond of emphasizing that a client spends 167 hours per week doing other things besides therapy. Norcross and Lambert (2019a) reiterated the estimate that

40% of overall change in therapy can be attributed to extratherapeutic change. Therapists who recognize this can focus clients on putting into practice what they have gained in therapy, applying it to their lives, and building confidence and a sense of mastery in their lives. Therapists do not live their lives for their clients; rather, they help them to grow in ways that will enable them to live their lives in healthy and meaningful ways. Therapists focus clients on their own power and aim for clients to gain self-efficacy outside of the therapy office.

In this chapter, we first provide an overview of the various concepts that refer to this notion of building competence, confidence, or self-efficacy in our clients. We then consider self-efficacy as a potential common factor through consideration of our inclusion and exclusion criteria. We then provide a CF therapy definition of self-efficacy that evolves from our conceptual discussion before turning to interventions that facilitate self-efficacy under three broad categories: application, liberation, and mastery (see Figure 6.1).

**FIGURE 6.1. Common Factors (CF) Therapy Model With Self-Efficacy Interventions**

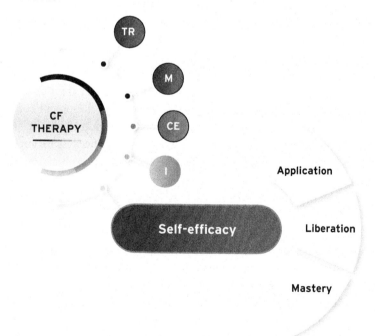

*Note.* TR = therapeutic relationship; M = motivation; CE = corrective experiencing; I = insight.

## OVERVIEW OF SELF-EFFICACY

Frank and Frank (1991) pointed out how all schools of psychotherapy build this sense of mastery and self-efficacy. The primary figure in self-efficacy theorizing and research for several decades was Albert Bandura (1997), who defined *self-efficacy* as follows: "Perceived self-efficacy refers to beliefs in one's capabilities to organize and execute the courses of action required to produce given attainments" (p. 3). From Bandura's perspective, humans are both shapers of their lives as well as are shaped by the environment and their behavior. For Bandura, the three determinants reciprocally influence one another: behavior; personal factors (factors that are internal to the person, including cognitive, affective, and biological factors); and the external environment. In terms of CF therapy, the personal factors related to change have largely been addressed in previous chapters (corrective experiencing and insight; see Chapters 4 and 5, this volume, respectively); this chapter focuses on the enacted behavior and the external environment in particular.

Self-efficacy is meaningfully distinct from other related concepts. Self-concept and self-esteem are related, but Bandura (1997) emphasized that self-efficacy differs by relating to "judgments of personal *capability* [emphasis added]" (p. 11). Locus of control differs from self-efficacy by relating more closely to how one's behaviors relate to expected outcomes. Bandura (1997) made a key distinction that self-efficacy is about the performance of the desired behavior (the athletic performance, the work project completed, the speaking up in a social setting) and not so much about the outcomes of the behavior (the trophy, the rejection, the praise, the disappointment that are consequences of the behavior). Making this distinction can be freeing, as in "I can do this, not because people will then like me, but because it's important for me to be able to do this regardless of the outcome." Humans can behave in their environment as effective persons, with or without continual reinforcement from the environment. In this way, the efficacy focuses on things that have controllability by personal means. According to Bandura's (1997) research, outcome expectations don't predict performance, but efficacy does. In the case when both efficacy and outcome expectations are associated statistically with performance, outcome expectation is a "redundant predictor" for performance above and beyond efficacy (Bandura, 1997, p. 24).

Self-efficacy also includes appraisal of one's capability to perform a desired behavior. The expectancy of completing a behavior needs to be accompanied by a possession of the skills to bring about the expected outcome. According to Bandura (1997), "People who regard outcomes as personally determined, but who lack requisite skills, would experience a low sense of efficacy and view the activities with a sense of futility" (p. 20). Without self-efficacy, demoralization seems a consequence. As Bandura (1997) wrote, "The pattern in which people perceive themselves as ineffectual but see others like them enjoying the benefits of successful effort is apt to give rise to self-disparagement and depression" (p. 21).

As emphasized in the CF therapy theory of pathology, demoralization is the target for intervention, and remoralization is the consequence hoped for by therapist and client. Depression really focuses on self-inefficacy, which includes despondence about the future, which can be reinforced by inactivity. Behavioral activation and new experiences of being effective can build this sense of efficacy. Depression can be seen as reflective of high expectancy around outcomes with low expectancy around self-efficacy (see Maddux & Lewis, 1995). With anxiety, self-efficacy seems most relevant in the perceived loss of control over one's experience (Maddux & Lewis, 1995). Bandura (1997) highlighted how guided mastery helps clients to have new experiences with stimuli (think corrective experiencing) and assist them in moving toward self-efficacy.

In our early deliberations of change principles to be included in CF therapy, it became clear that a principle was needed that incorporated extratherapeutic change. We considered using generalization as our focal term, because extratherapeutic change includes therapy interventions evoking similar responses to the stimuli of the home environment (Hughes, 2011). Psychoeducation was also proposed, given the tendency for therapists to give didactic instruction to clients, but this was superseded within the insight change principle. In similar fashion, practice, rehearsal, and action were considered. On the basis of Lambert's (2013) breakdown of common factors into support factors, learning factors, and action factors, it was clear that we needed an action factor in our model. Goldfried's (2019) model emphasized "*ongoing reality testing*" as a final factor and was described in Eubanks and Goldfried (2019) in this way:

> The ultimate goal of therapy is to help patients move to the stage of *unconscious competence*, in which adaptive behaviors become so well-learned that they no longer require deliberate effort. To reach this stage, patients need to engage in repeated corrective experiences. Patients may also need the therapist's help to process these new experiences: they may fail to detect, accept, or recall their success experiences because these experiences are inconsistent with their long-standing views of themselves. . . . The client's reality has changed, and the client recalibrates his or her expectations [*thought*] and self-view [*self-evaluation*] to be in line with this new reality. This process of ongoing reality testing represents the consolidation of change. (p. 95)

Application of content is a clear aspect of what this model is describing, as is the recalibration of expectations. We found the use of reality testing somewhat unusual, given its connection with the distorted reality experienced during psychosis. Similarly, the unconscious aspect of the description seemed somewhat problematic given the nature of our fourth factor, insight, which is typically conscious. Application of content and recalibration of expectations in favor of mastery seemed consistent with our favored term.

We finally landed on Bandura's favored term of *self-efficacy* because it encompassed many more of the concepts we hoped to capture within a change principle. His early definition, "beliefs in one's capabilities to organize and execute the courses of action required to produce given attainments," addressed the sense of application and mastery (Bandura, 1997, p. 3). Lambert's (2013) breakdown of possible common factors included cognitive mastery, mastery efforts, practice, reality testing, and success experiences. Self-efficacy encompassed these factors, in addition to such terms as self-actualization, emotional agility, psychological flexibility, effectiveness, resilience, mastery, hope, and confidence. It also reflected what Prochaska and DiClemente (2019) described as occurring in the late stages of therapy based on their transtheoretical model of therapy. Their "processes of change" included self-liberation, contingency management, counterconditioning, and stimulus control (p. 164). Their description of *self-liberation* included Bandura's term:

> During the action stage, clients act from a sense of *self-liberation*. They need to believe that they have the autonomy and to take responsibility to change their lives in key ways. Yet they also accept that coercive forces are as much a part of life as is autonomy. Self-liberation is based in part on a sense of self-efficacy (Bandura, 1977, 1982), the belief that one's own efforts play a crucial role in succeeding in the face of difficult situations.
>
> Self-liberation, however, requires more than an affective and cognitive foundation. Clients must also be effective using behavioral processes, such as *counterconditioning* and *stimulus control*, to cope with those external circumstances that can coerce them into relapsing.
>
> As they best prepare for the action stage, clients act from a sense of self-liberation or will-power. They need to believe that they possess the autonomy and power to change their lives in key ways. (Prochaska & DiClemente, 2019, p. 165; see also Prochaska & Norcross, 2018, p. 426)

They went on to point out that this self-liberation is based on a sense of self-efficacy as described by Bandura, or "the belief that one's own efforts play a critical role in succeeding in the face of difficult situations" (Prochaska & Norcross, 2018, p. 426).

Self-efficacy became, for us, a term for a construct that resided between the self-liberation that humanistic therapists may prize (for its resonance with self-actualization) and the generalization that behavioral therapists may prize (for the focus on applicability). Psychodynamic therapists would likely embrace the term for its relation to mastery following corrective experiencing. It evokes the positive psychology concept of hope or belief that one can move toward one's desired goals (see Snyder et al., 2002). Self-efficacy encapsulates the key elements of a CF therapy focus on remoralization, harkening back to Frank and Frank's (1991) contextual model.

One may ask whether self-efficacy is not a change principle but rather a psychotherapy outcome. This would be a fair critique, given that it reflects a significant hope for the eventual state of the client at the end of treatment. Indeed, our examination of research on self-efficacy gave promising evidence for self-efficacy as a mediator of outcome. Self-efficacy seems closely associated with remoralization, to the degree that it is difficult to distinguish the terms. However, as Goldfried and Robins (1982) pointed out from Bandura's (1977) work, the distinction between *outcome expectancies*—"a person's estimate that a given behavior will lead to certain outcomes"—and *efficacy expectancies*—"the conviction that one can successfully execute the behavior required to produce the outcomes" (Goldfried & Robins, 1982, p. 363)—is important. Assisting clients with building this capacity, applying content from their therapy experiences, helping them feel empowered, and gaining a sense of mastery all appear to be tasks that can occur during therapy. The identification of self-efficacy as an outcome need not undermine its importance as a change principle to occur during treatment, especially in the approach to the end of treatment.

A word of caution is needed here regarding the potential risk for using self-efficacy to dignify one cultural perspective over another. Self-efficacy, because it includes "self" in the term, could mistakenly be equated with an individualistic cultural perspective. Perhaps it is easier to see how self-efficacy can be applied therapeutically for individuals in this perspective. However, Bandura (1997) pointed out that efficacy is just as essential when individuals in collectivistic cultural settings are engaged in group pursuits. Contribution to collective aims can be an especially meaningful aspect of efficacy. As Bandura (1997) wrote,

> Personal efficacy is valued not because of reverence for individualism but because a strong sense of personal efficacy is vital for successful adaptation and change regardless of whether they are achieved individually or by group members putting their personal capabilities to the best collective use. . . . Members are respected for their personal contributions to group accomplishments. (p. 32)

Now that we have described self-efficacy as a general change principle involving the building of capacity and belief in one's capacity to perform desired tasks, we subject it to greater scrutiny as a CF therapy change principle. By doing so, we emphasize the need for a shift toward empowerment and liberation. We also emphasize the importance of extratherapeutic factors in change and the need for CF therapists to recognize the efficacy of clients in the world outside the therapy office. Whereas self-efficacy can be felt and built throughout the course of treatment, we recognize the change principle as an important bridge as the client moves toward the end of treatment.

## INCLUSION CRITERIA FOR SELF-EFFICACY

Here we take each of the criteria from Chapter 1 and use them to evaluate how self-efficacy aligns with our requirements for an element in CF therapy.

### Research Evidence in Support of Self-Efficacy

The research evidence for the association between self-efficacy and outcome is strong and should be understood conceptually. As the construct of self-efficacy is not primarily the province of psychotherapy research, it has been associated with the behavioral outcomes of numerous psychosocial interventions (e.g., education, athletic performance). Broadly understood, the research evidence supports self-efficacy beliefs as mediating outcomes, specifically mediating the relationship between the intervention and the target outcome.

A glance at Bandura's (1997) major self-efficacy volume shows self-efficacy is associated with health-promoting behavior and positive outcomes in learning environments. Bandura and Locke (2003) reviewed how self-efficacy is associated with performance in many settings and on many important constructs and outcomes, including both laboratory and field studies, psychosocial functioning in children and adolescents, academic achievement and persistence, health functioning, athletic performance, and perceived collective efficacy in group functioning. Maddux and Gosselin (2012) reviewed self-efficacy and its role in influencing the relationship between stressful events and physical symptoms, coping with traumatic life events, avoiding relapse with substance abuse concerns, and treating eating disorders. Reviewing only experimental data, Sheeran et al. (2016) used meta-analysis to examine changes in health-related intentions and behaviors. They found very strong evidence that interventions that address self-efficacy are effective in promoting health behavior change, making a strong causal argument.

Specifically with mental health studies, the data focuses on more structured interventions, especially cognitive behavior and substance abuse treatments.

In a meta-analysis of self-efficacy and smoking cessation, there was a reliable relationship between SE and future smoking, but it was modest (.21 standard deviation units; Gwaltney et al., 2009). Fentz et al. (2014) reviewed several studies and found support for "panic self-efficacy" as a mediator in outcome in cognitive behavior therapy (CBT) for panic disorder. In a similar study, Goldin et al. (2012) found strong evidence for "cognitive reappraisal self-efficacy" mediating the effects of CBT for social anxiety disorder. Gallagher et al. (2020) used self-efficacy as a "positive expectancy" and found in a meta-analysis of 154 studies that it was associated with lower posttraumatic stress disorder symptoms. Backenstrass et al. (2006) found evidence in a smaller study for self-efficacy not as a predictor of improvement in CBT for depression but as a mediator of therapy-induced change.

Similar to motivation (see Chapter 3), self-efficacy may often reflect a theory in practice rather than an explicit, articulated aspect of the therapy as it often coincides with preparing clients for the end of treatment (see the section on ending therapy in Chapter 2). As such, it has not received as much research attention as a specified common factor. Rather, the research evidence supports it as an outcome and as a mediator of outcome. Although self-efficacy may occupy liminal space as intervention, outcome, and mediator of outcome, there is not a shortage of research on the principle of self-efficacy's importance in positive behavioral change. Sufficient research evidence exists to support the inclusion of self-efficacy in CF therapy.

## Self-Efficacy Is Conceptually Present in Most Therapies

From their description of the contextual model, Frank and Frank's (1991) last two elements were that all therapies work by "enhancing the patient's sense of mastery or self efficacy" (p. 48) and by "providing opportunities for practice" (p. 50). Both of these principles are embedded in our conception of self-efficacy as a CF therapy change principle. Regarding their idea of self-efficacy, Frank and Frank joined these two ideas into one: "All schools of psychotherapy bolster the patient's sense of mastery or self-efficacy in at least two ways" (p. 48). Whereas one of the ways is by simply using the contextual model (i.e., by offering the client a myth and a ritual to address demoralization), the second is "by providing occasions for the patient to experience success" (p. 48). Overall, self-efficacy can be thought of as embedded in all therapies as they help the client build a sense of mastery and effectiveness.

Though therapists of various schools may not use the term explicitly, the concept of self-efficacy can be seen as an inherent aspect of therapies. In more conceptual work on self-efficacy based on Bandura's work, Goldfried and

Robins (1982) reviewed how self-efficacy was present in Adlerian therapy, Glasser's reality therapy, A. T. Beck's cognitive therapy, Ellis's rational emotive behavior therapy, and Frankl's logotherapy. Given how Bandura came from a behavioral background, it is perhaps easiest to see how self-efficacy fits in a behavioral model of treatment, as behavior therapy trains in coping and increasing personal mastery.

Humanistic and psychodynamic therapies focus on the self in ways that can be consistent with self-efficacy. Rogers wrote of an actualizing tendency, a potential for the self to move in the direction of self-actualization or growth or fulfillment, with the removal of barriers to this tendency constituting a primary purpose of therapy (Thorne, 1992). Crits-Christoph et al. (2013) wrote from a psychodynamic perspective that therapists look for changes in self-understanding through the process of therapy. Levenson (1995) wrote about time-limited dynamic therapy using a case in which the primary goals were increasing self-efficacy and the patient's understanding of their role in relational interactions. Increasing understanding, confidence in the self, and feeling a sense of mastery all seem congruent with the self-liberation spoken of by Prochaska and Norcross (2018) as a general principle of their "action stage" of therapy (p. 426).

Self-efficacy differs from but seems conceptually related to Goldfried's (2019) emphasis on ongoing reality testing as a change principle common to therapies. The emphasis is on helping clients to notice a discrepancy between past functioning (early treatment) and current, more effective functioning such that the client "recalibrates [their] expectations . . . and self-view . . . to be in line with this new reality," thus bringing about "the consolidation of change" (Eubanks & Goldfried, 2019, p. 95). Application of content, enacting practice, revising the view of the self—these all seem highly congruent with self-efficacy beliefs and behaviors.

In summary, self-efficacy may not be explicitly described as an aspect of a therapy, but it is implied and supported in therapies across the board. Furthermore, it is identified as a common factor by Frank and Frank (1991) and is conceptually consistent with Goldfried's (2019) model of change principles. It passes this criterion for inclusion in CF therapy.

## EXCLUSION CRITERIA FOR SELF-EFFICACY

The exclusion criterion of nonredundancy may be the most difficult to argue for self-efficacy, given the large number of related concepts. Competing lists of common factors have included self-efficacy—most notably the Frank and Frank (1991) list—but most have included several closely related ideas.

As noted previously, Lambert's (2013) list of common factors included cognitive mastery, mastery efforts, practice, reality testing, and success experiences. Prochaska and Norcross (2018) included terms in their action stage that relate, including counterconditioning, stimulus control, self-liberation, self-efficacy, contingency management, and social liberation. Goldfried (2019) used different terms for relevant change principles at the end of therapy: ongoing reality testing and unconscious competence.

Self-efficacy seemed to us a superordinate concept for many of these terms. Because self-efficacy can be used to refer to an outcome, it can conceptually supersede interventions that build efficacy beliefs (i.e., counterconditioning, stimulus control, contingency management, mastery efforts, practice, and success experiences). Because self-efficacy emphasizes the building of the self in the face of challenges outside of the therapy office, it can conceptually supersede terms that emphasize application (e.g., generalization, reality testing, mastery efforts, practice). Because self-efficacy usually refers to internalized beliefs that are empowering, the term can conceptually supersede ideas that convey mastery and similar beliefs (e.g., self-liberation, social liberation, unconscious competence, cognitive mastery).

In addition, the term self-efficacy conveys conceptual closeness to terms that are held dear in many therapeutic frameworks, including self-actualization, psychological flexibility, and resilience. Using the term to represent an outcome as well as interventions to bring about an outcome allows greater flexibility with the term. In keeping with CF therapy aims, the potential redundancy is acknowledged and self-efficacy is selected as the most comprehensive and inclusive of the available terms. In light of the breadth of possible definitions and the potential for the term to become overly broad in understanding, the following section addresses the specific elements to be included for CF therapy.

## DEFINITION OF SELF-EFFICACY

As described earlier, our definition of self-efficacy from a CF therapy perspective is based on Bandura's more global definition and Frank and Frank's transtheoretical description of the clinical application of self-efficacy. Tailoring these definitions also requires an acknowledgement of the role of liberation and empowerment in therapy.

Bandura's (1997) definition is as follows: "Perceived self-efficacy refers to beliefs in one's capabilities to organize and execute the courses of action required to produce given attainments" (p. 3). Note the emphasis on beliefs and the focus on the self in terms of capabilities to perform tasks. The definition also emphasizes specific actions as the targets of the belief, though these are anticipated actions. The definition implies confidence in taking effective action.

Applying the term clinically, Frank and Frank (1991) wrote, "All schools of psychotherapy bolster the patient's sense of mastery or self-efficacy in at least two ways: by providing the patient with [the theory of change, rationale and procedure] and by providing occasions for the patient to experience success" (p. 48). Note that their conditions for bolstering self-efficacy (which they use interchangeably with "mastery" in this section) include pointing to the overall therapeutic myth and ritual. This implies that in CF therapy, self-efficacy can arise from corrective experiencing and insight. Their second condition emphasizes helping the client to have success, which implies application and practice.

Tailoring a definition to CF therapy, given our review of the literature, also requires an acknowledgment of how liberation and empowerment occur in therapy. The confidence implied by Bandura's definition of self-efficacy can also include the empowerment of the client, helping clients to believe in their "autonomy and power to change their lives" (Prochaska & Norcross, 2018, p. 26). Changes in self-understanding can be liberating in ways that build self-efficacy. Social liberation can follow when clients are empowered, including learning social advocacy and garnering support in interpersonal relationships to better meet needs and reflect healthy living.

These elements all belie the reality that clients take their therapeutic gains (i.e., insights, new experiences) into their lived experience outside of therapy. Though this often occurs without direct therapist instruction, therapists can directly address application and practice in ways that build self-efficacy. The application of therapy content extratherapeutically need not be neglected, especially as therapists assist their clients to prepare for the end of treatment.

Finally, all of the definitions for CF therapy change principles include that demoralization is the target. Remoralization and self-efficacy are closely related concepts, making it straightforward to meet the requirement, especially as Frank and Frank (1991) explored this relation to remoralization at length.

For the purposes of CF therapy, we use the following definition of self-efficacy.

## COMMON FACTORS DEFINITION OF SELF-EFFICACY

Therapists encourage their client to apply therapy content and practice toward experiences that build a believable sense of empowerment, liberation, and mastery outside of therapy consistent with remoralization.

## INTERVENTION CONCEPTS FOR SELF-EFFICACY

Translating the CF metatheory to specific interventions requires not merely that self-efficacy be a change principle but that it be translated into specific, actionable interventions for use by CF therapists. As with the other change principles (therapeutic relationship, motivation, corrective experiencing, and insight), this intervention approach emphasizes attention to the change principle as the lens of CF therapy. The CF therapist seeks to employ specific interventions to evoke this change principle with their client. In this section, we give an overview of self-efficacy intervention, followed by outlines of specific interventions to evoke this change principle with a client. The broad categories of self-efficacy interventions include application, liberation, and mastery. We also offer deliberate practice exercises for the aspiring CF therapist to hone their skills with the interventions.

Therapists can use self-efficacy, as with any of the guiding change principles of CF therapy, as a heuristic (see Lazarus & Wachtel, 2018). Think of heuristics as practical mental shortcuts to more complex ideas, like a general guideline. In work with clients, the change principles can readily come to mind to guide intervention decisions. As clients progress in therapy (and therapists use routine outcome monitoring to continuously assess progress), therapists can use the rubric of CF therapy change principles to determine how to apply interventions.

We offer several questions to guide therapists in the use of the heuristic of self-efficacy:

- What is my client's life like outside of therapy? What social support can my client count on as they make the changes we are discussing? What practices can they take home with them?

- How does my client perceive their ability to enact the changes we are discussing? If they doubt their ability, what kinds of experiences could help to address this perception? What abilities can they reasonably gain to increase their capability and belief in their capability?

- What ideas or power structures keep my client feeling limited? Are there barriers that they see that together we can undermine to help them feel empowered or liberated? In the face of power structures, what choices does my client have that can help them feel empowered?

- How is my client feeling about handling the challenges in their life, especially after therapy has ended? Can we predict potential challenges and help them prepare for handling them?

Questions like these may prompt therapists to choose interventions that promote self-efficacy. As a client experiences the emotions and improved perceptions, they are likely to feel an increase in confidence in their ability to manage the challenges in their life. Therapists can ask directly about support outside of therapy and preparing for anticipated challenges. Through application, liberation, and mastery, the client feels empowered in their life and remoralized. Each of the following interventions is designed to build this sense of remoralization, the inverse of demoralization.

## Application

PRINCIPLE 6.1

Clients make progress as emotional and cognitive realizations are applied in both therapeutic and extratherapeutic settings, resulting in increased belief in their capability of change.

Clients make gains as they have new emotional experiences (see the discussion of corrective experiencing in Chapter 4 of this volume) and cognitive experiences (see the discussion of insight in Chapter 5). These experiences themselves can serve as success experiences that can build a client's self-efficacy, though it may benefit the client if the therapist explicitly encourages application of insight and gains. *Application* as the header for this category of interventions that build self-efficacy covers a rather broad range of ideas that could also be described using words such as mastery, competence, self-realization, capability, self-reliance, and so on, all of which are increased through putting therapy experiences into practice. For example, one of Bandura's (1997) identified primary sources of self-efficacy is "enactive mastery experiences that serve as indicators of capability" (p. 79). (As a relevant aside, he also noted physiological and affective states as contributing to self-efficacy—these states seeming to directly reflect what we have described in Chapters 4 and 5 in this book as both the emotional and cognitive aspects of corrective experiencing and insight.) Bandura highlighted how these are performance accomplishments, not the outcomes of those performances. The distinction matters, as therapists can help clients focus less on outcomes that are not within their control (e.g., how my family will respond, how my boss will respond, how the medicine will cure my pain) and more on controllable performances (e.g., how I learn to speak to my family assertively, how I do my job effectively, how I engage in pain management practices). Therefore, as clients begin to have experiences in therapy that feel helpful, therapists can support by encouraging ongoing shifts consistent with these experiences and helping clients to be realistic and attribute control and success appropriately. Table 6.1 summarizes interventions that therapists can use to help clients apply emotional and cognitive insights.

Application can be most helpful when the therapist keeps self-efficacy in mind, emphasizing (whether privately in their own mind or saying it aloud to clients) that ongoing therapy itself is not the goal. Rather, the client is aiming to build competency on their own. A neat summary of self-efficacy interventions can be found in Maddux and Lewis (1995):

> Interventions can be better directed toward increasing self-efficacy by helping clients view success experiences more constructively, by increasing client involvement in planning interventions, by setting concrete goals, by encouraging adaptive distortions of self and world, and by providing clients with a variety of coping and control strategies. (p. 63)

Generalization is a common way that therapists speak about the application aspect of self-efficacy. For example, a description of CBT for panic disorder and agoraphobia emphasizes that self-directed exposure "encourages independence and generalization of the skills learned in treatment to conditions in which the therapist is not present" (Craske & Barlow, 2014, p. 10). Relapse prevention also emphasizes anticipating how depression, substance abuse, eating disorders, or other concerns may play out in real life and planning for their eventuality (see Marlatt & Donovan, 2005). Normalizing

**TABLE 6.1. Example Application Interventions**

| Intervention | Broad theoretical categories | Specific theoretical approaches | Additional resources |
|---|---|---|---|
| Generalization | Behavioral | Interoceptive exposure | Craske & Barlow (2014), "Panic Disorder and Agoraphobia" |
| Relapse prevention | Cognitive behavior | Substance abuse treatment, among others | Marlatt & Donovan (2005), *Relapse Prevention: Maintenance Strategies in the Treatment of Addictive Behaviors* (2nd ed.) |
| Contingency management | Cognitive behavior | Substance abuse treatment | Petry (2012), *Contingency Management for Substance Abuse Treatment: A Guide to Implementing This Evidence-Based Practice* |
| Homework | Cognitive behavior, among others | Dialectical behavioral therapy (DBT) | Linehan (2015), *DBT Skills Training Handouts and Worksheets* (2nd ed.) |

relapse can be especially helpful, including identifying potential triggers and how progress can be maintained (for an example with eating disorders, see Fairburn & Cooper, 2014). Contingency management is another way to describe this, planning for how to maintain gains by forming contingency plans. Having realistic plans that are consistent with these application strategies can help the client feel confident in managing challenges outside of treatment (Petry, 2012).

Homework represents one mechanism by which cognitive behavior therapists typically implement generalization. Whereas sometimes homework can be designed to address corrective experiencing or insight, often the client builds self-efficacy through a successful completion. In a study of CBT for anxiety disorders, homework compliance was predictive of treatment outcome, but treatment expectancy was not (LeBeau et al., 2013). This study does not necessarily contradict the expectancy literature we describe in Chapter 3 (e.g., Westra et al., 2007, found that early homework compliance mediated the relationship between expectancy and change), but it highlights the importance of carrying through with action outside of treatment. In a meta-analysis of 46 studies comparing treatments with or without homework in CBT, the evidence supported that homework enhanced outcome (Kazantzis et al., 2010).

Therapists can be thoughtful and intentional about making client homework completion more likely and more effective for the client. Cummings et al. (2014) highlighted several ways to help make homework assignments more effective when working with youth (which can be applied to clients generally, including adults). Their suggestions include providing a clear rationale for homework, congruent with treatment goals and collaboratively set with the client. They recommended flexibly tailoring homework tasks based on the uniqueness of the client. Involving loved ones can be appropriate. As barriers to completing homework arise, therapists work with the client to solve problems. These recommendations highlight the creative, adaptive approach therapists take to building self-efficacy by application.

Jacobson and Christensen (1996) had a similar approach to increasing homework completion with couples in their book on acceptance and change in couple therapy, including the following suggestions:

1. "Explain rationale and emphasize importance of the task." (p. 165)

2. "Involve the couple in the specifics of the assignment." (p. 165)

3. "Exaggerate the aversiveness of the task." (p. 166)

4. "Anticipate and pre-empt reasons for noncompliance." (p. 166)

5. "Make sure the task is understood." (p. 167)

6. Make sure to follow up and "use [the] homework in the subsequent session." (p. 168)

7. In rare instances, call the couple midweek in between sessions to encourage completion of the homework (see Jacobson & Christensen, 1996, pp. 168–169).

Given that most of these resources and concepts come from the behavioral and cognitive behavior frameworks for treatment, it appears significantly less likely for humanistic and psychodynamic approaches to actively encourage application through homework or relapse prevention. From a client-centered perspective, the inner experiencing of the client is the reference for all action throughout therapy and in the client's extratherapeutic environment. For this reason, it may seem less relevant to speak of application as an intervention. However, it is common for therapists to discuss the application of therapy content to a client's life outside of therapy. For this reason, it seems reasonable to consider this a common element even in the absence of direct humanistic theorizing around application or generalization.

One psychodynamic perspective highlights the concept of application, but indirectly. Levenson (1995) pointed out that the primary indirect benefit of therapy—and one of the indicators of the client's preparation for termination—was that the patient has "evidenced interactional changes with significant others in his or her life" (p. 219). Regarding termination, Levenson also noted how the therapist planning termination helps the patient believe that the therapist feels comfortable terminating, which brings a sense of confidence. The application of therapy-generated relational content to extratherapeutic relationships seems implied and focused on building the patient's confidence at termination.

To enact application interventions, notice opportunities to discuss homework or other plans to apply content after the session. Sometimes this can take concrete forms such as generalization, taking a specific skill (e.g., diaphragmatic breathing, assertiveness practice, meditation) and a specific timeline for practice (e.g., twice daily, three times this week). Sometimes this can begin in a more open-ended fashion and move toward being more concrete. For example, therapists can ask questions such as "Based on what we did today, what do you see as your next step?," "What are you going to take away from our time today?," or "What's next for you?" Clients may rarely offer concrete steps in response to these questions, but the therapist can help the client move from a more general sense of what's next to concrete steps the client can take to actualize their intention. Therapists can hold to a value of openness while also encouraging the client to be specific. Application can be especially important as therapy moves toward termination, encouraging a client to gain confidence that they have gained what they wanted from therapy.

In summary, many of the application interventions tend to come from more concrete approaches, especially behavioral or cognitive behavior formulations. CF therapists focus on the principle of application when addressing how therapy content, based on experiences and insights in session, can be practiced and related to the client's life. For help with enacting such interventions, please see the deliberate practice instructions for application interventions in Table 6.2.

## Liberation

### PRINCIPLE 6.2

Clients experience empowerment and liberation through their own actions. Therapists can support their clients' empowerment by highlighting the role of self in moving toward self-actualization, by recognizing power in systems, and by emphasizing how choice in the face of these factors moves toward remoralization.

*Liberation* refers to a movement out of captivity and in a psychological context refers to a feeling of movement into freedom, out from the thrall of limiting systems, perspectives, and situations. Prochaska and Norcross (2018) in their integrative approach placed liberation within the context of choice and recognized two types of liberation: self-liberation and social liberation. *Self-liberation* refers to the experience of being personally responsible for choosing as one becomes aware of alternatives, whereas *social liberation* refers to external situations changing that provide greater choice. We consider both in this section with the general assumption that an increase in self-efficacy can come as clients feel that their actions and experiences (inside and outside of therapy) are chosen by them. Therapy can enable this sense of choice and liberation. Table 6.3 lists interventions that therapists can use to empower clients and help them achieve both self-liberation and social liberation.

Without a perspective of liberation, self-efficacy runs the risk of being used by a therapist to blame a client. For example, consider the situation when a client expresses feeling helpless in their life, and the therapist sees

**TABLE 6.2. Deliberate Practice Suggestions for Application**

| Method | Descriptions |
|---|---|
| Video-assisted observation of your work | • Watch a session, especially the end of the session. Sessions near the end of a course of therapy, as therapy is moving toward termination, can be especially valuable for application interventions. Watch for the following:<br><br>– Identify moments when therapy is summed up, including specific insights or emotions, and when you can ask about how the client can take this with them.<br><br>– Watch out for discussions of the client's relationships, noticing the sources of support the client can rely on.<br><br>– Identify anticipation of events outside of therapy. These are moments when you can ask about how to prepare for these events in ways that are consistent with what has been discussed in therapy. Are relapse prevention concepts relevant in these situations?<br><br>– Identify opportunities for generalization. When there are specific tasks you are encouraging the client to take, notice how specific and clear the directions are.<br><br>– Notice opportunities for follow-up, including whether or not you bring up the specific tasks from the last session.<br><br>– When preparing for termination, notice how potential challenges are discussed. Consider contingency management, how the client feels ready to handle different challenges or relapses.<br><br>• Identify key moments to share with a consultant, trying to identify and move through any defensiveness you may feel about sharing this. |
| Getting consultant feedback[a] | • Determine whether your relationship with your consultant is sufficiently supportive and safe for soliciting feedback openly. Consider working through defensive reactions with your consultant.<br><br>• Watch the session with your consultant, asking for assistance to notice moments when application could be discussed. In moments when application is discussed, ask for help to ensure that the intended actions are specific.<br><br>• With your consultant, use a role play to practice initiating discussions around applying therapy content to the client's relationships, work, or other setting outside of therapy. Get feedback from the consultant and continue practicing. Focus on saying the words you would actually say to a client, not just talking about what you might say to a client. |
| Setting small incremental goals | • Perhaps with your consultant's help, identify your current comfort level and competence with application interventions. Then, identify a behavior to practice on your own that stretches you just beyond this comfort level. Try to ensure that your practice is neither too overwhelming nor too easy. Be as specific as possible when describing what you are going to practice. |

*(continues)*

**TABLE 6.2. Deliberate Practice Suggestions for Application (*Continued*)**

| Method | Descriptions |
|---|---|
| Solo deliberate practice | • Dedicate sufficient time to practice on your own.<br>• Use the session video to practice noticing moments when application would be helpful and can be initiated. Practice verbalizing these interventions aloud as if you are speaking to the client.<br>• Notice how comfortable/uncomfortable the practice is and adjust the practice as needed. |
| Feedback-informed treatment | • Use outcome measures at each session to determine how the client is progressing in treatment. When progress feedback shows client as not on track, checking in around social support outside of therapy can be helpful. A discussion of how therapy content is applied can be especially helpful for generalization. |

aWe use the word "consultant" in this and other deliberate practice tables for brevity. We mean this to refer to mentors, supervisors, trainers, colleagues, or other experts as appropriate to the skill being practiced.

**TABLE 6.3. Example Liberation Interventions**

| Intervention | Broad theoretical categories | Specific theoretical approaches | Additional resources |
|---|---|---|---|
| Self-actualization or self-determination | Humanistic | Client-centered therapy<br><br>Motivational interviewing | Rogers (1957/1992), "The Necessary and Sufficient Conditions of Therapeutic Personality Change"<br><br>W. R. Miller & Rollnick (2013), *Motivational Interviewing: Helping People Change* (3rd ed.) |
| Existential therapy | | Existential therapy | Yalom (1980), *Existential Psychotherapy* |
| Defusion, valued living | Third wave | Acceptance and commitment therapy (ACT) | Harris (2013), *Getting Unstuck in ACT: A Clinician's Guide to Overcoming Common Obstacles in Acceptance and Commitment Therapy* |
| Feminist therapy | Feminist | Feminist therapy | K. M. Evans et al. (2011), *Introduction to Feminist Therapy: Strategies for Social and Individual Change* |
| Multicultural orientation | Multicultural | Multicultural orientation | Hook et al. (2017), *Cultural Humility: Engaging Diverse Identities in Therapy*<br><br>https://www.multiculturalorientation.com<br><br>https://www.sentio.org/mcovideos |

primarily what the client is failing to put into action. The therapist may put the client in a victim's role for not showing more efficacy in their life. Certainly, practicing therapists are familiar with this attitude from case conference or treatment team settings, when a provider who is less familiar with the full context of the client's life jumps to rescue the struggling therapist by blaming the client for their distress. Here we remind you about how self-efficacy focuses on liberation rather than blame. As Bandura (1997) wrote, "Self-efficacy is concerned with human enablement, not with moral judgments" (p. 33). Our behavior is multidetermined, and a person is a causal actor but also one aspect of a complex system of causal factors.

Liberation, a term used in the common factors work of Prochaska and Norcross (2018), implies freedom from restrictions with thought or behavior. Liberation can be thought of as a synonym of emancipation or unshackling, a sort of freeing from limitations that a person experiences in their life. In order to be free in this sense, it appears essential for clients not just to notice the restrictions but to transcend them in some way. They must be empowered to move forward in spite of existing restrictions. This may be especially true when the restrictions are outside the person's control. For self-efficacy to be experienced, one must perceive a sense of mastery or empowerment, so these ideas may seem initially at odds with one another.

Self-actualization is believed to occur as barriers are removed, a self-liberation process. In humanistic approaches, such as client-centered therapy, the therapist trusts that the client will move in the direction of a fully functioning person, given the right conditions. The therapy offers these conditions (i.e., unconditional positive regard, genuineness, and empathy), so the client can move in this direction. The therapist recognizes the client's right to self-determination, to choose their own way, and works to create an environment in which they can explore their own way forward. "Self-authority and personal power" are the outcome of client-centered therapy over time (Raskin et al., 2008, p. 180). The internal barriers of demands can be undermined, and the client moves forward empowered. The overlap with motivational interviewing, focusing on self-determination, is obvious here.

Psychologist and memoir author Gottlieb (2019) used a metaphor from her own therapist to illustrate how self-liberation can work. In the metaphor (taken from a newspaper cartoon), a prisoner in a jail grapples with the bars on the window, obviously stuck. However, the prisoner does not notice that the door has been left open. The implication here is that we become emotionally stuck, and it often takes a new perspective to recognize the freedom that we possess to become unstuck and address the challenges in our lives. It evokes Seligman's (1972) research on learned helplessness from the 1970s, in which dogs stopped attempting to escape shocks even with a way to escape. The key is to see that we may be less stuck than things appear. Much like Dorothy at the beginning of the chapter, we can begin to recognize our power, feel empowered, and act in our own interest.

An existential approach to therapy also emphasizes liberation of the self through personal freedom. Waking up to the realities of death and the limits of our control can emphasize the range of choices available to us in our current state. As Mendelowitz and Schneider (2008) noted, "Freedom . . . has its limits, and we refer here to delimited freedom—a freedom that makes peace with the many things one is not free to change" (p. 315). In paradoxical fashion, grappling with the profound existential limits leaves us in a liberated state. Yalom (2002) also pointed out how when clients struggle, sometimes they persist in believing that their situation is outside of their control. The therapist can do well then to help the client examine the part of the situation where they may have some responsibility, then rise to assume that responsibility. This can be done only with significant validation and gentleness, as without this the client will likely feel blamed. Frank and Frank (1991) pointed out that it makes sense to encourage someone to take responsibility for changes only when they possess the ability to change it.

A similar sentiment comes from a third-wave cognitive behavior approach, acceptance and commitment therapy. In this approach a therapist can emphasize how control over one's thoughts and feelings is illusory and how our efforts to control them contribute to our distress (see Harris, 2013). Rather, acknowledging our thoughts and feelings allows us to be less controlled by them and see how we can actively move in valued directions. No longer in the thrall of debilitating emotions, we can engage in our lives more meaningfully.

Therapy itself focuses on self-determination as a deeply held ethical value. Working toward liberation as an aspect of self-determination is therefore embedded in every therapy to some degree (American Psychological Association, 2017). Therapists listen to clients' intentions and goals for therapy and discuss ways to approach these goals. Therapy's healthy respect for self-determination is part of what makes therapy healing.

In addition to self-liberation, a common thread for liberation is social liberation (Prochaska & Norcross, 2018). Based on their summary of the idea, social liberation can include "when patients seek social advocacy and interpersonal situations, like clubs or communities, that support their chosen lifestyles, thereby engendering a complete and deeper sense of themselves" (Prochaska & Norcross, 2018, p. 426). Clients often feel free to engage in interpersonal relationships in new ways that promote their health and well-being. Key examples could include practicing assertive communication, relating to others with empathy, or taking interpersonal risks in spite of anxiety. Such actions tend to build social connections. The role of perceived social support in undergirding mental health would suggest that these social connections are especially key for health following termination (see Wang et al., 2018).

Social liberation also implies freedom in the face of social oppression. Social liberation is an essential aspect of feminist therapy and multicultural orientation (see Chapter 2). Feminist therapy focuses on eliminating oppression—internal and external—not just for women, but for all people (see K. M. Evans et al., 2011). From this perspective the therapist trusts the lived experience of women and believes in the need for social change (K. M. Evans et al., 2011). Similar to the cultural opportunity concept within multicultural orientation, a feminist perspective emphasizes noticing the context in which the client lives and breathes. As one notices the context with cultural humility, gendered or racialized aspects of the client's interactions become more salient. Similarly, this orientation can be applied to homophobia, ableism, transphobia, or other oppressive and embedded ideologies. When one rejects male centering and White centering, one can see how systems that males and Whites experience as empowering tend to be disempowering for people who are not male and/or not White. People showing symptoms of pathology who exist in an oppressive system may actually be experiencing symptoms of disempowerment. As K. M. Evans et al. (2011) noted, "The source of pathology is social, not personal; external, not internal" (p. 15). The focus of change becomes the system, not the client, and the goal of therapy is to assist the client in being autonomous and active in their life, including actions toward social change. Feminist therapy addresses empowerment across multiple dimensions (Brown, 2018).

In short, therapy can be egalitarian, take into account the sociopolitical context, and recognize the role of power in systems and the dynamics of interactions. As addressed in Chapter 2, multicultural orientation can offer a perspective that allows therapists to work toward empowering clients within disempowering systems. The therapist seeking to work toward social liberation helps the client to see how they are situated relative to power, survey possible options that are within the client's grasp, and support the client as they move toward social change.

Overall, a common thread in self-liberation seems to be helping the client to notice how control (often a deference to distress, anxiety, or the authority of the therapist or others) is not serving them, then recognize their power to do otherwise, whereas another common thread in social liberation seems to be helping the client to notice how society (both generally as well as in specific relationships) is not necessarily set up to serve them, then recognize their power to interact differently with society and in relationships. CF therapists can use the liberation concept as a lens to assist their clients in working toward self-liberation as well as social liberation. Note the two different deliberate practice outlines in Tables 6.4 and 6.5, each focused on liberation in these two senses.

## Mastery

### PRINCIPLE 6.3

As clients apply the insights and experiences gained in therapy and feel empowered in their lives, they gain a sense of mastery or of being capable to navigate the challenges they will continue to face in their lives.

Perhaps the self-efficacy intervention that is most closely identified as synonymous with an outcome, mastery reflects the remoralization aspect of self-efficacy. Mastery reflects the sense of being capable and empowered as a result of the experiences of therapy. As clients understand their challenges, have language to describe them, and have actions to address them, then they gain confidence in their ability to meet their challenges. "Name it to tame it" has become a truism used popularly to describe this. Frank and Frank (1991) also illustrated this by alluding to fairy tales in which stating a name has the power to undo a curse. They pointed out also that "experiences of success" are embedded in all therapies and then this allows clients to "attribute [the performance] to their own efforts" (p. 49).

As clients have had success experiences during therapy, the role of the therapist becomes helping the client to attribute the success to the client and their efforts. "Verbal persuasion" is one of Bandura's (1997) methods for increasing self-efficacy (other methods include "physiological and affective states," for example). Goldfried and Robins (1982) suggested ways of doing this. For example, the therapist can help the client compare the past to the present. A discussion of what has changed since the initial session can serve to highlight the improvements the client has made. They also recommend reminding clients of the successes they have experienced over the course of therapy. As discussions of improvements occur, the client may tend to attribute the changes made to the therapist. Therapists may feel flattered by this and can resist the urge by acknowledging the client's gratitude and emphasizing the client's actions and successes.

**TABLE 6.4. Deliberate Practice Suggestions for Self-Liberation**

| Method | Descriptions |
|---|---|
| Video-assisted observation of your work | • Watch a session, looking for:<br>  – Moments when your client is expressing that they feel stuck or disempowered in some way.<br>    ○ Consider how your conceptualization of the case could help explain how they are stuck.<br>    ○ Consider how your client could take action if they felt less stuck.<br>    ○ Consider how to gently help them take responsibility in their lives without blame.<br>  – Moments when your client is deferential to the authority of you or the authority of others. Consider ways to help your client see this without needing to defer to you in doing so. Consider also how you may underestimate your client and how you may correct this.<br>  – Moments when your client feels stuck by being overwhelmed by thoughts/emotions. Consider ways to use acceptance and commitment therapy principles to help them defuse.<br>  – Moments that connect to your client's deeply held values. Consider helping your client explore their values or possible actions that connect to their values.<br>• Identify key moments to share with a consultant, trying to identify and move through any defensiveness you may feel about sharing this. |
| Getting consultant feedback | • Determine whether your relationship with your consultant is sufficiently supportive and safe for soliciting feedback openly. Consider working through defensive reactions with your consultant.<br>• Watch the session with your consultant, asking for assistance to notice moments when client is stuck or disempowered. Ask for help with identifying how the power dynamic plays out between you and your client.<br>• With your consultant, use a role play to practice initiating discussions around helping your client feel empowered and liberated. Get feedback from the consultant and continue practicing. Focus on saying the words you would actually say to a client, not just talking about what you might say to a client. |
| Setting small incremental goals | • Perhaps with your consultant's help, identify your current comfort level and competence with self-liberation interventions. Then, identify a behavior to practice on your own that stretches you just beyond this comfort level. Try to ensure that your practice is neither too overwhelming nor too easy. Be as specific as possible when describing what you are going to practice. |

*(continues)*

**TABLE 6.4. Deliberate Practice Suggestions for Self-Liberation (*Continued*)**

| Method | Descriptions |
|---|---|
| Solo deliberate practice | • Dedicate sufficient time to practice on your own. |
| | • Use the session video to practice noticing moments when to focus on empowering ideas with your client. Practice verbalizing these interventions aloud as if you are speaking to your client. |
| | • Notice how comfortable/uncomfortable the practice is, and adjust the practice as needed. |
| Feedback-informed treatment | • Use outcome measures at each session to determine how your client is progressing in treatment. When progress feedback shows your client as not on track, consider discussing their sense of control or mastery in their life, helping them know that therapy progresses on their terms. |

**TABLE 6.5. Deliberate Practice Suggestions for Social Liberation**

| Method | Descriptions |
|---|---|
| Video-assisted observation of your work | • Watch a session, looking for: |
| | – How your client responds to you that may be related to how you and your client identify with regard to gender, race, ability, sexual orientation, or any other relevant status. Consider how this may reflect unspoken dynamics around power. |
| | – Culturally relevant content, verbal and nonverbal. Consider also how power plays out in the content your client shares. |
| | – How your client describes relationships with others and support or lack of support in those relationships. Consider how your client can take action in the direction of increased support. |
| | – How your client tends to advocate for or disregard the need to advocate for themselves. Consider how your client can take action in the direction of increased advocacy for themselves or others, recognizing the cultural dimensions of the client's context. |
| | • Identify key moments to share with a consultant, trying to identify and move through any defensiveness you may feel about sharing this. |
| Getting consultant feedback | • Determine whether your relationship with your consultant is sufficiently supportive and safe for soliciting feedback openly. Consider working through defensive reactions with your consultant. |
| | • Watch the session with your consultant, asking for assistance to notice cultural opportunities. Pay particular attention to moments when you are helping your client to consider how to get support and/or take action. Get feedback on the cultural appropriateness of interventions. |
| | • With your consultant, use a role play to practice discussions focused on social liberation, including action in the direction of increased social support or other advocacy. |

**TABLE 6.5. Deliberate Practice Suggestions for Social Liberation (*Continued*)**

| Method | Descriptions |
|---|---|
| Setting small incremental goals | • Perhaps with your consultant's help, identify your current comfort level and competence with social liberation interventions. Then, identify a behavior to practice on your own that stretches you just beyond this comfort level. Try to ensure that your practice is neither too overwhelming nor too easy. Be as specific as possible when describing what you are going to practice. |
| Solo deliberate practice | • Dedicate sufficient time to practice on your own. |
| | • Use the session video to practice noticing how you speak to relevant social liberation discussions. Practice verbalizing these interventions aloud as if you are speaking to the client. |
| | • Notice how comfortable/uncomfortable the practice is and adjust the practice as needed. |
| Feedback-informed treatment | • Use outcome measures at each session to determine how your client is progressing in treatment. When progress feedback shows a client as not on track, checking in around perceived social support can be especially helpful. Consider how your client understands their distress, encouraging a contextual consideration of their distress that does not excessively pathologize the individual within the context. |

Mastery does not need to imply that the therapist flatters the client with untrue or inaccurate perceptions of their ability. Mastery reflects actual competence and the perception of actual competence. As the client engages in practice (application) during therapy and gains confidence and a sense of empowerment (liberation), then mastery seems likely to follow. In this sense, mastery reflects the other two elements of self-efficacy as both the actual building of competence through practice and the empowerment through appraising that competence.

Mastery, as remoralization, becomes generative toward ongoing change and improvement in the client's life. Bandura (1997) described self-efficacy as a "generative capability" (p. 36). Clients, as they near termination, report a sense that sounds something like "I know I'm going to have more challenges in my life, but I feel ready for them." They feel they do not necessarily need a prescribed course of action for every possible eventuality (though, for many, contingency management can be essential). Rather, there is a remoralized confidence in their ability to meet future challenges. This sense can be a helpful marker for the client's preparation for termination; indeed, clients often express this sense when they are also indicating their readiness for ending treatment. As discussed in Chapter 2's section on ending therapy,

Goode et al. (2017) recommended helping the client take ownership for gains, recognizing their role in the change.

The interventions for mastery involve these two main ideas: checking for mastery and assisting the client with attributing change. CF therapists can use these as a rubric for enhancing mastery throughout the course of therapy or for preparing a client for termination.

## SUMMARY

Self-efficacy and remoralization are closely related ideas. As CF therapists focus on building self-efficacy through application, they look for ways for clients to practice therapy content outside of therapy and develop the confidence needed to move forward. As they focus on liberation, they consider ways to empower their clients by seeing how control can be superseded in the direction of self-actualization. They can seek social liberation through helping clients to advocate for themselves in relationships and society generally. These actions help clients feel a sense of mastery, one of the signs that clients are moving toward remoralization. Overall, self-efficacy interventions help clients to build competence and perceive their own competence in their lives. This change principle forms a lens through which CF therapists can select interventions from across possible therapeutic orientations and perspectives as they assist clients in their movement toward remoralization.

# EPILOGUE

*The Future of Common Factors Therapy*

From our initial chapter, we endeavored to describe how common factors (CF) therapy can exist with specified components. Acknowledging that it is no longer a metatheory alone, we developed a conceptual framework for transforming the CF hypothesis into a bona fide treatment approach. Our conceptual framework is consistent with the contextual model of Frank and Frank (1991) in that it includes a theory of change, a theory of pathology, and specified rituals or actions to evoke change. Our CF therapy framework is also consistent with Goldfried's (2019) work in that we have focused on change principles that are shared across therapeutic orientations. We have used our previously established criteria (Bailey & Ogles, 2019) to propose five change principles as supported by research evidence and consistent with extant models (e.g., Anderson et al., 2010; Frank & Frank, 1991; Goldfried, 2019; Lambert, 2013; Wampold & Imel, 2015), evident across theoretical orientations, and as parsimonious or nonredundant factors.

Our five factors—the therapeutic relationship, motivation, corrective experiencing, insight, and self-efficacy—represent a model that we hope is sufficiently comprehensive in scope that therapists can legitimately follow it and

https://doi.org/10.1037/0000343-008
*Common Factors Therapy: A Principle-Based Treatment Framework*, by R. J. Bailey and B. M. Ogles

call themselves CF therapists. We hope also that the focus on change principles allows for therapists to flexibly apply concepts that they find in any theoretical orientation to their clinical work. In this way, our model can be generative and innovative rather than limiting and restrictive. Therapists can use the resources we have pointed to in each chapter to deepen their understanding of each change principle.

We reiterate that the CF therapy model we presented can be considered as an open model, one that can change based on new evidence and persuasive arguments regarding change principles that have not yet been considered or even discovered. Our model is far from the first, and it seems unlikely to be the last model. However, reviewing a few other models can show how consistency may give our model some staying power. For example, consider Frank and Frank's (1991) model of change principles:

- "combating the patient's sense of alienation and strengthening the therapeutic relationship" (p. 44),
- "inspiring and maintaining the patient's expectation of help" (p. 44),
- "providing new learning experiences" (p. 45),
- "arousing emotions" (p. 46),
- "enhancing the patient's sense of mastery or self-efficacy" (p. 48), and
- "providing opportunities for practice" (p. 50).

Our model is similar with a few notable exceptions. Item 5 on their list, self-efficacy, is in our model, but our model subsumes both Items 5 and 6. Items 3 and 4 are more clearly distinguished, focusing on insight ("new learning experiences" in Item 3) and corrective experiencing (emphasizing emotional experiencing) as closely related but distinct. Items 1 and 2 are closely related but given greater detail. Frank and Frank's (1991) model bears similarity to Goldfried's (2019) model, first proposed in the 1980s, which includes five principles of change that cross theoretical boundaries:

- promoting client expectation and motivation that therapy can help,
- establishing an optimal therapeutic alliance,
- facilitating client awareness of the factors associated with his or her difficulties,
- encouraging the client to engage in corrective experiences, and
- emphasizing ongoing reality testing in the client's life.

Our model is in a slightly different order from Goldfried's list, and our fifth element, self-efficacy, uses different conceptual framing than his term, *ongoing reality testing*. As noted previously, our similarity to Goldfried's (2019) proposal is intentional. Perhaps the greatest difference lies in the nomenclature we landed on as we detailed each change principle. We hope that our model represents a refinement and extension of Goldfried's ideas.

Lambert's (2013) grouping of common factors into support, learning, and action factors is relevant here. Our first two factors, therapeutic relationship and motivation, together form a foundation as support factors. Clearly, corrective experiencing and insight fit within the learning category of common factors, whereas self-efficacy caps the treatment with its emphasis on practice and action. We used the metaphor of a house earlier, considering how these factors fit together cohesively as the structure of therapy. Perhaps Lambert's categorization of common factors fits well with our breakdown of five factors.

Moving forward with CF therapy for researchers could involve subjecting the key elements of the therapy to empirical inquiries. This could include studies of whether the common factors act as change principles that are active in all therapies. We welcome and encourage the ongoing exploration of common factors across theoretical orientations. We do not exclude the possibility that data-driven investigations of the factors could lead to a revision of the change principles we have included, which would be a welcome eventuality. Empirical research could also include clinical trials of CF therapy, with the caution that most therapies tend to be shown as effective generally.

Moving forward with CF therapy for therapists could involve beginning to identify as a CF therapist. We feel this identification is appropriate when therapists conceptualize and guide their treatment with these change principles as their guideposts. If identifying as a CF therapist seems a bridge too far, all therapists reading this volume could use its contents to enhance their practice relative to the common factors. Supervisors could move forward with using the contents of the volume to enhance their training, using the common factors as a lens for training therapists.

It is our hope that CF therapy can add to the rich clinical literature guiding the work of psychotherapy. Every time a therapist works to increase their empathy while practicing reflective listening, considers how they can assist their client to confront difficult emotions, or designs a valuable way to practice a skill they learned in therapy, the therapist is invoking common factors. May they continue to do so in ways that relieve human suffering.

# References

Abramowitz, J. S., Deacon, B. J., & Whiteside, S. P. H. (2019). *Exposure therapy for anxiety: Principles and practice* (2nd ed.). Guilford Press.

Alexander, F., & French, T. M. (1946). *Psychoanalytic therapy: Principles and application.* Ronald Press.

American Psychiatric Association. (2022). *Diagnostic and statistical manual of mental disorders* (5th ed., text rev.). https://doi.org/10.1176/appi.books.9780890425787

American Psychological Association. (2017). *Ethical principles of psychologists and code of conduct* (2002, amended effective June 1, 2010, and January 1, 2017). https://www.apa.org/ethics/code

Anderson, T., Crowley, M. E. J., Himawan, L., Holmberg, J. K., & Uhlin, B. D. (2016). Therapist facilitative interpersonal skills and training status: A randomized clinical trial on alliance and outcome. *Psychotherapy Research, 26*(5), 511–529. https://doi.org/10.1080/10503307.2015.1049671

Anderson, T., Lunnen, K. M., & Ogles, B. M. (2010). Putting models and techniques in context. In B. L. Duncan, S. D. Miller, B. E. Wampold, & M. A. Hubble (Eds.), *The heart and soul of change: Delivering what works in therapy* (2nd ed., pp. 143–166). American Psychological Association. https://doi.org/10.1037/12075-005

Anderson, T., McClintock, A. S., Himawan, L., Song, X., & Patterson, C. L. (2016). A prospective study of therapist facilitative interpersonal skills as a predictor of treatment outcome. *Journal of Consulting and Clinical Psychology, 84*(1), 57–66. https://doi.org/10.1037/ccp0000060

Anderson, T., Ogles, B. M., Heckman, B. D., & MacFarlane, P. (2012). Varieties of corrective experiencing in context: A study of contrasts. In L. G. Castonguay & C. E. Hill (Eds.), *Transformation in psychotherapy: Corrective experiences across cognitive behavioral, humanistic, and psychodynamic approaches* (pp. 281–316). American Psychological Association. https://doi.org/10.1037/13747-014

Anderson, T., Ogles, B. M., Patterson, C. L., Lambert, M. J., & Vermeersch, D. A. (2009). Therapist effects: Facilitative interpersonal skills as a predictor of therapist success. *Journal of Clinical Psychology, 65*(7), 755–768. https://doi.org/10.1002/jclp.20583

Anderson, T., Perlman, M. R., McCarrick, S. M., & McClintock, A. S. (2020). Modeling therapist responses with structured practice enhances facilitative interpersonal skills. *Journal of Clinical Psychology, 76*(4), 659–675. https://doi.org/10.1002/jclp.22911

Arkowitz, H. (1992). A common factors therapy for depression. In J. C. Norcross & M. R. Goldfried (Eds.), *Handbook of psychotherapy integration* (pp. 402–432). Basic Books.

Backenstrass, M., Schwarz, T., Fiedler, P., Joest, K., Reck, C., Mundt, C., & Kronmueller, K.-T. (2006). Negative mood regulation expectancies, self-efficacy beliefs, and locus of control orientation: Moderators or mediators of change in the treatment of depression? *Psychotherapy Research, 16*(2), 250–258. https://doi.org/10.1080/10503300500485474

Bailey, R. J., & Ogles, B. M. (2019). Common factors as a therapeutic approach: What is required? *Practice Innovations, 4*(4), 241–254. https://doi.org/10.1037/pri0000100

Bandura, A. (1977). Self-efficacy: Toward a unifying theory of behavioral change. *Psychological Review, 84*(2), 191–215. https://doi.org/10.1037/0033-295X.84.2.191

Bandura, A. (1982). Self-efficacy mechanism in human agency. *American Psychologist, 37*(2), 122–147. https://doi.org/10.1037/0003-066X.37.2.122

Bandura, A. (1989). Human agency in social cognitive theory. *American Psychologist, 44*(9), 1175–1184. https://doi.org/10.1037/0003-066X.44.9.1175

Bandura, A. (1997). *Self-efficacy: The exercise of control.* W. H. Freeman.

Bandura, A., & Locke, E. A. (2003). Negative self-efficacy and goal effects revisited. *Journal of Applied Psychology, 88*(1), 87–99. https://doi.org/10.1037/0021-9010.88.1.87

Barlow, D. H. (Ed.). (2014). *Clinical handbook of psychological disorders: A step-by-step treatment manual* (5th ed.). Guilford Press. https://doi.org/10.1093/oxfordhb/9780199328710.001.0001

Barlow, D. H. (2020). *Clinical handbook of psychological disorders: A step-by-step treatment manual* (6th ed.). Guilford Press.

Barlow, D. H., & Craske, M. G. (2022). *Mastery of your anxiety and panic: Workbook* (5th ed.). Oxford University Press.

Barlow, D. H., Ellard, K. K., & Fairholme, C. P. (2010). *Unified protocol for transdiagnostic treatment of emotional disorders: Workbook.* Oxford University Press.

Barrett, L. F. (2017). *How emotions are made: The secret life of the brain.* Houghton Mifflin Harcourt.

Bathje, G. J., Pillersdorf, D., & Eddir, H. (2022). Multicultural competence as a common factor in the process and outcome of counseling. *Journal of*

*Humanistic Psychology*. Advance online publication. https://doi.org/10.1177/00221678221099679

Beck, A. T. (2005). The current state of cognitive therapy: A 40-year retrospective. *Archives of General Psychiatry, 62*(9), 953–959. https://doi.org/10.1001/archpsyc.62.9.953

Beck, A. T., Emery, G., & Greenberg, R. L. (2005). *Anxiety disorders and phobias: A cognitive perspective*. Basic Books.

Beck, A. T., & Freeman, E. (1990). *Cognitive therapy of personality disorders*. Guilford Press.

Beck, A. T., Rush, A. J., Shaw, B. F., & Emery, G. (1979). *Cognitive therapy of depression*. Guilford Press.

Beck, A. T., Wright, F. D., Newman, C. F., & Liese, B. S. (1993). *Cognitive therapy of substance abuse*. Guilford Press.

Beck, J. S. (2005). *Cognitive therapy for challenging problems: What to do when the basics don't work*. Guilford Press.

Beck, J. S. (2011). *Cognitive therapy: Basics and beyond* (2nd ed.). Guilford Press.

Beck, J. S. (2021). *Cognitive behavior therapy: Basics and beyond* (3rd ed.). Guilford Press.

Beutler, L. E., Moleiro, C., & Talebi, H. (2002). Resistance in psychotherapy: What conclusions are supported by research. *Journal of Clinical Psychology, 58*(2), 207–217. https://doi.org/10.1002/jclp.1144

Bhatia, A., & Gelso, C. J. (2017). The termination phase: Therapists' perspective on the therapeutic relationship and outcome. *Psychotherapy, 54*(1), 76–87. https://doi.org/10.1037/pst0000100

Biello, D. (2006, December 8). Fact or fiction? Archimedes coined the term "Eureka!" in the bath. *Scientific American*. https://www.scientificamerican.com/article/fact-or-fiction-archimede

Bordin, E. S. (1979). The generalizability of the psychoanalytic concept of the working alliance. *Psychotherapy: Theory, Research, & Practice, 16*(3), 252–260. https://doi.org/10.1037/h0085885

Boswell, J. F., Bentley, K. H., & Barlow, D. H. (2017). Motivation facilitation in the unified protocol for transdiagnostic treatment of emotional disorders. In H. Arkowitz, W. R. Miller, & S. Rollnick (Eds.), *Motivational interviewing in the treatment of psychological problems* (2nd ed., pp. 33–57). Guilford Press.

Brady, J. P., Davison, G. C., Dewald, P. A., Egan, G., Fadiman, J., Frank, J. D., Gill, M. M., Hoffman, I., Kempler, W., Lazarus, A. A., Raimy, V., Rotter, J. B., & Strupp, H. H. (1980). Some views on effective principles of psychotherapy. *Cognitive Therapy and Research, 4*(3), 271–306.

Brown, L. S. (2018). *Feminist therapy* (2nd ed.). American Psychological Association. https://doi.org/10.1037/0000092-000

Burnette, J. L., O'Boyle, E. H., VanEpps, E. M., Pollack, J. M., & Finkel, E. J. (2013). Mind-sets matter: A meta-analytic review of implicit theories and self-regulation. *Psychological Bulletin, 139*(3), 655–701. https://doi.org/10.1037/a0029531

Burns, D. D. (1999). *The feeling good handbook*. Plume.

Burns, D. D. (2020). *Feeling great: The revolutionary new treatment for depression and anxiety.* PESI Publishing.

Butcher, J. N., Graham, J. R., Tellegen, A., & Kaemmer, B. (1989). *Manual for the restandardized Minnesota Multiphasic Personality Inventory: MMPI-2.* University of Minnesota Press.

Cahill, S. P., Rauch, S. A., Hembree, E. A., & Foa, E. B. (2003). Effect of cognitive-behavioral treatments for PTSD on anger. *Journal of Cognitive Psychotherapy, 17*(2), 113–131. https://doi.org/10.1891/jcop.17.2.113.57434

Cameron, K., Ogrodniczuk, J., & Hadjipavlou, G. (2014). Changes in alexithymia following psychological intervention: A review. *Harvard Review of Psychiatry, 22*(3), 162–178. https://doi.org/10.1097/HRP.0000000000000036

Campbell, J. (2008). *The hero with a thousand faces* (3rd ed.). New World Library. (Original work published 1949)

Carbonell, D. (2022, May 22). *A breathing exercise to calm panic attacks.* The Anxiety Coach. https://www.anxietycoach.com/breathingexercise.html

Carona, C., Handford, C., & Fonseca, A. (2021). Socratic questioning put into clinical practice. *BJPsych Advances, 27*(6), 424–426. https://doi.org/10.1192/bja.2020.77

Carroll, L. (2020). *Alice's adventures in wonderland* (A. Rackham, Illus.). Project Gutenberg. https://www.gutenberg.org/files/28885/28885-h/28885-h.htm (Original work published 1865)

Carryer, J. R., & Greenberg, L. S. (2010). Optimal levels of emotional arousal in experiential therapy of depression. *Journal of Consulting and Clinical Psychology, 78*(2), 190–199. https://doi.org/10.1037/a0018401

Caspar, F., & Berger, T. (2012). Corrective experiences: What can we learn from different models and research in basic psychology? In L. G. Castonguay & C. E. Hill (Eds.), *Transformation in psychotherapy: Corrective experiences across cognitive behavioral, humanistic, and psychodynamic approaches* (pp. 141–157). American Psychological Association. https://doi.org/10.1037/13747-009

Castonguay, L. G., Eubanks, C. F., Goldfried, M. R., Muran, J. C., & Lutz, W. (2015). Research on psychotherapy integration: Building on the past, looking to the future. *Psychotherapy Research, 25*(3), 365–382. https://doi.org/10.1080/10503307.2015.1014010

Castonguay, L. G., & Hill, C. E. (Eds.). (2007). *Insight in psychotherapy.* American Psychological Association. https://doi.org/10.1037/11532-000

Castonguay, L. G., & Hill, C. E. (2012). Corrective experiences in psychotherapy: An introduction. In L. G. Castonguay & C. E. Hill (Eds.), *Transformation in psychotherapy: Corrective experiences across cognitive behavioral, humanistic, and psychodynamic approaches* (pp. 3–9). American Psychological Association. https://doi.org/10.1037/13747-001

Cautela, J. H. (1965). Desensitization and insight. *Behaviour Research and Therapy, 3*(1), 59–64. https://doi.org/10.1016/0005-7967(65)90042-2

Chow, D. (2018). *The first kiss: Undoing the intake model and igniting the first sessions in psychotherapy.* Correlate Press.

Codd, R. T. (Ed.). (2018). *Practice-based research: A guide for clinicians*. Taylor & Francis/Routledge. https://doi.org/10.4324/9781315524610

Colloca, L., Jonas, W. B., Killen, J., Jr., Miller, F. G., & Shurtleff, D. (2015). Reevaluating the placebo effect in medical practice. *Zeitschrift für Psychologie*, *222*(3), 124–127. https://doi.org/10.1027/2151-2604/a000177

Connolly Gibbons, M. B., Crits-Christoph, P., Barber, J. P., & Schamberger, M. (2007). Insight in psychotherapy: A review of empirical literature. In L. G. Castonguay & C. Hill (Eds.), *Insight in psychotherapy* (pp. 143–165). American Psychological Association. https://doi.org/10.1037/11532-007

Constantino, M. J., Coyne, A. E., Boswell, J. F., Iles, B. R., & Vîslă, A. (2019). Promoting treatment credibility. In J. C. Norcross & M. J. Lambert (Eds.), *Psychotherapy relationships that work: Vol. 1. Evidence-based therapist contributions* (3rd ed., pp. 495–521). Oxford University Press. https://doi.org/10.1093/med-psych/9780190843953.003.0014

Constantino, M. J., Vîslă, A., Coyne, A. E., & Boswell, J. F. (2019). Cultivating positive outcome expectations. In J. C. Norcross & M. J. Lambert (Eds.), *Psychotherapy relationships that work: Vol. 1. Evidence-based therapist contributions* (3rd ed., pp. 461–494). Oxford University Press. https://doi.org/10.1093/med-psych/9780190843953.003.0013

Constantino, M. J., & Westra, H. A. (2012). An expectancy-based approach to facilitating corrective experiences in psychotherapy. In L. G. Castonguay & C. E. Hill (Eds.), *Transformation in psychotherapy: Corrective experiences across cognitive behavioral, humanistic, and psychodynamic approaches* (pp. 121–139). American Psychological Association. https://doi.org/10.1037/13747-008

Cormier, S., & Nurius, P. S. (2003). *Interviewing and change strategies for helpers* (5th ed.). Brooks/Cole.

Coyne, A. E., Constantino, M. J., Gaines, A. N., Laws, H. B., Westra, H. A., & Antony, M. M. (2021). Association between therapist attunement to patient outcome expectation and worry reduction in two therapies for generalized anxiety disorder. *Journal of Counseling Psychology*, *68*(2), 182–193. https://doi.org/10.1037/cou0000457

Craske, M. G., & Barlow, D. H. (2014). Panic disorder and agoraphobia. In D. H. Barlow (Ed.), *Clinical handbook of psychological disorders: A step-by-step treatment manual* (5th ed., pp. 1–61). Guilford Press.

Crits-Christoph, P., Connolly Gibbons, M. B., & Mukherjee, D. (2013). Psychotherapy process-outcome research. In M. J. Lambert (Ed.), *Bergin and Garfield's handbook of psychotherapy and behavior change* (6th ed., pp. 298–340). Wiley.

Cuijpers, P. (1998). A psychoeducational approach to the treatment of depression: A meta-analysis of Lewinsohn's "coping with depression" course. *Behavior Therapy*, *29*(3), 521–533. https://doi.org/10.1016/S0005-7894(98)80047-6

Cuijpers, P., Driessen, E., Hollon, S. D., van Oppen, P., Barth, J., & Andersson, G. (2012). The efficacy of non-directive supportive therapy for adult depression: A meta-analysis. *Clinical Psychology Review*, *32*(4), 280–291. https://doi.org/10.1016/j.cpr.2012.01.003

Cuijpers, P., van Straten, A., & Warmerdam, L. (2007). Behavioral activation treatments of depression: A meta-analysis. *Clinical Psychology Review, 27*(3), 318–326. https://doi.org/10.1016/j.cpr.2006.11.001

Cummings, C. M., Kazantzis, N., & Kendall, P. C. (2014). Facilitation homework and generalization of skills to the real world. In E. S. Sburlati, H. J. Lyneham, C. A. Schniering, & R. M. Rapee (Eds.), *Evidence-based CBT for anxiety and depression in children and adolescents: A competencies-based approach* (pp. 141–155). Wiley. https://doi.org/10.1002/9781118500576.ch11

Davis, D. E., DeBlaere, C., Brubaker, K., Owen, J., Jordan, T. A., II, Hook, J. N., & Van Tongeren, D. R. (2016). Microaggressions and perceptions of cultural humility in counseling. *Journal of Counseling and Development, 94*(4), 483–493. https://doi.org/10.1002/jcad.12107

de Jong, K., Conijn, J. M., Gallagher, R. A. V., Reshetnikova, A. S., Heij, M., & Lutz, M. C. (2021). Using progress feedback to improve outcomes and reduce drop-out, treatment duration, and deterioration: A multilevel meta-analysis. *Clinical Psychology Review, 85*(2021), 102002. https://doi.org/10.1016/j.cpr.2021.102002

Del Re, A. C., Flückiger, C., Horvath, A. O., Symonds, D., & Wampold, B. E. (2012). Therapist effects in the therapeutic alliance-outcome relationship: A restricted-maximum likelihood meta-analysis. *Clinical Psychology Review, 32*(7), 642–649. https://doi.org/10.1016/j.cpr.2012.07.002

Del Re, A. C., Flückiger, C., Horvath, A. O., & Wampold, B. E. (2021). Examining therapist effects in the alliance–outcome relationship: A multilevel meta-analysis. *Journal of Consulting and Clinical Psychology, 89*(5), 371–378. https://doi.org/10.1037/ccp0000637

Donker, T., Griffiths, K. M., Cuijpers, P., & Christensen, H. (2009). Psychoeducation for depression, anxiety and psychological distress: A meta-analysis. *BMC Medicine, 7*(1), 79. https://doi.org/10.1186/1741-7015-7-79

Edwards, C. J., Beutler, L. E., & Someah, K. (2019). Reactance level. In J. C. Norcross & B. E. Wampold, *Psychotherapy relationships that work: Vol. 2. Evidence-based therapist responsiveness* (3rd ed., pp. 188–211). Oxford. https://doi.org/10.1093/med-psych/9780190843960.003.0007

Eells, T. D. (Ed.). (2022). *Handbook of psychotherapy case formulation* (3rd ed.). Guilford Press.

Elliott, R. (2007). Decoding insight talk: Discourse analyses of insight in ordinary language and in psychotherapy. In L. G. Castonguay & C. Hill (Eds.), *Insight in psychotherapy* (pp. 167–185). American Psychological Association. https://doi.org/10.1037/11532-008

Elliott, R., Bohart, A. C., Watson, J. C., & Murphy, D. (2018). Therapist empathy and client outcome: An updated meta-analysis. *Psychotherapy, 55*(4), 399–410. https://doi.org/10.1037/pst0000175

Elliott, R., Shapiro, D. A., Firth-Cozens, J., Stiles, W. B., Hardy, G. E., Llewelyn, S. P., & Margison, F. R. (2001). Comprehensive process analysis of insight events in cognitive-behavioral and psychodynamic-interpersonal psychotherapies. In C. E. Hill (Ed.), *Helping skills: The empirical foundation* (pp. 309–333). American Psychological Association. https://doi.org/10.1037/10412-019

Elliott, R., Watson, J. C., Goldman, R. N., & Greenberg, L. S. (2004). *Learning emotion-focused therapy: The process-experiential approach to change.* American Psychological Association. https://doi.org/10.1037/10725-000

Emmelkamp, P. M. G. (2013). Behavior therapy with adults. In M. J. Lambert (Ed.), *Bergin and Garfield's handbook of psychotherapy and behavior change* (6th ed., pp. 343–392). Wiley.

Ericsson, K. A., Krampe, R. T., & Tesch-Römer, C. (1993). The role of deliberate practice in the acquisition of expert performance. *Psychological Review, 100*(3), 363–406. https://doi.org/10.1037/0033-295X.100.3.363

Eubanks, C. F., & Goldfried, M. R. (2019). A principle-based approach to psychotherapy integration. In J. C. Norcross & M. R. Goldfried (Eds.), *Handbook of psychotherapy integration* (3rd ed., pp. 88–105). Oxford University Press.

Evans, C., & Carlyle, J. (2021). *Outcome measures and evaluation in counselling and psychotherapy.* Sage.

Evans, K. M., Kincade, E. A., & Seem, S. R. (2011). *Introduction to feminist therapy: Strategies for social and individual change.* Sage. https://doi.org/10.4135/9781483387109

Fairburn, C. G., & Cooper, Z. (2014). Panic disorder and agoraphobia. In D. H. Barlow (Ed.), *Clinical handbook of psychological disorders: A step-by-step treatment manual* (5th ed., pp. 670–702). Guilford Press.

Fentz, H. N., Arendt, M., O'Toole, M. S., Hoffart, A., & Hougaard, E. (2014). The mediational role of panic self-efficacy in cognitive behavioral therapy for panic disorder: A systematic review and meta-analysis. *Behaviour Research and Therapy, 60*, 23–33. https://doi.org/10.1016/j.brat.2014.06.003

Fineman, B., & Wiita, C. (Hosts). (2020, October 12). VBT in focus: Dr. Don Meichenbaum on CBT and hype (No. 67) [Audio podcast episode]. In *Very bad therapy.* Very Bad Therapy Inc. https://www.verybadtherapy.com/episodes/vbt-in-focus-dr-don-meichenbaum-on-cbt-and-hype

Finn, S. E. (1996). *Manual for using the MMPI-2 as a therapeutic intervention.* University of Minnesota Press.

Finn, S. E., Fischer, C. T., & Handler, L. (Eds.). (2012). *Collaborative/therapeutic assessment: A casebook and guide.* John Wiley & Sons.

Finsrud, I., Nissen-Lie, H. A., Vrabel, K., Høstmælingen, A., Wampold, B. E., & Ulvenes, P. G. (2022). It's the therapist and the treatment: The structure of common therapeutic relationship factors. *Psychotherapy Research, 32*(2), 139–150. https://doi.org/10.1080/10503307.2021.1916640

Fisch, R., Weakland, J. H., & Segal, L. (1982). *The tactics of change: Doing therapy briefly.* Jossey-Bass Publishers.

Fish, J. M. (1973). *Placebo therapy: A practical guide to social influence in psychotherapy.* Jossey-Bass Publishers.

Flückiger, C., Del Re, A. C., Wampold, B. E., & Horvath, A. O. (2018). The alliance in adult psychotherapy: A meta-analytic synthesis. *Psychotherapy*, *55*(4), 316–340. https://doi.org/10.1037/pst0000172

Foa, E. B., Hembree, E. A., Olasov Rothbaum, B., & Rauch, S. A. M. (2019). *Prolonged exposure therapy for PTSD: Emotional processing of traumatic experiences* (2nd ed.). Oxford University Press. https://doi.org/10.1093/med-psych/9780190926939.001.0001

Foa, E. B., Huppert, J. D., & Cahill, S. P. (2006). Emotional processing theory: An update. In B. O. Rothbaum (Ed.), *Pathological anxiety: Emotional processing in etiology and treatment* (pp. 3–24). Guilford Press.

Foa, E. B., Yadin, E., & Lichner, T. K. (2012). *Exposure and response (ritual) prevention for obsessive–compulsive disorder: Therapist guide*. Oxford University Press. https://doi.org/10.1093/med:psych/9780195335286.001.0001

Forbes, M. K., Tackett, J. L., Markon, K. E., & Krueger, R. F. (2016). Beyond comorbidity: Toward a dimensional and hierarchical approach to understanding psychopathology across the life span. *Development and Psychopathology*, *28*(4pt1), 971–986. https://doi.org/10.1017/S0954579416000651

Forsyth, J. P., & Eifert, G. H. (2016). *The mindfulness and acceptance workbook for anxiety: A guide to breaking free from anxiety, phobias, and worry using acceptance and commitment therapy*. New Harbinger Publications.

Fosha, D. (2000). *The transforming power of affect: A model for accelerated change*. Basic Books.

Fosha, D. (2009). Emotion and recognition at work: Energy, vitality, pleasure, truth, desire & the emergent phenomenology of transformational experience. In D. Fosha, D. J. Siegel, & M. Solomon (Eds.), *The healing power of emotion: Affective neuroscience, development, and clinical practice* (pp. 172–203). Norton.

Fosha, D., Paivio, S. C., Gleiser, K., & Ford, J. D. (2009). Experiential and emotion-focused therapy. In C. A. Courtois & J. D. Ford (Eds.), *Treating complex traumatic stress disorders: An evidence-based guide* (pp. 286–311). Guilford Press.

Frank, J. D. (1961). *Persuasion and healing: A comparative study of psychotherapy*. Johns Hopkins University Press.

Frank, J. D. (1973). *Persuasion and healing: A comparative study of psychotherapy*. Schocken Books.

Frank, J. D., & Frank, J. B. (1991). *Persuasion and healing: A comparative study of psychotherapy* (3rd ed.). Johns Hopkins University Press.

Fraser, J. S., & Solovey, A. D. (2007). *Second-order change in psychotherapy: The golden thread that unifies effective treatments*. American Psychological Association. https://doi.org/10.1037/11499-000

Gallagher, M. W., Long, L. J., & Phillips, C. A. (2020). Hope, optimism, self-efficacy, and posttraumatic stress disorder: A meta-analytic review of the protective effects of positive expectancies. *Journal of Clinical Psychology*, *76*(3), 329–355. https://doi.org/10.1002/jclp.22882

Gelso, C. J. (2009). The real relationship in a postmodern world: Theoretical and empirical explorations. *Psychotherapy Research, 19*(3), 253–264. https://doi.org/10.1080/10503300802389242

Gelso, C. J., & Carter, J. A. (1994). Components of the psychotherapy relationship: Their interaction and unfolding during treatment. *Journal of Counseling Psychology, 41*(3), 296–306. https://doi.org/10.1037/0022-0167.41.3.296

Gendlin, E. T. (1981). *Focusing*. Bantam Dell.

Gilbert, P. (2010). *Compassion focused therapy*. Routledge. https://doi.org/10.4324/9780203851197

Gilbert, P. (2019). *The compassionate mind (compassion focused therapy)*. Robinson.

Gilbert, P., & Choden. (2014). *Mindful compassion*. New Harbinger Publications.

Goldfried, M. R. (1980). Toward the delineation of therapeutic change principles. *American Psychologist, 35*(11), 991–999. https://doi.org/10.1037/0003-066X.35.11.991

Goldfried, M. R. (2012). The corrective experience: A core principle for therapeutic change. In L. G. Castonguay & C. E. Hill (Eds.), *Transformation in psychotherapy: Corrective experiences across cognitive behavioral, humanistic, and psychodynamic approaches* (pp. 13–29). American Psychological Association. https://doi.org/10.1037/13747-002

Goldfried, M. R. (2019). Obtaining consensus in psychotherapy: What holds us back? *American Psychologist, 74*(4), 484–496. https://doi.org/10.1037/amp0000365

Goldfried, M. R., & Robins, C. (1982). On the facilitation of self-efficacy. *Cognitive Therapy and Research, 6*(4), 361–379. https://doi.org/10.1007/BF01184004

Goldin, P. R., Ziv, M., Jazaieri, H., Werner, K., Kraemer, H., Heimberg, R. G., & Gross, J. J. (2012). Cognitive reappraisal self-efficacy mediates the effects of individual cognitive-behavioral therapy for social anxiety disorder. *Journal of Consulting and Clinical Psychology, 80*(6), 1034–1040. https://doi.org/10.1037/a0028555

Gollwitzer, P. M. (1999). Implementation intentions: Strong effects of simple plans. *American Psychologist, 54*(7), 493–503. https://doi.org/10.1037/0003-066X.54.7.493

Goode, J., Park, J., Parkin, S., Tompkins, K. A., & Swift, J. K. (2017). A collaborative approach to psychotherapy termination. *Psychotherapy, 54*(1), 10–14. https://doi.org/10.1037/pst0000085

Gottlieb, L. (2019). *Maybe you should talk to someone*. Houghton Mifflin Harcourt.

Greenberg, L. S. (2012). Emotions, the great captains of our lives: Their role in the process of change in psychotherapy. *American Psychologist, 67*(8), 697–707. https://doi.org/10.1037/a0029858

Greenberg, L. S. (2016). The clinical application of emotion in psychotherapy. In L. Feldman Barrett, M. Lews, & J. M. Haviland-Jones (Eds.), *Handbook of emotions* (4th ed., pp. 670–684). Guilford Press.

Greenberg, L. S. (2021). *Changing emotion with emotion: A practitioner's guide.* American Psychological Association. https://doi.org/10.1037/0000248-000

Greenberg, R. P., Constantino, M. J., & Bruce, N. (2006). Are patient expectations still relevant for psychotherapy process and outcome? *Clinical Psychology Review, 26*(6), 657–678. https://doi.org/10.1016/j.cpr.2005.03.002

Greenson, R. R. (1967). *The technique and practice of psychoanalysis* (Vol. 1). International Universities Press.

Grencavage, L. M., & Norcross, J. C. (1990). Where are the commonalities among the therapeutic common factors? *Professional Psychology, Research and Practice, 21*(5), 372–378. https://doi.org/10.1037/0735-7028.21.5.372

Grosse Holtforth, M., & Flückiger, C. (2012). The stream of corrective experiences in action: Big bang and constant dripping. In L. G. Castonguay & C. E. Hill (Eds.), *Transformation in psychotherapy: Corrective experiences across cognitive behavioral, humanistic, and psychodynamic approaches* (pp. 317–333). American Psychological Association. https://doi.org/10.1037/13747-015

Gwaltney, C. J., Metrik, J., Kahler, C. W., & Shiffman, S. (2009). Self-efficacy and smoking cessation: A meta-analysis. *Psychology of Addictive Behaviors, 23*(1), 56–66. https://doi.org/10.1037/a0013529

Hammer, E. (1990). *Reaching the affect: Style in the psychodynamic therapies.* Jason Aronson.

Hannan, C., Lambert, M. J., Harmon, C., Nielsen, S. L., Smart, D. W., Shimokawa, K., & Sutton, S. W. (2005). A lab test and algorithms for identifying clients at risk for treatment failure. *Journal of Clinical Psychology, 61*(2), 155–163. https://doi.org/10.1002/jclp.20108

Harris, R. (2008). *The happiness trap: How to stop struggling and start living: A guide to ACT.* Trumpeter Books.

Harris, R. (2013). *Getting unstuck in ACT: A clinician's guide to overcoming common obstacles in acceptance and commitment therapy.* New Harbinger Publications.

Harris, R. (2019). *ACT made simple: An easy-to-read primer on acceptance and commitment therapy.* New Harbinger Publications.

Hayes, A. M., Beck, J. G., & Yasinski, C. (2012). A cognitive behavioral perspective on corrective experiences. In L. G. Castonguay & C. E. Hill (Eds.), *Transformation in psychotherapy: Corrective experiences across cognitive behavioral, humanistic, and psychodynamic approaches* (pp. 69–83). American Psychological Association. https://doi.org/10.1037/13747-005

Hayes, A. M., Beevers, C. G., Feldman, G. C., Laurenceau, J. P., & Perlman, C. (2005). Avoidance and processing as predictors of symptom change and positive growth in an integrative therapy for depression. *International Journal of Behavioral Medicine, 12*(2), 111–122. https://doi.org/10.1207/s15327558ijbm1202_9

Hayes, S. C., & Lillis, J. (2012). *Acceptance and commitment therapy.* American Psychological Association.

Heatherton, T. F. (2011). Neuroscience of self and self-regulation. *Annual Review of Psychology, 62*(1), 363–390. https://doi.org/10.1146/annurev.psych.121208. 131616

Hill, C. E. (1986). An overview of the Hill counselor and client verbal response modes category systems. In L. Greenberg & W. Pinsof (Eds.), *The psychotherapeutic process: A research handbook* (pp. 131–160). Guilford.

Hill, C. E. (Ed.). (2004). *Dream work in therapy: Facilitating exploration, insight, and action.* American Psychological Association. https://doi.org/10.1037/10624-000

Hill, C. E. (2020). *Helping skills: Facilitating exploration, insight, and action* (5th ed.). American Psychological Association. https://doi.org/10.1037/0000147-000

Hill, C. E., Castonguay, L. G., Angus, L., Arnkoff, D. B., Barber, J. P., Bohart, A. C., Borkovec, T. D., Bowman, E. A., Caspar, F., Gibbons, M. B. C., Crits-Christoph, P., Cruz, J. M., Elliott, R., Friedlander, M. L., Gelso, C. J., Glass, C. R., Goldfried, M. R., Greenberg, L. S., Holtforth, M. G., & Wampold, B. E. (2007). Insight in psychotherapy: Definitions, processes, consequences, and research directions. In L. G. Castonguay & C. Hill (Eds.), *Insight in psychotherapy* (pp. 441–454). American Psychological Association. https://doi.org/10.1037/11532-021

Hill, C. E., Castonguay, L. G., Farber, B. A., Knox, S., Stiles, W. B., Anderson, T., Angus, L. E., Barber, J. P., Beck, J. G., Bohart, A. C., Caspar, F., Constantino, M. J., Elliott, R., Friedlander, M. L., Goldfried, M. R., Greenberg, L. S., Grosse Holtforth, M., Hayes, A. M., Hayes, J. A., & Sharpless, B. A. (2012). Corrective experiences in psychotherapy: Definitions, processes, consequences, and research directions. In L. G. Castonguay & C. E. Hill (Eds.), *Transformation in psychotherapy: Corrective experiences across cognitive behavioral, humanistic, and psychodynamic approaches* (pp. 355–370). American Psychological Association. https://doi.org/10.1037/13747-017

Hill, C. E., Thompson, B. J., & Mahalik, J. R. (1989). *Therapist techniques and client outcomes: Eight cases of brief psychotherapy.* Sage.

Hook, J. N., Davis, D., Owen, J., & DeBlaere, C. (2017). *Cultural humility: Engaging diverse identities in therapy.* American Psychological Association. https://doi.org/10.1037/0000037-000

Horvath, A. O., Del Re, A. C., Flückiger, C., & Symonds, D. (2011). Alliance in individual psychotherapy. *Psychotherapy, 48*(1), 9–16. https://doi.org/10.1037/a0022186

Howard, K. I., Kopta, S. M., Krause, M. S., & Orlinsky, D. E. (1986). The dose-effect relationship in psychotherapy. *American Psychologist, 41*(2), 159–164. https://doi.org/10.1037/0003-066X.41.2.159

Howard, K. I., Lueger, R. J., Maling, M. S., & Martinovich, Z. (1993). A phase model of psychotherapy outcome: Causal mediation of change. *Journal of Consulting and Clinical Psychology, 61*(4), 678–685. https://doi.org/10.1037/0022-006X.61.4.678

Hubble, M. A., Duncan, B. L., & Miller, S. D. (Eds.). (1999). *The heart and soul of change: What works in therapy*. American Psychological Association. https://doi.org/10.1037/11132-000

Hughes, J. W. (2011). Stimulus generalization. In J. S. Kreutzer, J. DeLuca, & B. Caplan (Eds.), *Encyclopedia of clinical neuropsychology*. Springer. https://doi.org/10.1007/978-0-387-79948-3_2118

Hugo, V. (2021, July 20). *Les Misérables*. Project Gutenberg. https://www.gutenberg.org/files/135/135-h/135-h.htm#link2HCH0026 (Original work published 1887)

Ittaman, S. V., VanWormer, J. J., & Rezkalla, S. H. (2014). The role of aspirin in the prevention of cardiovascular disease. *Clinical Medicine & Research, 12*(3–4), 147–154. https://doi.org/10.3121/cmr.2013.1197

Jacobson, N. S., & Christensen, A. (1996). *Integrative couple therapy: Promoting acceptance and change*. W. W. Norton & Co.

Jaycox, L. H., & Foa, E. B. (1996). Obstacles in implementing exposure therapy for PTSD: Case discussions and practical solutions. *Clinical Psychology & Psychotherapy, 3*(3), 176–184. https://doi.org/10.1002/(SICI)1099-0879(199609)3:3<176::AID-CPP100>3.0.CO;2-1

Jaycox, L. H., Foa, E. B., & Morral, A. R. (1998). Influence of emotional engagement and habituation on exposure therapy for PTSD. *Journal of Consulting and Clinical Psychology, 66*(1), 185–192. https://doi.org/10.1037/0022-006X.66.1.185

Jennissen, S., Huber, J., Ehrenthal, J. C., Schauenburg, H., & Dinger, U. (2018). Association between insight and outcome of psychotherapy: Systematic review and meta-analysis. *The American Journal of Psychiatry, 175*(10), 961–969. https://doi.org/10.1176/appi.ajp.2018.17080847

Kaner, A., & Prelinger, E. (2005). *The craft of psychodynamic psychotherapy*. Jason Aronson.

Kanfer, F. H., & Schefft, B. K. (1988). *Guiding the process of therapeutic change*. Research Press.

Kazantzis, N., Whittington, C., & Dattilio, F. (2010). Meta-analysis of homework effects in cognitive and behavioral therapy: A replication and extension. *Clinical Psychology: Science and Practice, 17*(2), 144–156. https://doi.org/10.1111/j.1468-2850.2010.01204.x

Kegan, R. (1982). *The evolving self: Problem and process in human development*. Harvard University Press. https://doi.org/10.4159/9780674039414

Khoury, B., Lecomte, T., Fortin, G., Masse, M., Therien, P., Bouchard, V., Chapleau, M. A., Paquin, K., & Hofmann, S. G. (2013). Mindfulness-based therapy: A comprehensive meta-analysis. *Clinical Psychology Review, 33*(6), 763–771. https://doi.org/10.1016/j.cpr.2013.05.005

Kirmayer, L. J. (1990). Resistance, reactance, and reluctance to change: A cognitive attributional approach to strategic interventions. *Journal of Cognitive Psychotherapy, 4*(2), 83–104. https://doi.org/10.1891/0889-8391.4.2.83

Klerman, G. L., Weissman, M. M., Rounsaville, B. J., & Chevron, E. S. (1984). *Interpersonal psychotherapy of depression*. Rowman & Littlefield Publishers.

Knapp, S. J., VandeCreek, L. D., & Fingerhut, R. (2017). *Practical ethics for psychologists: A positive approach* (3rd ed.). American Psychological Association. https://doi.org/10.1037/0000036-000

Krebs, P., Norcross, J. C., Nicholson, J. M., & Prochaska, J. O. (2019). Stages of Change. In J. C. Norcross & B. E. Wampold (Eds.), *Psychotherapy relationships that work: Vol. 2. Evidence-based therapist responsiveness* (3rd ed., pp. 296–328). Oxford. https://doi.org/10.1093/med-psych/9780190843960.003.0010

Krypotos, A. M., Effting, M., Kindt, M., & Beckers, T. (2015). Avoidance learning: A review of theoretical models and recent developments. *Frontiers in Behavioral Neuroscience, 9*, 189. https://doi.org/10.3389/fnbeh.2015.00189

Lambert, M. J. (2013). The efficacy and effectiveness of psychotherapy. In M. J. Lambert (Ed.), *Bergin and Garfield's handbook of psychotherapy and behavior change* (6th ed., pp. 169–218). Wiley.

Lambert, M. J. (2015). Progress feedback and the OQ-system: The past and the future. *Psychotherapy, 52*(4), 381–390. https://doi.org/10.1037/pst0000027

Lambert, M. J., Bailey, R., Kimball, K., Shimokawa, K., Harmon, S. C., & Slade, K. (2007). *Clinical support tool manual—brief version—40*. OQ Measures.

Lambert, M. J., & Bergin, A. E. (1992). Achievements and limitations of psychotherapy research. In D. K. Freedheim, H. J. Freudenberger, J. W. Kessler, S. B. Messer, D. R. Peterson, H. H. Strupp, & P. L. Wachtel (Eds.), *History of psychotherapy: A century of change* (pp. 360–390). American Psychological Association. https://doi.org/10.1037/10110-010

Lambert, M. J., & Ogles, B. M. (2004). The efficacy and effectiveness of psychotherapy. In M. J. Lambert (Ed.), *Bergin and Garfield's handbook of psychotherapy and behavior change* (5th ed., pp. 139–193). Wiley.

Lambert, M. J., & Ogles, B. M. (2014). Common factors: Post hoc explanation or empirically based therapy approach? *Psychotherapy, 51*(4), 500–504. https://doi.org/10.1037/a0036580

Lambert, M. J., Whipple, J. L., & Kleinstäuber, M. (2018). Collecting and delivering progress feedback: A meta-analysis of routine outcome monitoring. *Psychotherapy, 55*(4), 520–537. https://doi.org/10.1037/pst0000167

Lambert, M. J., Whipple, J. L., & Kleinstäuber, M. (2019). Collecting and delivering client feedback. In J. C. Norcross & M. J. Lambert, *Psychotherapy relationships that work* (3rd ed., Vol. 1., pp. 580–630). Oxford.

Langer, D. A., Mooney, T. K., & Wills, C. E. (2015). Shared decision-making for treatment planning in mental health care: Theory, evidence, and tools. *Oxford Handbook Topics in Psychology*. https://doi.org/10.1093/oxfordhb/9780199935291.013.7

Langer, E. J. (2009). *Counterclockwise: Mindful health and the power of possibility*. Ballantine Books.

Langs, R. (1981). *The technique of psychoanalytic psychotherapy* (Vol. 1). Jason Aronson.

Lantz, M. M., Pieterse, A. L., & Taylor, T. O. (2018). A social dominance theory perspective on multicultural competence. *Counselling Psychology Quarterly, 33*(2), 142–162. https://doi.org/10.1080/09515070.2018.1500352

Laska, K. M., Gurman, A. S., & Wampold, B. E. (2014). Expanding the lens of evidence-based practice in psychotherapy: A common factors perspective. *Psychotherapy: Theory, Research, & Practice, 51*(4), 467–481. https://doi.org/10.1037/a0034332

Laska, K. M., & Wampold, B. E. (2014). Ten things to remember about common factor theory. *Psychotherapy, 51*(4), 519–524. https://doi.org/10.1037/a0038245

Lazarus, A., & Wachtel, P. (2018). Integrative therapies. In J. O. Prochaska & J. C. Norcross (Eds.), *Systems of psychotherapy* (9th ed., pp. 388–413). Oxford University Press.

LeBeau, R. T., Davies, C. D., Culver, N. C., & Craske, M. G. (2013). Homework compliance counts in cognitive-behavioral therapy. *Cognitive Behaviour Therapy, 42*(3), 171–179. https://doi.org/10.1080/16506073.2013.763286

Lenkowsky, R. S. (1987). Bibliotherapy: A review and analysis of the literature. *The Journal of Special Education, 21*(2), 123–132. https://doi.org/10.1177/002246698702100211

Levenson, H. (1995). *Time-limited dynamic psychotherapy: A guide to clinical practice.* Basic Books.

Levy, S. T. (1990). *Principles of interpretation: Mastering clear and concise interventions in psychotherapy.* Jason Aronson.

Lewinsohn, P. M., Steinmetz, J. L., Antonuccio, D., & Teri, L. (1984). Group therapy for depression: The coping with depression course. *International Journal of Mental Health, 13*(3–4), 8–33. https://doi.org/10.1080/00207411.1984.11448974

Linehan, M. M. (2014). *DBT skills training manual* (2nd ed.). Guilford Press.

Linehan, M. M. (2015). *DBT skills training handouts and worksheets* (2nd ed.). Guilford Press.

Lingiardi, V., Filippucci, L., & Baiocco, R. (2005). Therapeutic alliance evaluation in personality disorders psychotherapy. *Psychotherapy Research, 15*(1–2), 45–53. https://doi.org/10.1080/10503300512331327047

Littell, J. H., & Girvin, H. (2002). Stages of Change. A critique. *Behavior Modification, 26*(2), 223–273. https://doi.org/10.1177/0145445502026002006

Luborsky, L. (1984). *Principles of psychoanalytic psychotherapy: A manual for supportive-expressive treatment.* Basic Books.

Lundahl, B. W., Kunz, C., Brownell, C., Tollefson, D., & Burke, B. L. (2010). A meta-analysis of motivational interviewing: Twenty-five years of empirical studies. *Research on Social Work Practice, 20*(2), 137–160. https://doi.org/10.1177/1049731509347850

Lundh, L. G. (2014). The search for common factors in psychotherapy: Two theoretical models, with different empirical implications. *Psychology and Behavioral Sciences, 3*(5), 131–150. https://doi.org/10.11648/j.pbs.20140305.11

Lunnen, K. M., & Ogles, B. M. (1998). A multiperspective, multivariable evaluation of reliable change. *Journal of Consulting and Clinical Psychology, 66*(2), 400–410. https://doi.org/10.1037/0022-006X.66.2.400

Lunnen, K. M., Ogles, B. M., & Pappas, L. N. (2008). A multi-perspective comparison of satisfaction, symptomatic change, perceived change, and end-point functioning. *Professional Psychology, Research and Practice, 39*(2), 145–152. https://doi.org/10.1037/0735-7028.39.2.145

Maddux, J. E., & Gosselin, J. T. (2012). Self-efficacy. In M. R. Leary & J. P. Tangney (Eds.), *Handbook of self and identity* (pp. 198–224). Guilford Press.

Maddux, J. E., & Lewis, J. (1995). Self-efficacy and adjustment: Basic principles and issues. In J. E. Maddux (Ed.), *Self-efficacy, adaptation, and adjustment: Theory, research, and application* (pp. 37–68). Plenum Press. https://doi.org/10.1007/978-1-4419-6868-5_2

Mains, J. A., & Scogin, F. R. (2003). The effectiveness of self-administered treatments: A practice-friendly review of the research. *Journal of Clinical Psychology, 59*(2), 237–246. https://doi.org/10.1002/jclp.10145

Marlatt, G. A., & Donovan, D. M. (Eds.). (2005). *Relapse prevention: Maintenance strategies in the treatment of addictive behaviors* (2nd ed.). Guilford Press.

Martell, C. R., Dimidjian, S., & Herman-Dunn, R. (2022). *Behavioral activation for depression: A clinician's guide* (2nd ed.). Guilford Press.

Martin, D. J., Garske, J. P., & Davis, M. K. (2000). Relation of the therapeutic alliance with outcome and other variables: A meta-analytic review. *Journal of Consulting and Clinical Psychology, 68*(3), 438–450. https://doi.org/10.1037/0022-006X.68.3.438

Mausbach, B. T., Moore, R., Roesch, S., Cardenas, V., & Patterson, T. L. (2010). The relationship between homework compliance and therapy outcomes: An updated meta-analysis. *Cognitive Therapy and Research, 34*(5), 429–438. https://doi.org/10.1007/s10608-010-9297-z

McCabe, G. A., & Widiger, T. A. (2020). A comprehensive comparison of the *ICD-11* and *DSM-5* section III personality disorder models. *Psychological Assessment, 32*(1), 72–84. https://doi.org/10.1037/pas0000772

McCulliss, D. (2012). Bibliotherapy: Historical and research perspectives. *Journal of Poetry Therapy, 25*(1), 23–38. https://doi.org/10.1080/08893675.2012.654944

McSmith, A. (2008, February 12). Fond farewell to the genius of Miles Kington. *Independent.* https://www.independent.co.uk/news/uk/this-britain/fond-farewell-to-the-genius-of-miles-kington-781024.html

Mendelowitz, E., & Schneider, K. (2008). Existential therapy. In R. J. Corsini & D. Wedding (Eds.), *Current psychotherapies* (8th ed., pp. 295–327). Thomson Brooks/Cole.

Merriam-Webster. (n.d.). Insight. In *Merriam-Webster.com dictionary.* Retrieved March 9, 2022, from https://www.merriam-webster.com/dictionary/insight

Messer, S. B. (2002). A psychodynamic perspective on resistance in psychotherapy: Vive la résistance. Journal of Clinical Psychology, 58(2), 157–163. https://doi.org/10.1002/jclp.1139

Messer, S. B., & McWilliams, N. (2007). Insight in psychodynamic therapy: Theory and assessment. In L. G. Castonguay & C. Hill (Eds.), Insight in psychotherapy (pp. 9–29). American Psychological Association. https://doi.org/10.1037/11532-001

Miller, S. B. (1992). Insight and other psychotherapy change processes. The Journal of the American Academy of Psychoanalysis, 20(4), 611–632. https://doi.org/10.1521/jaap.1.1992.20.4.611

Miller, S. D., Duncan, B. L., & Hubble, M. A. (1997). Escape from Babel: Toward a unifying language for psychotherapy practice. Norton.

Miller, W. R. (1983). Motivational interviewing with problem drinkers. Behavioural Psychotherapy, 11(2), 147–172. https://doi.org/10.1017/S0141347300006583

Miller, W. R., & Rollnick, S. (2002). Motivational interviewing: Preparing people for change (2nd ed.). Guilford Press.

Miller, W. R., & Rollnick, S. (2013). Motivational interviewing: Helping people change (3rd ed.). Guilford Press.

Miller, W. R., & Rose, G. S. (2009). Toward a theory of motivational interviewing. American Psychologist, 64(6), 527–537. https://doi.org/10.1037/a0016830

Miller, W. R., & Tonigan, J. S. (1997). Assessing drinkers' motivation for change: The Stages of Change Readiness and Treatment Eagerness Scale (SOCRATES). In G. A. Marlatt & G. R. VandenBos (Eds.), Addictive behaviors: Readings on etiology, prevention, and treatment (pp. 355–369). (Reprinted from "Psychology of Addictive Behaviors," 10, 1996, pp. 81–89). American Psychological Association. https://doi.org/10.1037/10248-014

Monson, C. M., Resick, P. A., & Rizvi, S. L. (2014). Posttraumatic stress disorder. In D. H. Barlow (Ed.), Clinical handbook of psychological disorders: A step-by-step treatment manual (5th ed., pp. 62–113). Guilford Press.

Moonshine, C., & Schaefer, S. (2019). Dialectical behavior therapy: Vol. 1. The clinician's guidebook for acquiring competency in DBT (2nd ed.). PESI Publishing & Media.

Muran, J. C., Eubanks, C. F., & Samstag, L. W. (2021). One more time with less jargon: An introduction to "Rupture Repair in Practice." Journal of Clinical Psychology, 77(2), 361–368. https://doi.org/10.1002/jclp.23105

Naar, S., & Safren, S. A. (2017). Motivational interviewing and CBT: Combining strategies for maximum effectiveness. Guilford Press.

Najavits, L. M. (2001). Seeking safety: A treatment manual for PTSD and substance abuse. Guilford Press.

National Aeronautics and Space Administration. (2017, August 7). New Horizons sees Pluto and Charon. https://www.nasa.gov/image-feature/new-horizons-sees-pluto-and-charon

Neff, K., & Germer, C. (2018). The mindful self-compassion workbook: A proven way to accept yourself, build inner strength, and thrive. Guilford Press.

Norcross, J. C. (1986). Eclectic psychotherapy: An introduction and overview. In J. C. Norcross (Ed.), *Handbook of eclectic psychotherapy* (1st ed., pp. 3–24). Brunner/Mazel.

Norcross, J. C. (2005). A primer on psychotherapy integration. In M. R. Goldfried & J. C. Norcross (Eds.), *Handbook of psychotherapy integration* (2nd ed., pp. 3–23). Oxford University Press. https://doi.org/10.1093/med:psych/9780195165791.003.0001

Norcross, J. C., Krebs, P. M., & Prochaska, J. O. (2011). Stages of change. *Journal of Clinical Psychology, 67*(2), 143–154. https://doi.org/10.1002/jclp.20758

Norcross, J. C., & Lambert, M. J. (2019a). Evidence-based psychotherapy relationship: The third task force. In J. C. Norcross & M. J. Lambert (Eds.), *Psychotherapy relationships that work: Vol. 1. Evidence-based therapist contributions* (3rd ed.). Oxford University Press.

Norcross, J. C., & Lambert, M. J. (Eds.). (2019b). *Psychotherapy relationships that work: Vol. 1. Evidence-based therapist contributions* (3rd ed.). Oxford University Press.

Norcross, J. C., & Newman, C. F. (2003). Psychotherapy integration: Setting the context. In J. C. Norcross & M. R. Goldfried (Eds.), *Handbook of psychotherapy integration* (pp. 3–45). Oxford University Press.

Norcross, J. C., & Wampold, B. E. (2011). Evidence-based therapy relationships: Research conclusions and clinical practices. *Psychotherapy, 48*(1), 98–102. https://doi.org/10.1037/a0022161

Norcross, J. C., & Wampold, B. E. (2019). *Psychotherapy relationships that work: Vol. 2. Evidence-based therapist responsiveness* (3rd ed.). Oxford University Press.

Norman, H., Marzano, L., Coulson, M., & Oskis, A. (2019). Effects of mindfulness-based interventions on alexithymia: A systematic review. *Evidence-Based Mental Health, 22*(1), 36–43. https://doi.org/10.1136/ebmental-2018-300029

O'Donohue, W. T., & Cummings, N. A. (2008). *Evidence-based adjunctive treatments.* Elsevier Academic Press.

Ogles, B. M., Lambert, M. J., & Fields, S. (2002). *Essentials of outcome assessment.* Wiley.

Ogles, B. M., Wood, D. S., Weidner, R. O., & Brown, S. D. (2021). *Motivational interviewing in higher education: A primer for academic advisors and student affairs professionals.* Charles C Thomas.

Orlinsky, D. E. (2009). The "generic model of psychotherapy" after 25 years: Evolution of a research-based metatheory. *Journal of Psychotherapy Integration, 19*(4), 319–339. https://doi.org/10.1037/a0017973

Orlinsky, D. E., & Howard, K. I. (1978). The relation of process to outcome in psychotherapy. In S. L. Garfield & A. E. Bergin (Eds.), *Handbook of psychotherapy and behavior change: An empirical analysis* (2nd ed., pp. 283–330). John Wiley & Sons.

Orlinsky, D. E., & Howard, K. I. (1987). A generic model of psychotherapy. *International Journal of Eclectic Psychotherapy, 6,* 6–27.

Owen, J. (2013). Early career perspectives on psychotherapy research and practice: Psychotherapist effects, multicultural orientation, and couple interventions. *Psychotherapy, 50*(4), 496–502. https://doi.org/10.1037/a0034617

Owen, J. J., Tao, K., Leach, M. M., & Rodolfa, E. (2011). Clients' perceptions of their psychotherapists' multicultural orientation. *Psychotherapy, 48*(3), 274–282. https://doi.org/10.1037/a0022065

Page, A. C., & Stritzke, W. G. (2015). *Clinical psychology for trainees*. Cambridge University Press.

Pascual-Leone, A., & Yeryomenko, N. (2017). The client "experiencing" scale as a predictor of treatment outcomes: A meta-analysis on psychotherapy process. *Psychotherapy Research, 27*(6), 653–665. https://doi.org/10.1080/10503307.2016.1152409

Payne, L. A., Ellard, K. K., Farchione, T. J., Fairholme, C. P., & Barlow, D. H. (2014). Emotional disorders: A unified transdiagnostic protocol. In D. H. Barlow (Ed.), *Clinical handbook of psychological disorders: A step-by-step treatment manual* (5th ed., pp. 237–274). Guilford Press.

Peluso, P. R., & Freund, R. R. (2018). Therapist and client emotional expression and psychotherapy outcomes: A meta-analysis. *Psychotherapy, 55*(4), 461–472. https://doi.org/10.1037/pst0000165

Peluso, P. R., & Freund, R. R. (2019). Emotional expression. In J. C. Norcross & M. J. Lambert (Eds.), *Psychotherapy relationships that work: Vol. 1. Evidence-based therapist contributions* (3rd ed., pp. 421–460). Oxford University Press. https://doi.org/10.1093/med-psych/9780190843953.003.0012

Persons, J. B. (1989). *Cognitive therapy in practice: A case formulation approach*. W. W. Norton & Company.

Petry, N. M. (2012). *Contingency management for substance abuse treatment: A guide to implementing this evidence-based practice*. Routledge.

Pfammatter, M. (2015). A classification of common therapeutic factors in psychotherapy based on their associations with treatment techniques. *European Psychiatry, 30*(Suppl. 1), 337. https://doi.org/10.1016/S0924-9338(15)30265-0

Polk, K. L., & Schoendorff, B. (Eds.). (2014). *The ACT matrix: A new approach to building psychological flexibility across settings & populations*. New Harbinger Publications.

Pos, A. E., Paolone, D. A., Smith, C. E., & Warwar, S. H. (2017). How does client expressed emotional arousal relate to outcome in experiential therapy for depression? *Person-Centered & Experiential Psychotherapies, 16*, 173–190. https://doi.org/10.1080/14779757.2017.1323666

Poston, J. M., & Hanson, W. E. (2010). Meta-analysis of psychological assessment as a therapeutic intervention. *Psychological Assessment, 22*(2), 203–212. https://doi.org/10.1037/a0018679

Powell, D. H. (1996). Behavior therapy generated insight. In J. R. Cautela & W. Ishaq (Eds.), *Contemporary issues in behavior therapy: Improving the human condition* (pp. 301–314). Plenum Press. https://doi.org/10.1007/978-1-4757-9826-5_16

Prochaska, J. O., & DiClemente, C. C. (1984). *The transtheoretical approach: Crossing traditional boundaries of therapy.* Dow Jones-Irwin.

Prochaska, J. O., & DiClemente, C. C. (2019). The transtheoretical approach. In J. C. Norcross & M. R. Goldfried (Eds.), *Handbook of psychotherapy integration* (3rd ed., pp. 161–183). Oxford University Press.

Prochaska, J. O., & Norcross, J. C. (2018). Comparative conclusions: Toward a transtheoretical therapy. In J. O. Prochaska & J. C. Norcross (Eds.), *Systems of psychotherapy* (9th ed., pp. 414–440). Oxford University Press.

Raskin, N. J., Rogers, C. R., & Witty, M. C. (2008). Client-centered therapy. In R. J. Corsini & D. Wedding (Eds.), *Current psychotherapies* (8th ed., pp. 141–186). Thomson Brooks/Cole.

Riggenbach, J. (2012). *The CBT toolbox: A workbook for clients and clinicians.* PESI Publishing & Media.

Rogers, C. (1961). *On becoming a person.* Houghton Mifflin Company.

Rogers, C. R. (1959). A theory of therapy, personality, and interpersonal relationships as developed in the client-centered framework. In S. Koch (Ed.), *Psychology: The study of a science: Vol. 3. Formulations of the person and the social context* (pp. 184–256). McGraw-Hill.

Rogers, C. R. (1975). Empathic: An unappreciated way of being. *The Counseling Psychologist, 5*(2), 2–10. https://doi.org/10.1177/001100007500500202

Rogers, C. R. (1986). Reflection of feelings. *Person-Centered Review, 1*(4), 375–377.

Rogers, C. R. (1992). The necessary and sufficient conditions of therapeutic personality change. *Journal of Consulting and Clinical Psychology, 60*(6), 827–832. https://doi.org/10.1037/0022-006X.60.6.827 (Original work published 1957)

Rosen, G. M., & Davison, G. C. (2003). Psychology should list empirically supported principles of change (ESPs) and not credential trademarked therapies or other treatment packages. *Behavior Modification, 27*(3), 300–312. https://doi.org/10.1177/0145445503027003003

Rosenzweig, S. (1936). Some implicit common factors in diverse methods of psychotherapy. *American Journal of Orthopsychiatry, 6*(3), 412–415. https://doi.org/10.1111/j.1939-0025.1936.tb05248.x

Rotter, J. B. (1954). *Social learning and clinical psychology.* Prentice-Hall. https://doi.org/10.1037/10788-000

Rousmaniere, T. (2016). *Deliberate practice for psychotherapists: A guide to improving clinical effectiveness.* Taylor & Francis. https://doi.org/10.4324/9781315472256

Rousmaniere, T., Goodyear, R. K., Miller, S. D., & Wampold, B. E. (2017). Introduction. In T. Rousmaniere, R. K. Goodyear, S. D. Miller, & B. E. Wampold (Eds.), *The cycle of excellence: Using deliberate practice to improve supervision and training* (pp. 3–22). Wiley-Blackwell. https://doi.org/10.1002/9781119165590.ch1

Ruini, C., & Mortara, C. C. (2022). Writing technique across psychotherapies—From traditional expressive writing to new positive psychology interventions: A narrative review. *Journal of Contemporary Psychotherapy, 52*(1), 23–34. https://doi.org/10.1007/s10879-021-09520-9

Ryan, R. M., & Deci, E. L. (2017). *Self-determination theory: Basic psychological needs in motivation, development, and wellness.* Guilford Press. https://doi.org/10.1521/978.14625/28806

Ryan, R. M., & Deci, E. L. (2019). Brick by brick: The origins, development, and future of self-determination theory. *Advances in Motivation Science, 6,* 111–156. https://doi.org/10.1016/bs.adms.2019.01.001

Safran, J. D., & Muran, J. C. (2000). *Negotiating the therapeutic alliance: A relational treatment guide.* Guilford Press.

Safran, J. D., Muran, J. C., & Eubanks-Carter, C. (2011). Repairing alliance ruptures. *Psychotherapy, 48*(1), 80–87. https://doi.org/10.1037/a0022140

Sclabassi, S. H. (1973). Literature as a therapeutic tool. A review of the literature on bibliotherapy. *American Journal of Psychotherapy, 27*(1), 70–77. https://doi.org/10.1176/appi.psychotherapy.1973.27.1.70

Seligman, M. E. P. (1972). Learned helplessness. *Annual Review of Medicine, 23*(1), 407–412. https://doi.org/10.1146/annurev.me.23.020172.002203

Shapiro, F. (2018). *Eye movement desensitization and reprocessing (EMDR) therapy* (3rd ed.). Guilford Press.

Shear, M. K., Bjelland, I., Beesdo, K., Gloster, A. T., & Wittchen, H. U. (2007). Supplementary dimensional assessment in anxiety disorders. *International Journal of Methods in Psychiatric Research, 16*(S1), S52–S64. https://doi.org/10.1002/mpr.215

Sheeran, P., Maki, A., Montanaro, E., Avishai-Yitshak, A., Bryan, A., Klein, W. M., Miles, E., & Rothman, A. J. (2016). The impact of changing attitudes, norms, and self-efficacy on health-related intentions and behavior: A meta-analysis. *Health Psychology, 35*(11), 1178–1188. https://doi.org/10.1037/hea0000387

Siegel, D. J. (2009). Emotion as integration: A possible answer to the question, What is an emotion? In D. Fosha, D. J. Siegel, & M. Solomon (Eds.), *The healing power of emotion: Affective neuroscience, development, and clinical practice* (pp. 145–171). Norton.

Sijercic, I., Button, M. L., Westra, H. A., & Hara, K. M. (2016). The interpersonal context of client motivational language in cognitive-behavioral therapy. *Psychotherapy, 53*(1), 13–21. https://doi.org/10.1037/pst0000017

Snyder, C. R., Rand, K. L., & Sigmon, D. R. (2002). Hope theory. In C. R. Snyder & S. J. Lopez (Eds.), *Handbook of positive psychology* (pp. 257–276). Oxford University Press.

Sommers, J. L. (2013, August 27). *My journey to hell and back, a personal experience with CBT and ERP.* International OCD Foundation. https://iocdf.org/blog/2013/08/27/my-journey-to-hell-and-back-a-personal-experience-with-cbt-and-erp

Sotsky, S. M., Glass, D. R., Shea, M. T., Pilkonis, P. A., Collins, J. F., Elkin, I., Watkins, J. T., Imber, S. D., Leber, W. R., & Moyer, J. (1991). Patient predictors of response to psychotherapy and pharmacotherapy: Findings in the NIMH Treatment of Depression Collaborative Research Program. *The American Journal of Psychiatry, 148*(8), 997–1008. https://doi.org/10.1176/ajp.148.8.997

Sperry, L., & Sperry, J. (2012). *Case conceptualization: Mastering this competency with ease and confidence.* Routledge. https://doi.org/10.4324/9780203110010

Starreveld, A. (2021). MAGIC: A proposed model based on common factors. *Integrative Psychological & Behavioral Science, 55*(3), 582–592. https://doi.org/10.1007/s12124-020-09599-0

Steinberg, M. P., & Miller, W. R. (2015). *Motivational interviewing in diabetes care.* Guilford Press.

Stephens, R. S., Babor, T. F., Kadden, R., Miller, M., & the Marijuana Treatment Project Research Group. (2002). The Marijuana Treatment Project: Rationale, design and participant characteristics. *Addiction, 97*(s1), 109–124. https://doi.org/10.1046/j.1360-0443.97.s01.6.x

Stroebe, M., & Schut, H. (1999). The dual process model of coping with bereavement: Rationale and description. *Death Studies, 23*(3), 197–224. https://doi.org/10.1080/074811899201046

Strupp, H. H. (1993). The Vanderbilt psychotherapy studies: Synopsis. *Journal of Consulting and Clinical Psychology, 61*(3), 431–433. https://doi.org/10.1037/0022-006X.61.3.431

Strupp, H. H., & Binder, J. L. (1984). *Psychotherapy in a new key: A guide to time-limited dynamic psychotherapy.* Basic Books.

Sturmey, P. (Ed.). (2007). *Functional analysis in clinical treatment.* Academic Press.

Sue, D. W., & Sue, D. (2008). *Counseling the culturally diverse: Theory and practice.* John Wiley & Sons.

Sue, D. W., Sue, D., Neville, H. A., & Smith, L. (2019). *Counseling the culturally diverse: Theory and practice* (8th ed.). John Wiley & Sons.

Sutton, C. (n.d.). Elementary particles. In *Encyclopedia Britannica.* https://www.britannica.com/science/subatomic-particle/Elementary-particles

Swift, J. K., Callahan, J. I., Cooper, M., & Parkin, S. R. (2019). Preferences. In J. C. Norcross & B. E. Wampold, *Psychotherapy relationships that work: Vol. 2. Evidence-based therapist responsiveness* (3rd ed., pp. 157–187). Oxford.

Swift, J. K., & Derthick, A. O. (2013). Increasing hope by addressing clients' outcome expectations. *Psychotherapy, 50*(3), 284–287. https://doi.org/10.1037/a0031941

Tao, K. W. (2015, October 30). *Multicultural counseling* [Conference keynote presentation]. Utah University Counseling Centers Conference, Park City, UT, United States.

Thorne, B. (1992). *Carl Rogers.* Sage.

Thorp, S. R., Ayers, C. R., Nuevo, R., Stoddard, J. A., Sorrell, J. T., & Wetherell, J. L. (2009). Meta-analysis comparing different behavioral treatments for late-life anxiety. *The American Journal of Geriatric Psychiatry, 17*(2), 105–115. https://doi.org/10.1097/JGP.0b013e31818b3f7e

Tompkins, M. A. (2004). *Using homework in psychotherapy: Strategies, guidelines, and forms.* Guilford Press.

Tryon, G. S., Birch, S. E., & Verkuilen, J. (2019). Goal consensus and collaboration. In J. C. Norcross & M. J. Lambert (Eds.), *Psychotherapy relationships that work: Vol. 1. Evidence-based therapist contributions* (3rd ed., pp. 167–204). Oxford University Press. https://doi.org/10.1093/med-psych/9780190843953.003.0005

Tschacher, W., Junghan, U. M., & Pfammatter, M. (2014). Towards a taxonomy of common factors in psychotherapy-results of an expert survey. *Clinical Psychology & Psychotherapy, 21*(1), 82–96. https://doi.org/10.1002/cpp.1822

Vidor, K., Fleming, V., Cukor, G., Thorpe, R., Taurog, N., & LeRoy, M. (1939). *The Wizard of Oz.* Metro-Goldwyn-Mayer.

Wampold, B. E. (2001). *The great psychotherapy debate: Models, methods, and findings.* Lawrence Erlbaum.

Wampold, B. E., & Budge, S. L. (2012). The 2011 Leona Tyler Award Address: The relationship—and its relationship to the common and specific factors of psychotherapy. *The Counseling Psychologist, 40*(4), 601–623. https://doi.org/10.1177/0011000011432709

Wampold, B. E., & Imel, Z. (2015). *The great psychotherapy debate: The evidence for what makes psychotherapy work* (2nd ed.). Taylor & Francis Group. https://doi.org/10.4324/9780203582015

Wampold, B. E., Imel, Z. E., Bhati, K. S., & Johnson-Jennings, M. D. (2007). Insight as a common factor. In L. G. Castonguay & C. Hill (Eds.), *Insight in psychotherapy* (pp. 119–139). American Psychological Association. https://doi.org/10.1037/11532-006

Wampold, B. E., Mondin, G. W., Moody, M., Stich, F., Benson, K., & Ahn, H. (1997). A meta-analysis of outcome studies comparing bona fide psychotherapies: Empirically, 'all must have prizes.' *Psychological Bulletin, 122*(3), 203–215. https://doi.org/10.1037/0033-2909.122.3.203

Wampold, B. E., & Ulvenes, P. G. (2019). Integration of common factors and specific ingredients. In J. C. Norcross & M. R. Goldfried (Eds.), *Handbook of psychotherapy integration* (3rd ed., pp. 69–87). Oxford University Press.

Wang, J., Mann, F., Lloyd-Evans, B., Ma, R., & Johnson, S. (2018). Associations between loneliness and perceived social support and outcomes of mental health problems: A systematic review. *BMC Psychiatry, 18*(1), 156. https://doi.org/10.1186/s12888-018-1736-5

Watzlawick, P., Weakland, J. H., & Fisch, R. (1974). *Change: Principles of problem formation and problem resolution.* W. W. Norton.

Weinberger, J. (1995). Common factors aren't so common: The common factors dilemma. *Clinical Psychology: Science and Practice, 2*(1), 45–69. https://doi.org/10.1111/j.1468-2850.1995.tb00024.x

Weinberger, J. (2014). Common factors are not so common and specific factors are not so specified: Toward an inclusive integration of psychotherapy research. *Psychotherapy, 51*(4), 514–518. https://doi.org/10.1037/a0037092

Weinberger, J., & Eig, A. (1999). Expectancies: The ignored common factor in psychotherapy. In I. Kirsch (Ed.), *How expectancies shape experience* (pp. 357–382). American Psychological Association. https://doi.org/10.1037/10332-015

Weiner, I. B., & Bornstein, R. F. (2009). *Principles of psychotherapy: Promoting evidence-based psychodynamic practice* (3rd ed.). John Wiley.

Weissman, M. M. (2005). *Mastering depression through interpersonal psychotherapy: Patient workbook.* Oxford University Press.

Weissman, M. M., Markowitz, J. C., & Klerman, G. L. (2017). *The guide to interpersonal psychotherapy: Updated and expanded edition.* Oxford.

Westra, H. A., & Aviram, A. (2015). Integrating motivational interviewing into the treatment of anxiety. In H. Arkowitz, W. R. Miller, & S. Rollnick (Eds.), *Motivational interviewing in the treatment of psychological problems* (2nd ed., pp. 83–109). Guilford Press.

Westra, H. A., Constantino, M. J., & Antony, M. M. (2016). Integrating motivational interviewing with cognitive-behavioral therapy for severe generalized anxiety disorder: An allegiance-controlled randomized clinical trial. *Journal of Consulting and Clinical Psychology, 84*(9), 768–782. https://doi.org/10.1037/ccp0000098

Westra, H. A., Dozois, D. J. A., & Marcus, M. (2007). Expectancy, homework compliance, and initial change in cognitive-behavioral therapy for anxiety. *Journal of Consulting and Clinical Psychology, 75*(3), 363–373. https://doi.org/10.1037/0022-006X.75.3.363

Westra, H. A., Norouzian, N., Poulin, L., Coyne, A., Constantino, M. J., Hara, K., Olson, D., & Antony, M. M. (2021). Testing a deliberate practice workshop for developing appropriate responsivity to resistance markers. *Psychotherapy, 58*(2), 175–185. https://doi.org/10.1037/pst0000311

Wigman, J. T., de Vos, S., Wichers, M., van Os, J., & Bartels-Velthuis, A. A. (2017). A transdiagnostic network approach to psychosis. *Schizophrenia Bulletin, 43*(1), 122–132. https://doi.org/10.1093/schbul/sbw095

Williams, C. (2019). The hero's journey: A mudmap for change. *Journal of Humanistic Psychology, 59*(4), 522–539. https://doi.org/10.1177/0022167817705499

Wilson, G. T. (2008). Behavior therapy. In R. J. Corsini & D. Wedding (Eds.), *Current psychotherapies* (8th ed., pp. 223–262). Thomson Brooks/Cole.

Wolitzky, D. L. (2020). Contemporary Freudian psychoanalytic psychotherapy. In S. B. Messer & N. J. Kaslow (Eds.), *Essential psychotherapies* (4th ed., pp. 35–70). Guilford Press.

Wolpe, J. (1969). *The practice of behavior therapy.* Pergamon Press.

Woods, S. L., & Rockman, P. (2021). *Mindfulness-based stress reduction: Protocol, practice, and teaching skills.* New Harbinger Publications.

Worden, J. W. (2018). *Grief counseling and grief therapy: A handbook for the mental health practitioner* (5th ed.). Springer.

World Health Organization. (2019). *International classification of diseases* (11th ed.). https://icd.who.int

Yalom, I. D. (1980). *Existential psychotherapy*. Basic Books.

Yalom, I. D. (2000). *Love's executioner*. HarperCollins Publishers.

Yalom, I. D. (2002). *The gift of therapy: An open letter to a new generation of therapists and their patients*. HarperCollins.

Yalom, I. D., & Leszcz, M. (2005). *The theory and practice of group psychotherapy*. Basic Books.

# Index

# About the Authors

**Russell J. Bailey, PhD,** is an associate professor at Utah Valley University. He completed his doctoral training in clinical psychology at Brigham Young University, where he also previously practiced, taught, and researched as clinical faculty in Counseling and Psychological Services. He has actively practiced psychotherapy since his licensing in 2012 and has been fascinated by psychotherapy research—especially process and outcome research—since 2004, when he first attended a conference for the Society for Psychotherapy Research. He is a deliberate practice certified therapist.

**Benjamin M. Ogles, PhD,** is a professor in the clinical psychology doctoral program at Brigham Young University. He is the author or coauthor of several books in addition to dozens of book chapters and journal articles about psychotherapy process and outcome, with a particular emphasis on measures for assessing statistical and clinically meaningful change. Publications coauthored by Dr. Ogles have appeared in *Psychotherapy Research, Journal of Clinical Psychology, Clinical Psychology Review, Psychotherapy,* and *Psychology and Psychotherapy: Theory, Research and Practice,* among others. He was the lead author of the book *Essentials of Outcome Assessment,* written with Michael J. Lambert and Scott A. Fields. After 16 years serving as a dean at two universities, he is enjoying his return to teaching and research in clinical psychology.